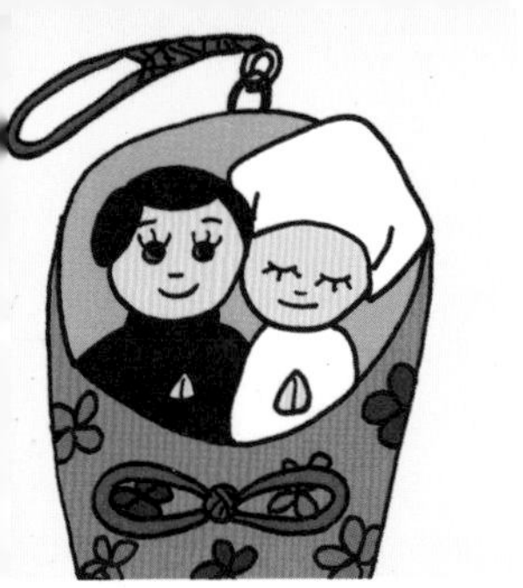

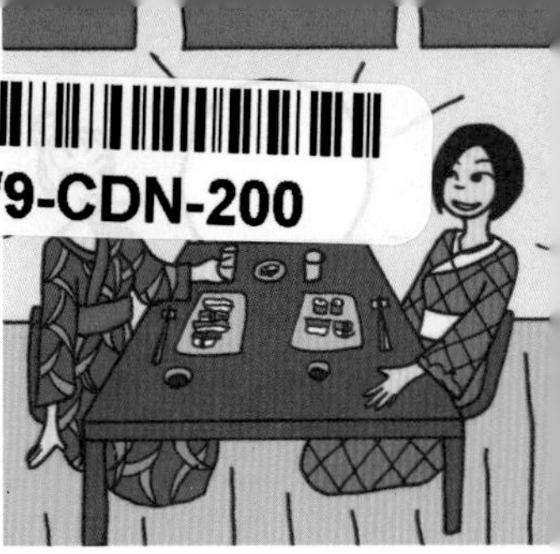

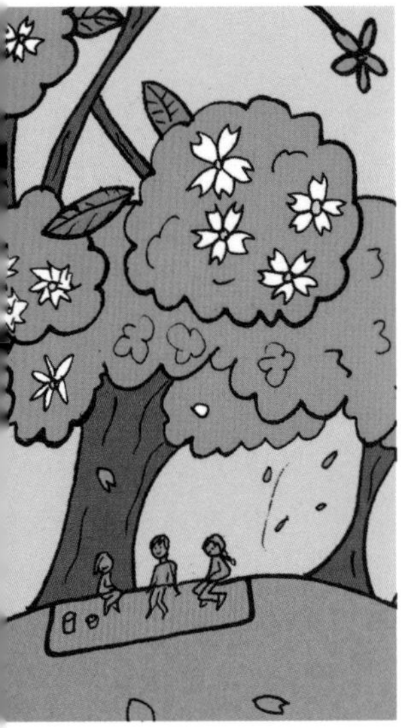

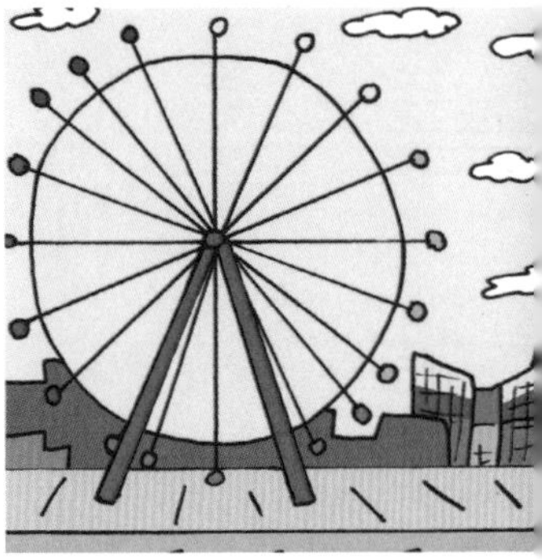

COOL JAPAN GUIDE

FUN IN THE LAND OF MANGA, LUCKY CATS AND RAMEN

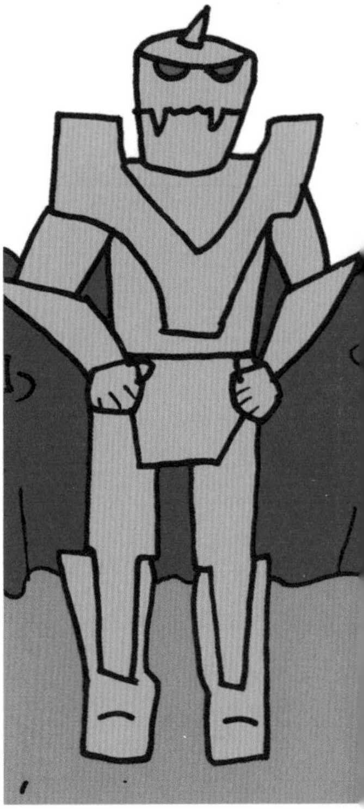

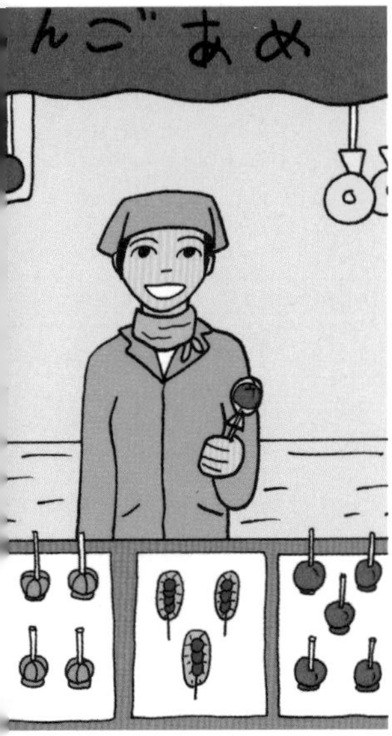
んごあめ

ABBY DENSON

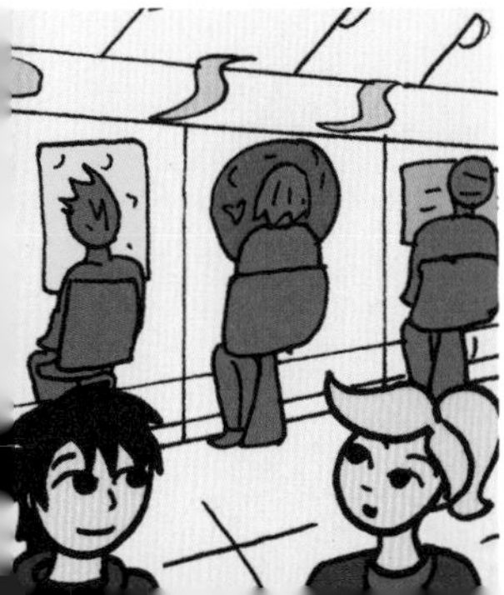

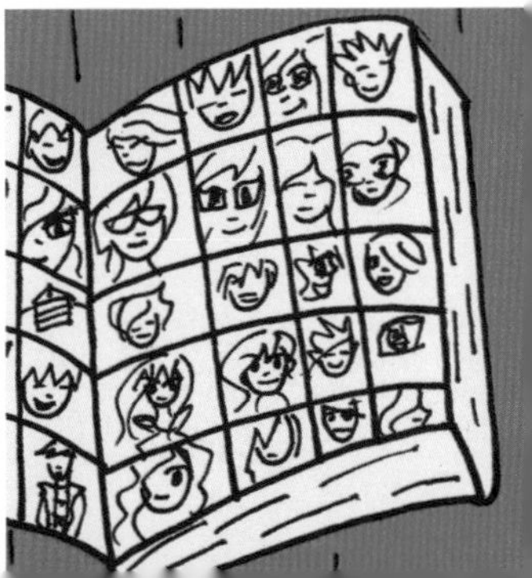

TUTTLE Publishing
Tokyo | Rutland, Vermont | Singapore

ACKNOWLEDGMENTS

My deepest gratitude goes out to all of my family members and friends for their support during this project.

Very special thanks go out to Matt Loux, Yuuko Koyama, Fusami Ogi, Yuji Nakagawa, Mika Sakki, Rodney Greenblat, Kate Williamson, Rie McClenny, Raina Telgemeier, Dave Roman, Kaneko Atsushi, Yoko Oikawa, Youri Morinaga, Chris Butcher, Masakazu Kigure, Xavier Lancel, Jeff Suon, Mina Monden and the countless others who have helped me feel welcome on my travels and offered valuable input for this book.

CONTENTS

INTRODUCTION

Hello!

Let me be your tour guide on a fun-filled journey to Japan! I'm an American cartoonist who has had a fascination with Japan for years. Anime and manga became part of my life when I was a teen. A comics fan already, I was instantly drawn to the diverse and exciting stories and art Japan's comics offered. Then, during my college years at Parsons School of Design in New York, I had a great opportunity to travel to Japan and complete a summer session at Sophia University in Tokyo, where I studied Japanese art and religion.

I adored my stay in Japan and collaborated on comics there with my friend Yuuko Koyama, a pen pal I had been corresponding with long before I ever made that first trip. To this day (over fifteen years later) we are still collaborating, and I try to visit Japan every year to have adventures with her. With me on my travels is my husband, Matt Loux, who is also an avid Japan traveler and very talented cartoonist!

Matt, Yuuko, and I will take you on a trip through some of our favorite places to go and things to do. Another character you'll meet is Kitty Sweet Tooth, my cartoon cat alter ego who likes to share new words and travel pointers.

I love visiting Japan so much that it's like another home to me. I'd like to share some of the things I love doing there, as well as some tips I've picked up along the way, with people who want to make the trek, or just want to have a little armchair adventure in one of the coolest countries in the world. I hope this book will come in handy for you when you're planning your trip or relaxing in your favorite chair.

Let's go!

PRONUNCIATION GUIDE

At the start of each chapter Kitty Sweet Tooth will teach you how to say some useful words and phrases. Here are a few basic rules of pronunciation.

In Japanese:

a is pronounced as in the word f<u>a</u>ther
e is pronounced as in the word s<u>e</u>t
i is pronounced ee as in the word s<u>ee</u>d
o is pronounced as in the word t<u>o</u>te
u is pronounced oo, as in the word s<u>oo</u>n

Most consonants are pronounced as in English. G is always hard, as in goat. F is a softer sound than in English, so try not to let your teeth touch your bottom lip when pronouncing it.
R is also a softer sound, like a gentle curl/roll of the tongue.
There is no l, q, v or x sound in Japanese.

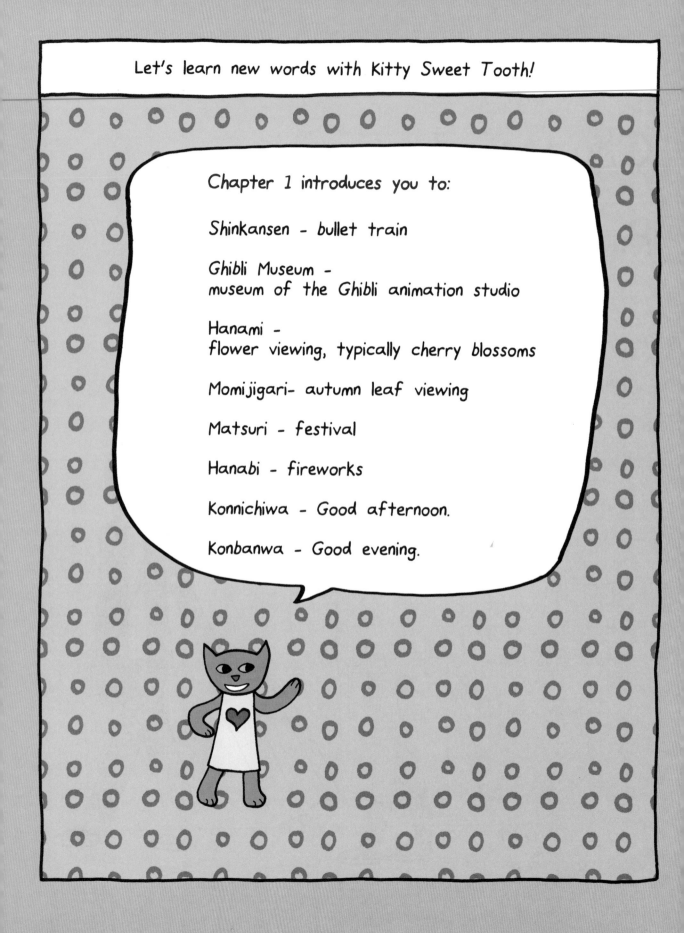

Let's learn new words with Kitty Sweet Tooth!

Chapter 1 introduces you to:

Shinkansen - bullet train

Ghibli Museum -
museum of the Ghibli animation studio

Hanami -
flower viewing, typically cherry blossoms

Momijigari- autumn leaf viewing

Matsuri - festival

Hanabi - fireworks

Konnichiwa - Good afternoon.

Konbanwa - Good evening.

Chapter 1
Prepare for Takeoff!

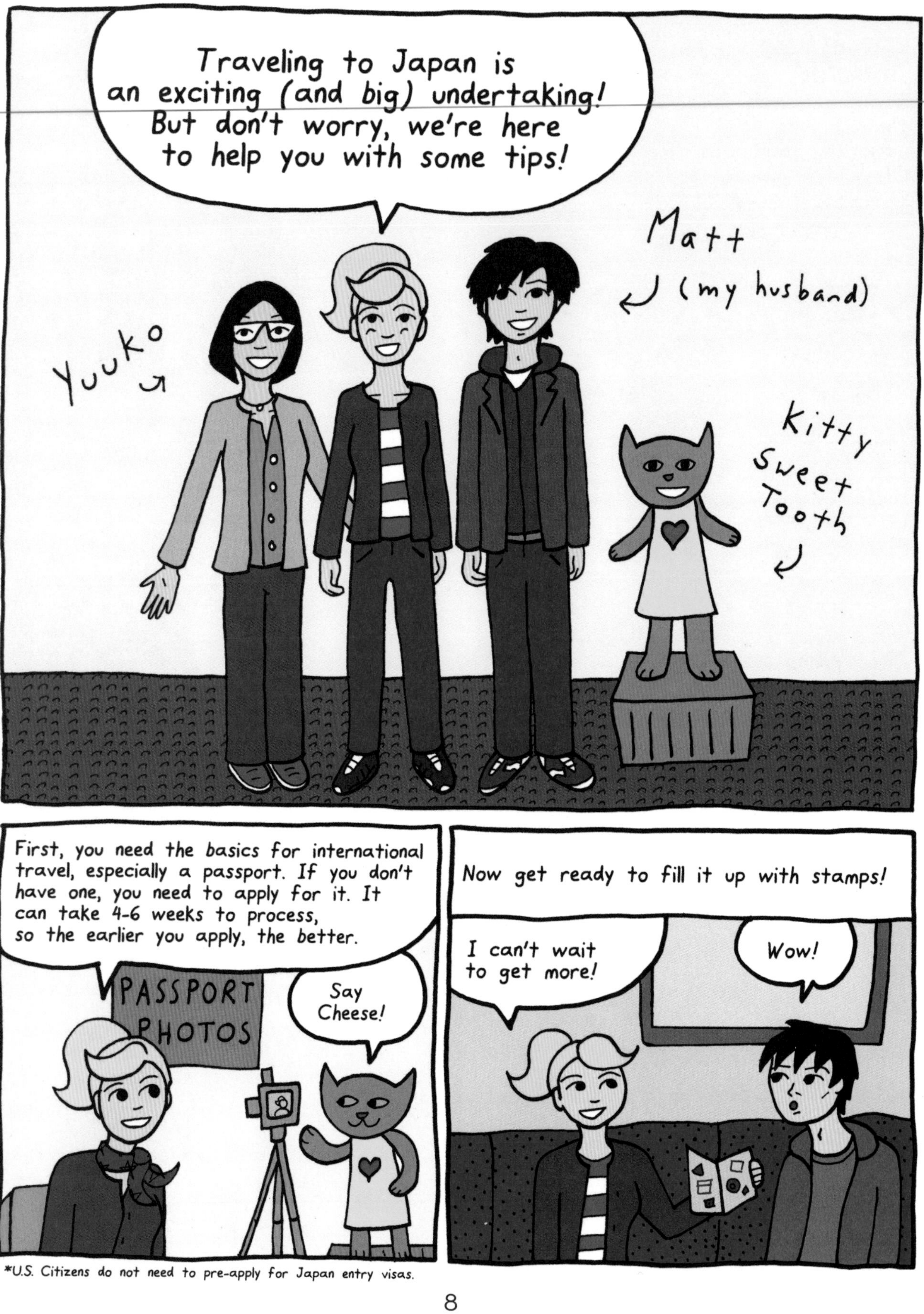
Traveling to Japan is an exciting (and big) undertaking! But don't worry, we're here to help you with some tips!
Matt
(my husband)
Yuuko
Kitty Sweet Tooth
First, you need the basics for international travel, especially a passport. If you don't have one, you need to apply for it. It can take 4-6 weeks to process, so the earlier you apply, the better.
PASSPORT PHOTOS
Say Cheese!
Now get ready to fill it up with stamps!
I can't wait to get more!
Wow!

*U.S. Citizens do not need to pre-apply for Japan entry visas.

How long are you going to be in Japan? I'd recommend at least ten days if possible. The flight from the U.S. can take 12-14 hours each way, and you'll need time to adjust. Of course, the longer your stay, the more you will see.

OCTOBER

3	4	5	6
10	11	12	13
17	18	19	20

Before traveling, think about whether or not you should buy a JR Railpass.

JAPAN RAIL PASS

This is a special discount pass for international visitors to Japan. It's purchased with a one-time fee and allows for unlimited use of JR's trains including most shinkansen (bullet trains). There are 1-week, 2-week and 3-week passes. If you're planning to travel cross-country in Japan this is a great way to do it, since individual shinkansen tickets can be pricey. If you're staying in one city, a pass probably isn't worthwhile.

You must purchase an exchange order for the JR pass before you leave. It can't be purchased in Japan, so you have to plan ahead. JR passes can be purchased online or through a travel agent that carries them. There's a list of those here at the JR website:
http://www.japanrailpass.net/eng/en001.html

TOPTOUR CORPORATION

Nº 027467

Exchange Order for JAPAN RAIL PASS

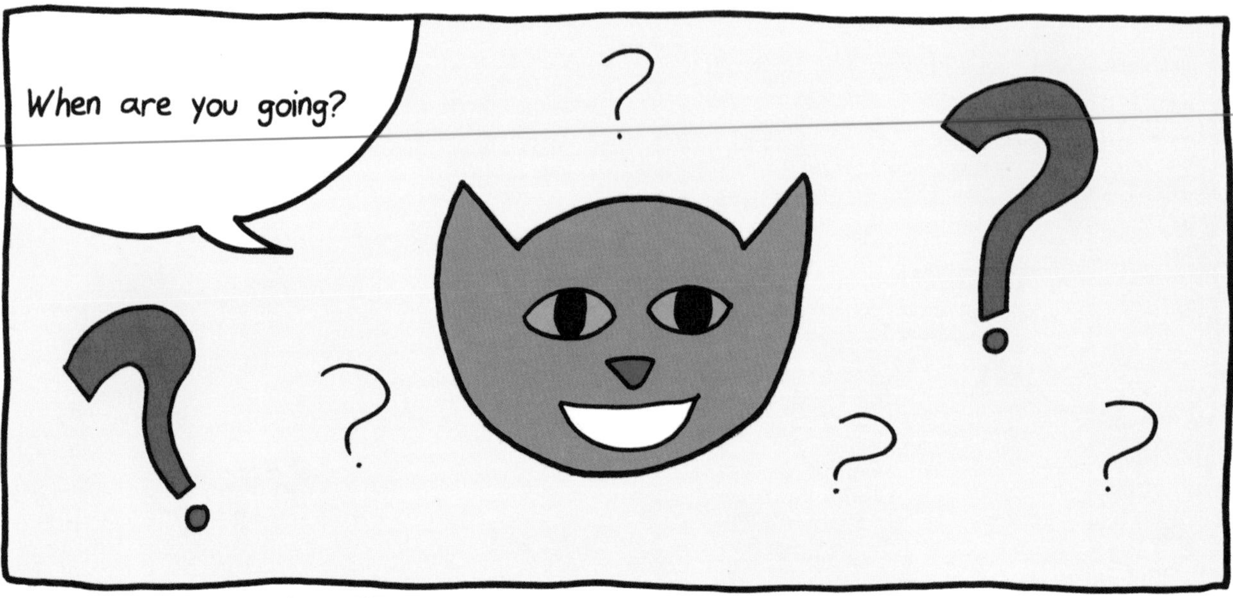
When are you going?

Japan has its charms year round, but depending on your interests, some seasons will appeal more than others. As you might expect, the more northern, mountainous areas tend to be cooler and the southern areas tend to be warmer.

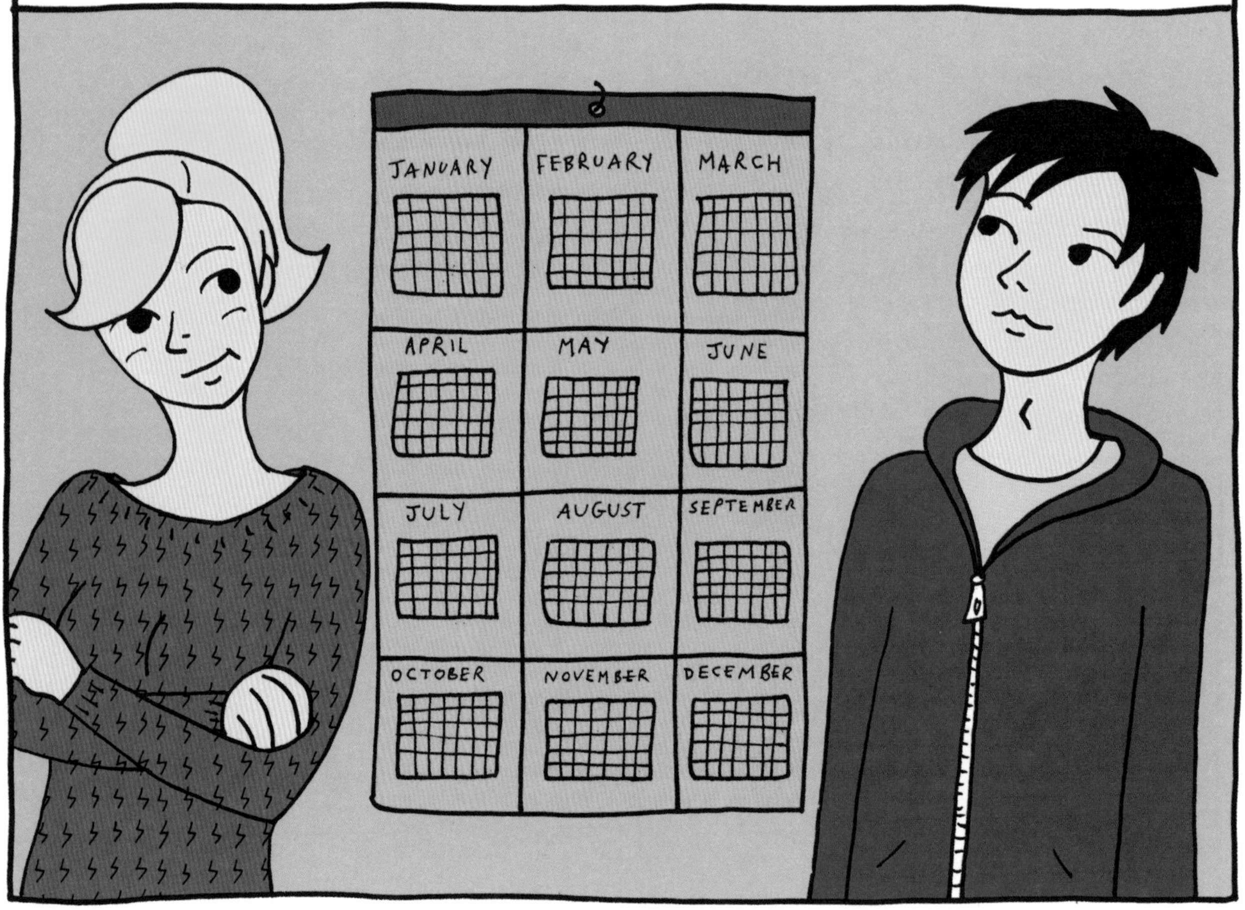
JANUARY
FEBRUARY
MARCH
APRIL
MAY
JUNE
JULY
AUGUST
SEPTEMBER
OCTOBER
NOVEMBER
DECEMBER

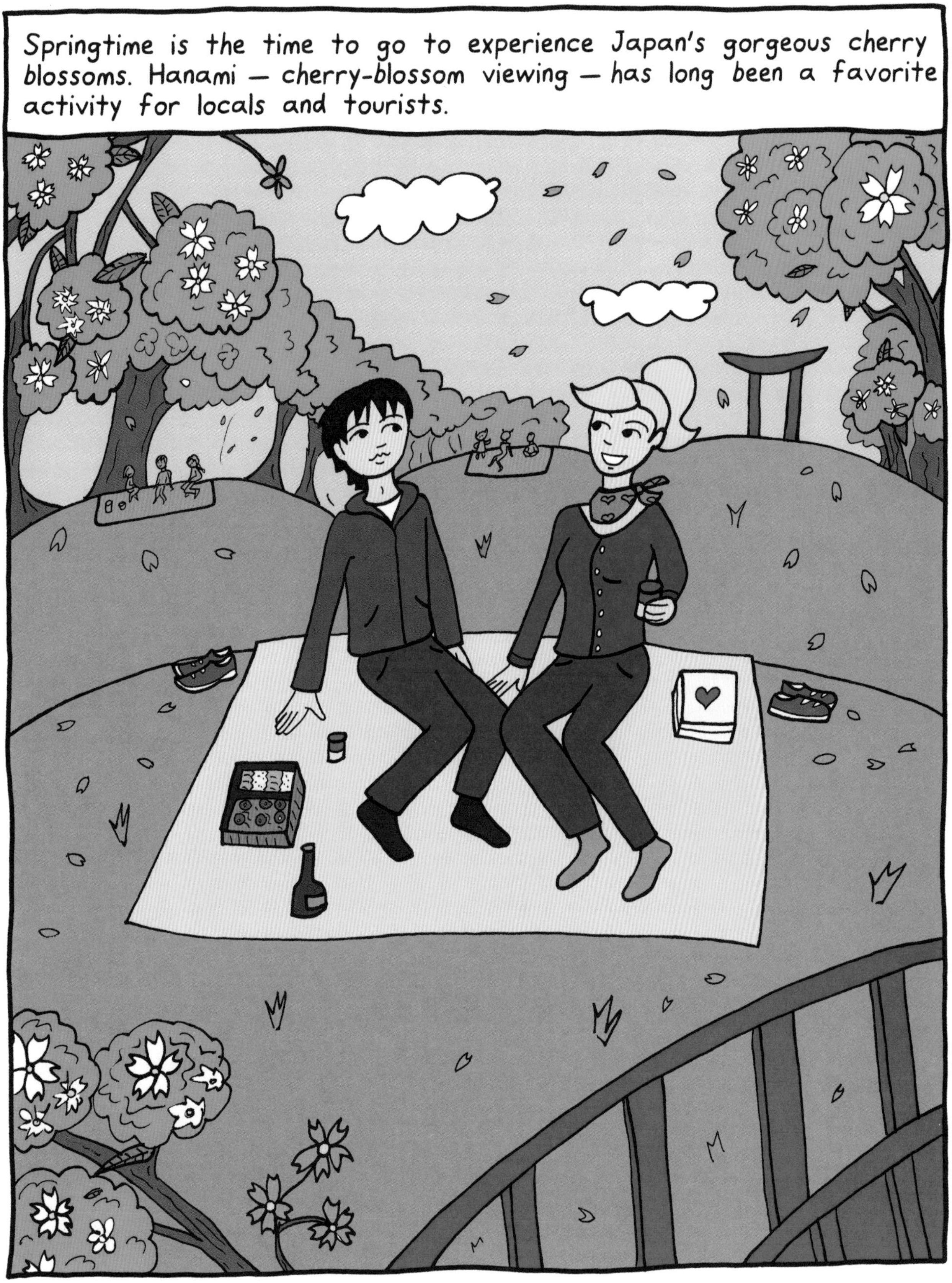
Springtime is the time to go to experience Japan's gorgeous cherry blossoms. Hanami — cherry-blossom viewing — has long been a favorite activity for locals and tourists.

Summertime in Japan is hot and humid, and it is also the peak time to experience Japan's festivals (matsuri) and fireworks (hanabi).

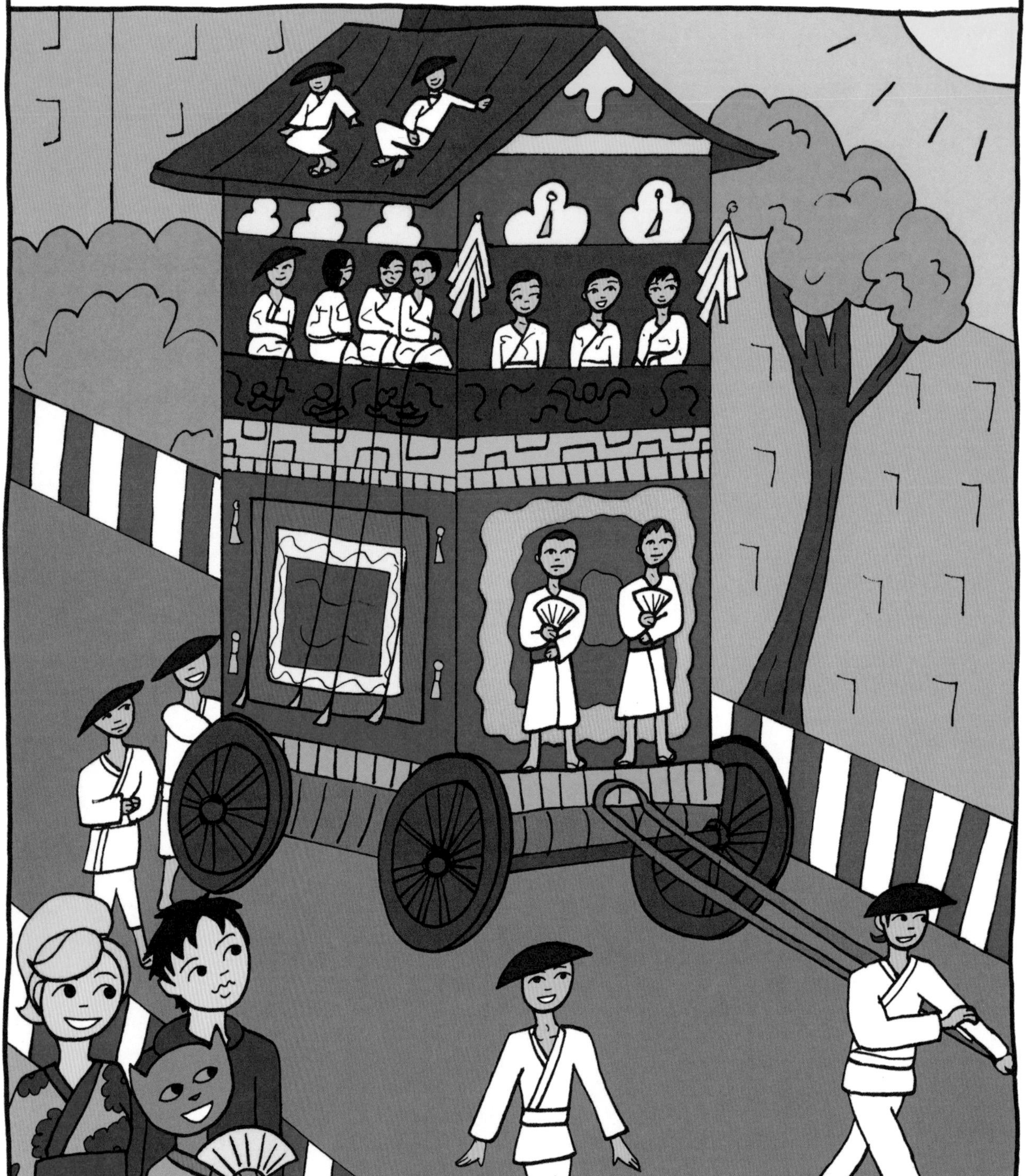

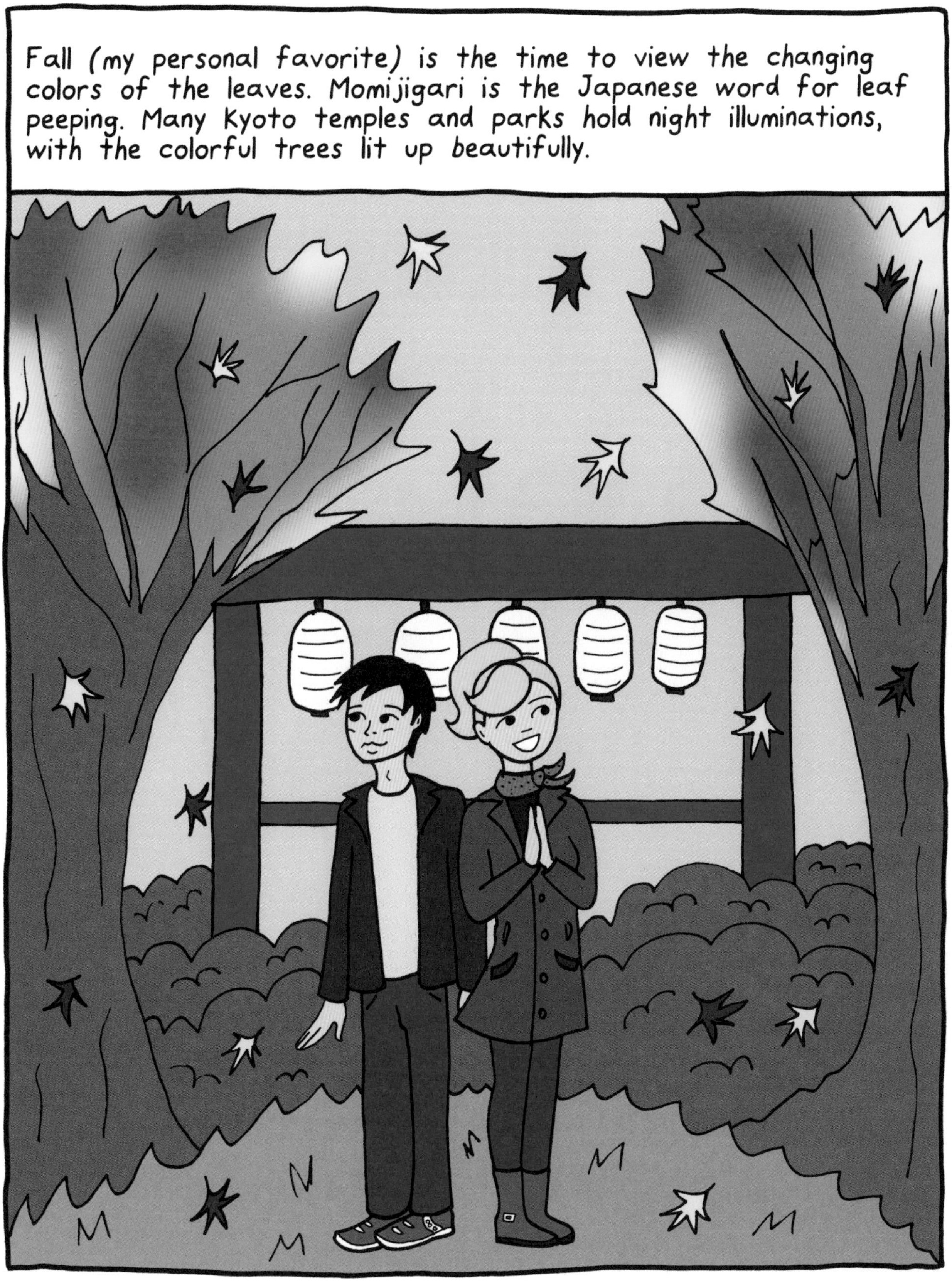
Fall (my personal favorite) is the time to view the changing colors of the leaves. Momijigari is the Japanese word for leaf peeping. Many Kyoto temples and parks hold night illuminations, with the colorful trees lit up beautifully.

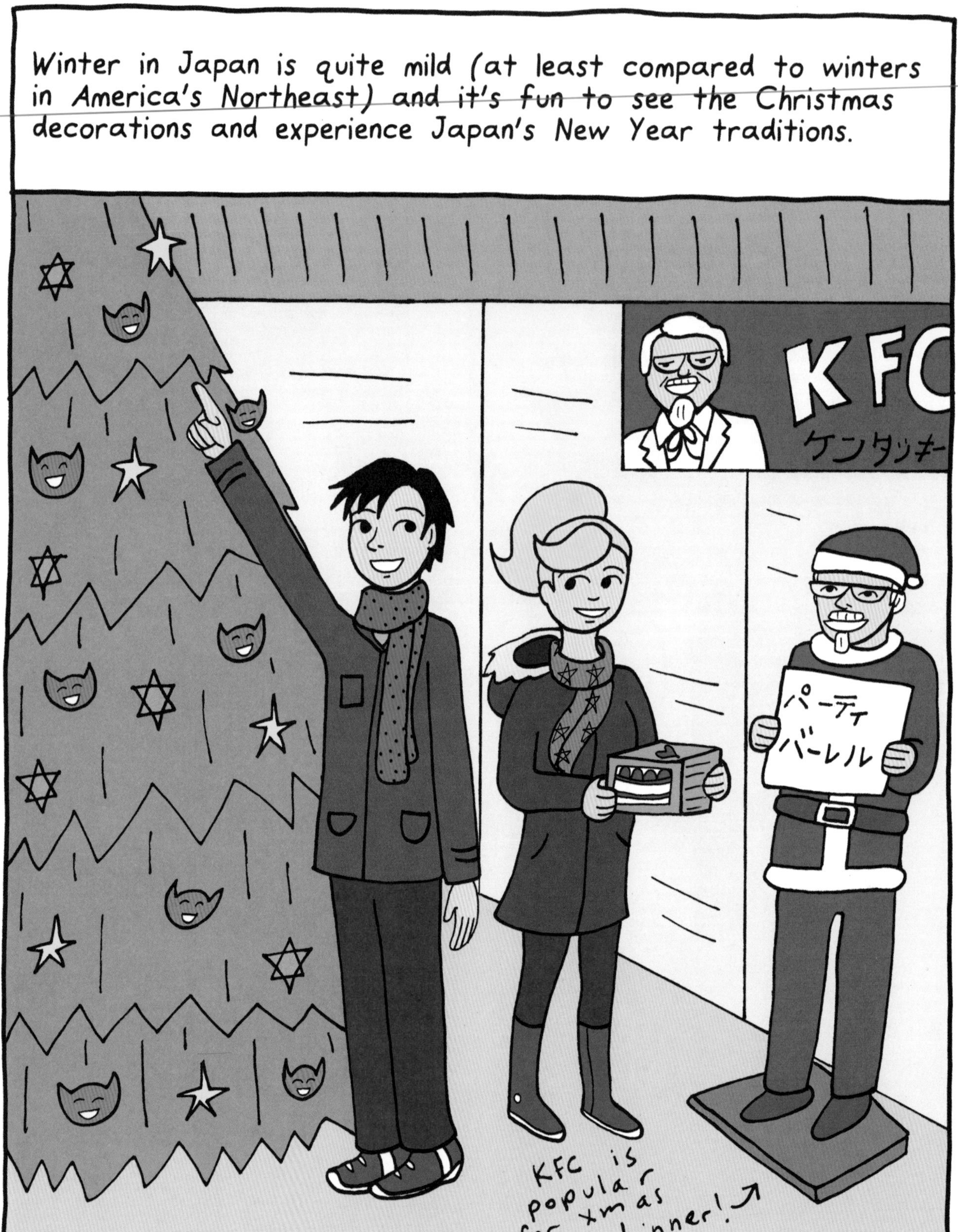
Winter in Japan is quite mild (at least compared to winters in America's Northeast) and it's fun to see the Christmas decorations and experience Japan's New Year traditions.
KFC
ケンタッキー
パーティ
バーレル
KFC is popular for xmas dinner!

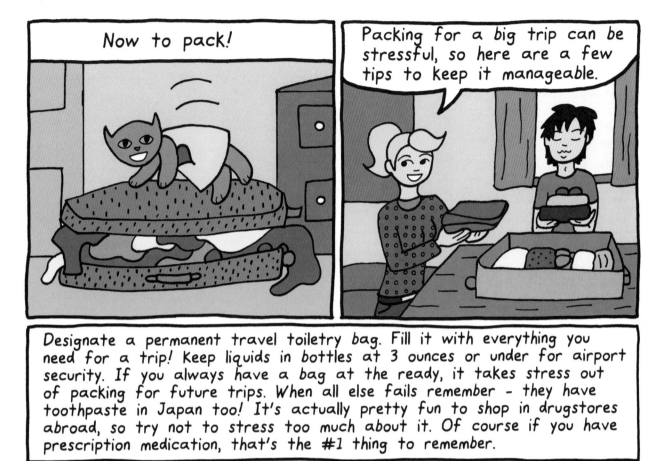

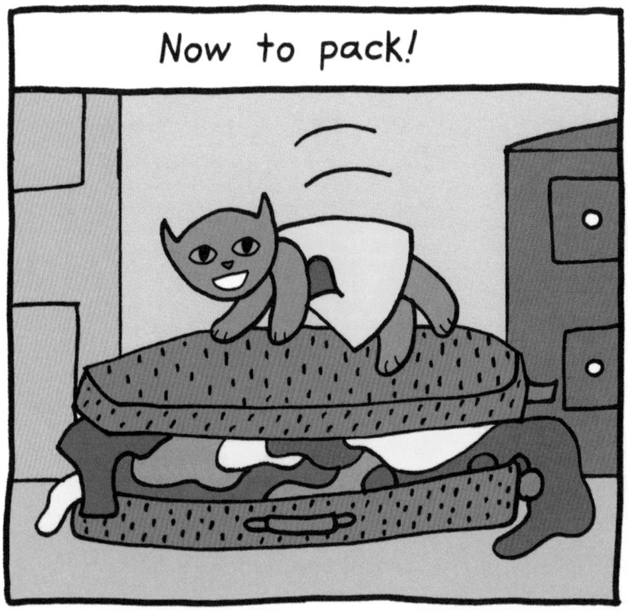
Now to pack!

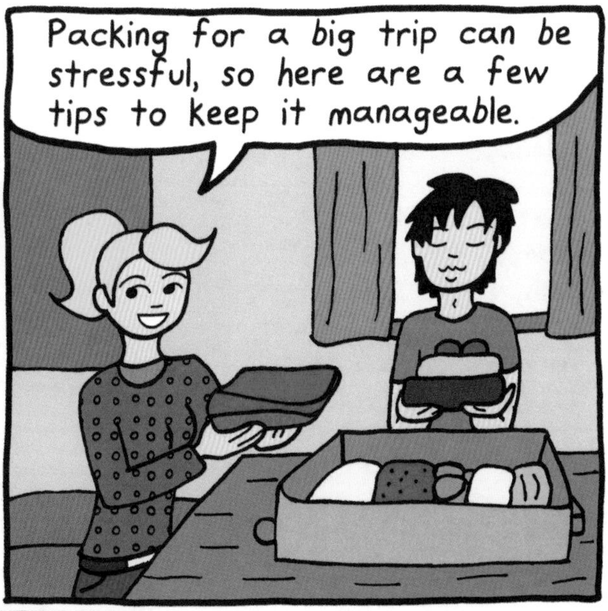
Packing for a big trip can be stressful, so here are a few tips to keep it manageable.

Designate a permanent travel toiletry bag. Fill it with everything you need for a trip! Keep liquids in bottles at 3 ounces or under for airport security. If you always have a bag at the ready, it takes stress out of packing for future trips. When all else fails remember - they have toothpaste in Japan too! It's actually pretty fun to shop in drugstores abroad, so try not to stress too much about it. Of course if you have prescription medication, that's the #1 thing to remember.

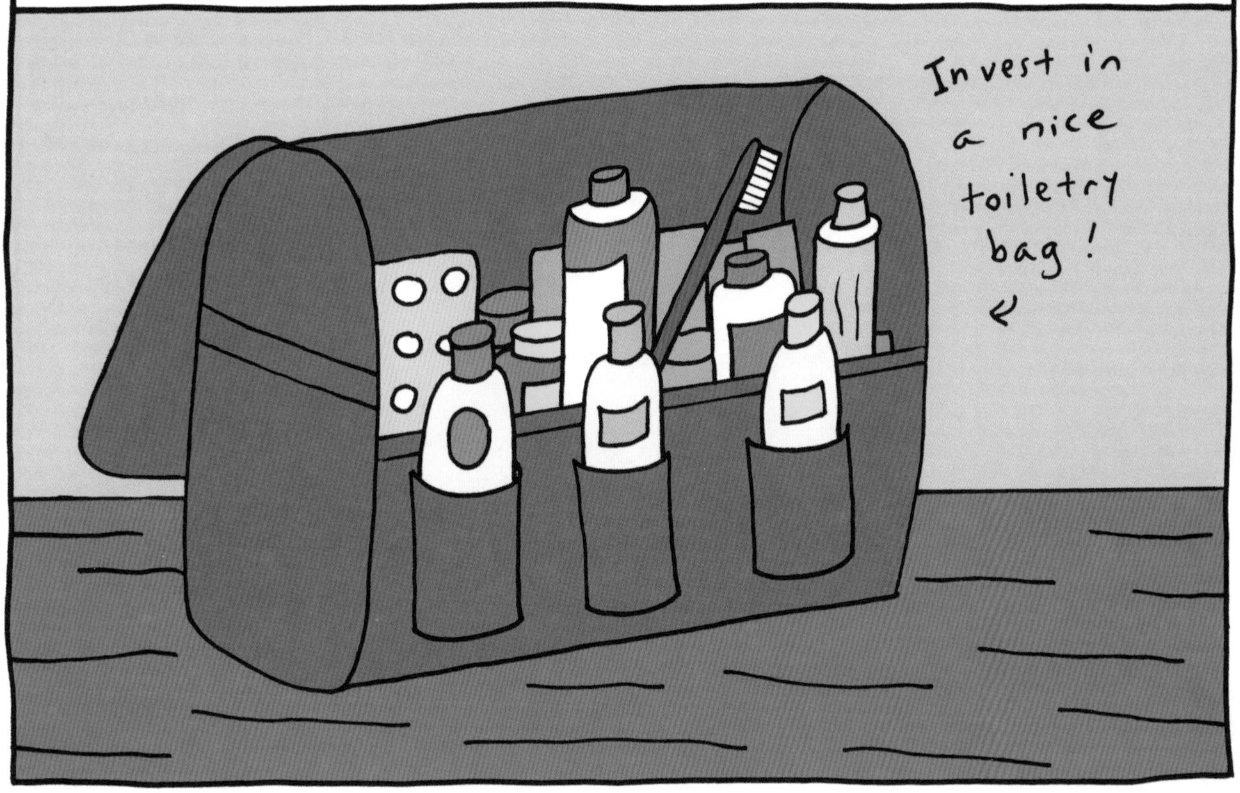
Invest in a nice toiletry bag!

Bring a spare foldable bag or duffle. I like to pack one rolling suitcase and one carry-on shoulder bag that can fit a laptop, sketchbook, pens, books, and whatever else I want to have on the plane. If you plan to buy souvenirs, an extra duffle that can be checked in for the return flight will be a big help. In a pinch, you can also pack your treasures in a box for the return flight.

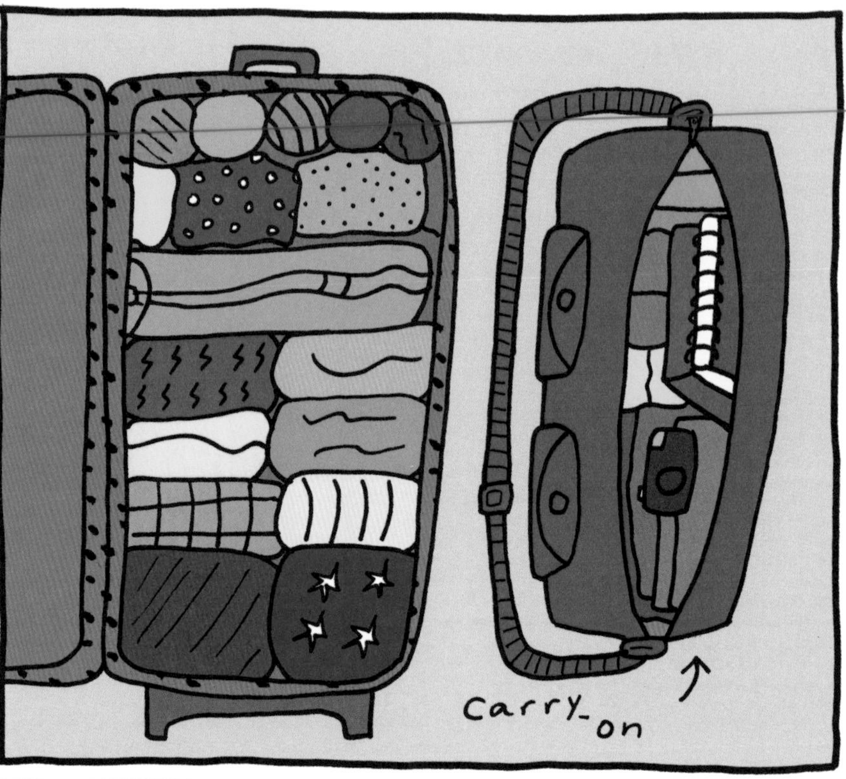
carry-on

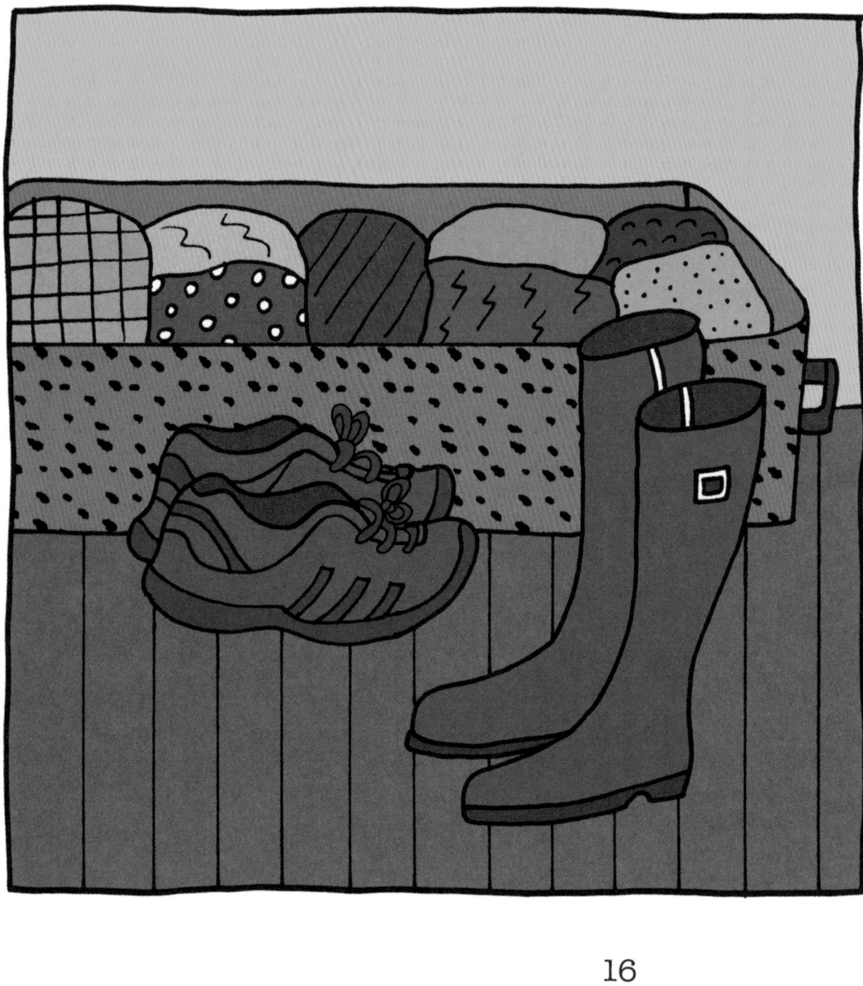

It's wise to pack one pair of boots (or rain-friendly footwear) and one pair of sneakers. If you think you might be going somewhere fancy, you can bring dress-shoes, though I've packed dressy clothes in the past only to regret the wasted packing space. I usually will wear my boots into the airport since they take less precious packing space and can slip on. Don't bother packing umbrellas, you can find them in any combini (convenience store).

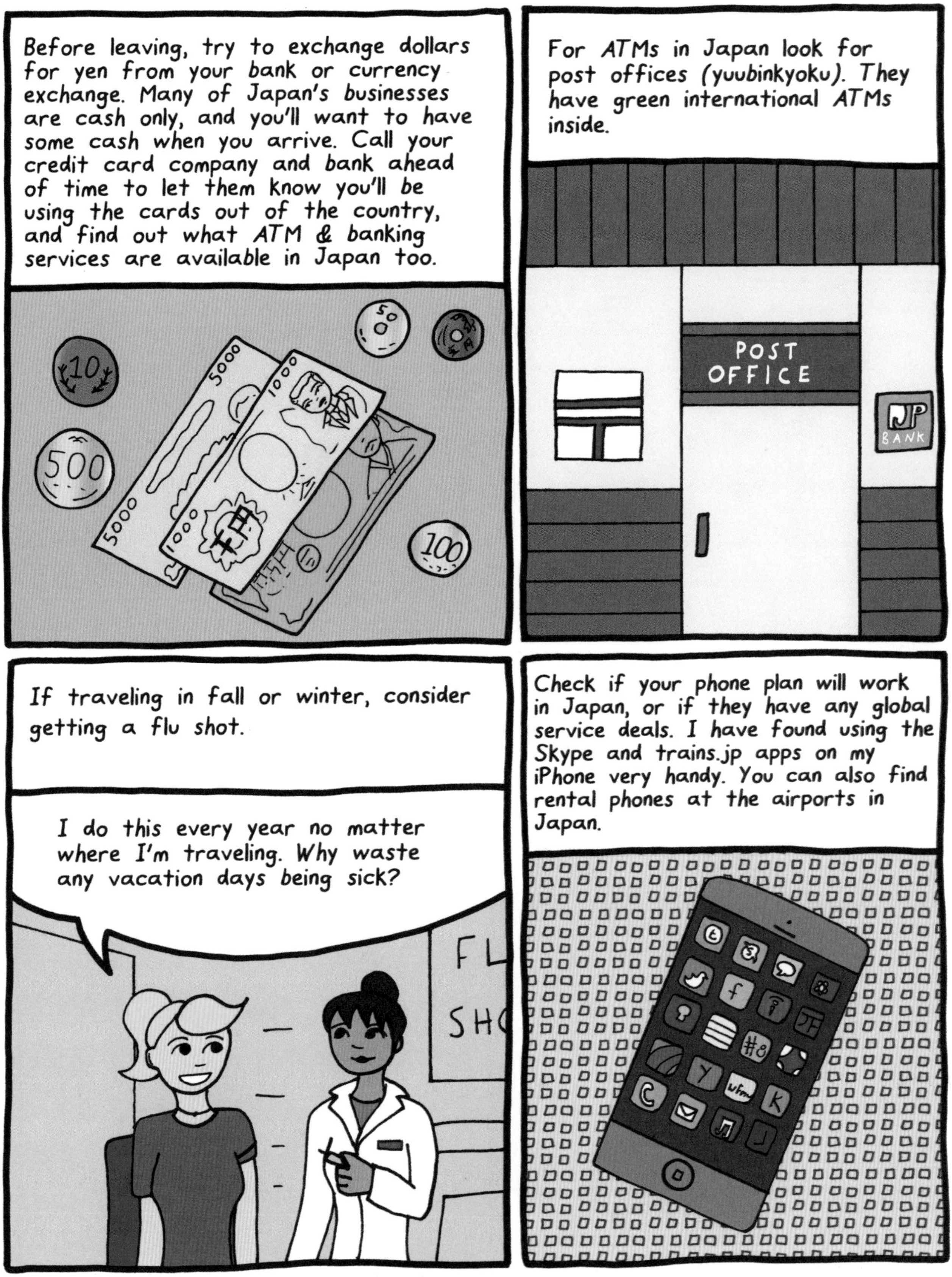
Before leaving, try to exchange dollars for yen from your bank or currency exchange. Many of Japan's businesses are cash only, and you'll want to have some cash when you arrive. Call your credit card company and bank ahead of time to let them know you'll be using the cards out of the country, and find out what ATM & banking services are available in Japan too.
For ATMs in Japan look for post offices (yuubinkyoku). They have green international ATMs inside.
POST OFFICE
JP BANK
If traveling in fall or winter, consider getting a flu shot.
I do this every year no matter where I'm traveling. Why waste any vacation days being sick?
Check if your phone plan will work in Japan, or if they have any global service deals. I have found using the Skype and trains.jp apps on my iPhone very handy. You can also find rental phones at the airports in Japan.

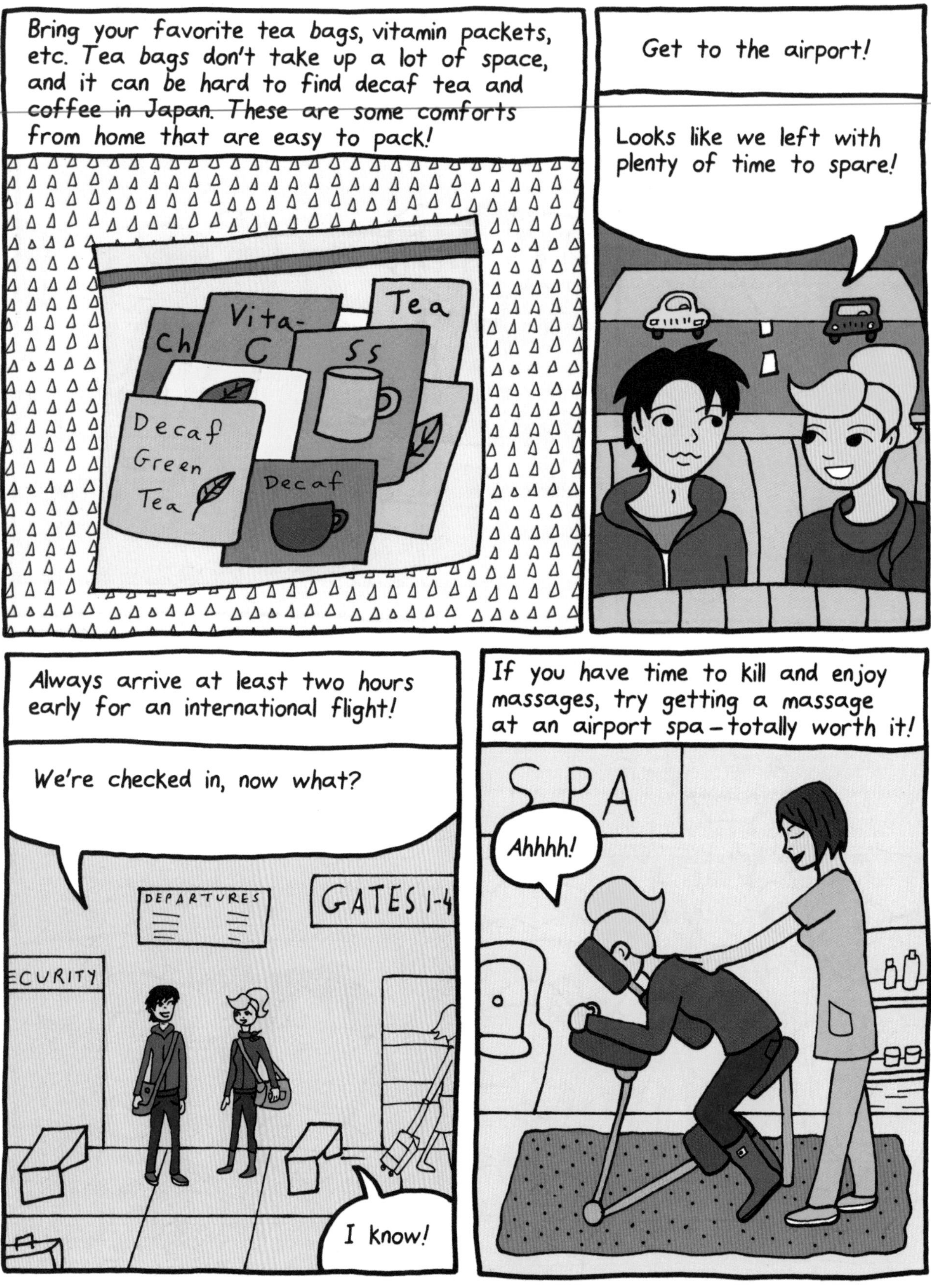
Bring your favorite tea bags, vitamin packets, etc. Tea bags don't take up a lot of space, and it can be hard to find decaf tea and coffee in Japan. These are some comforts from home that are easy to pack!
Ch
Vita-C
Ss
Tea
Decaf Green Tea
Decaf
Get to the airport!
Looks like we left with plenty of time to spare!
Always arrive at least two hours early for an international flight!
We're checked in, now what?
DEPARTURES
GATES 1-4
ECURITY
I know!
If you have time to kill and enjoy massages, try getting a massage at an airport spa—totally worth it!
SPA
Ahhhh!

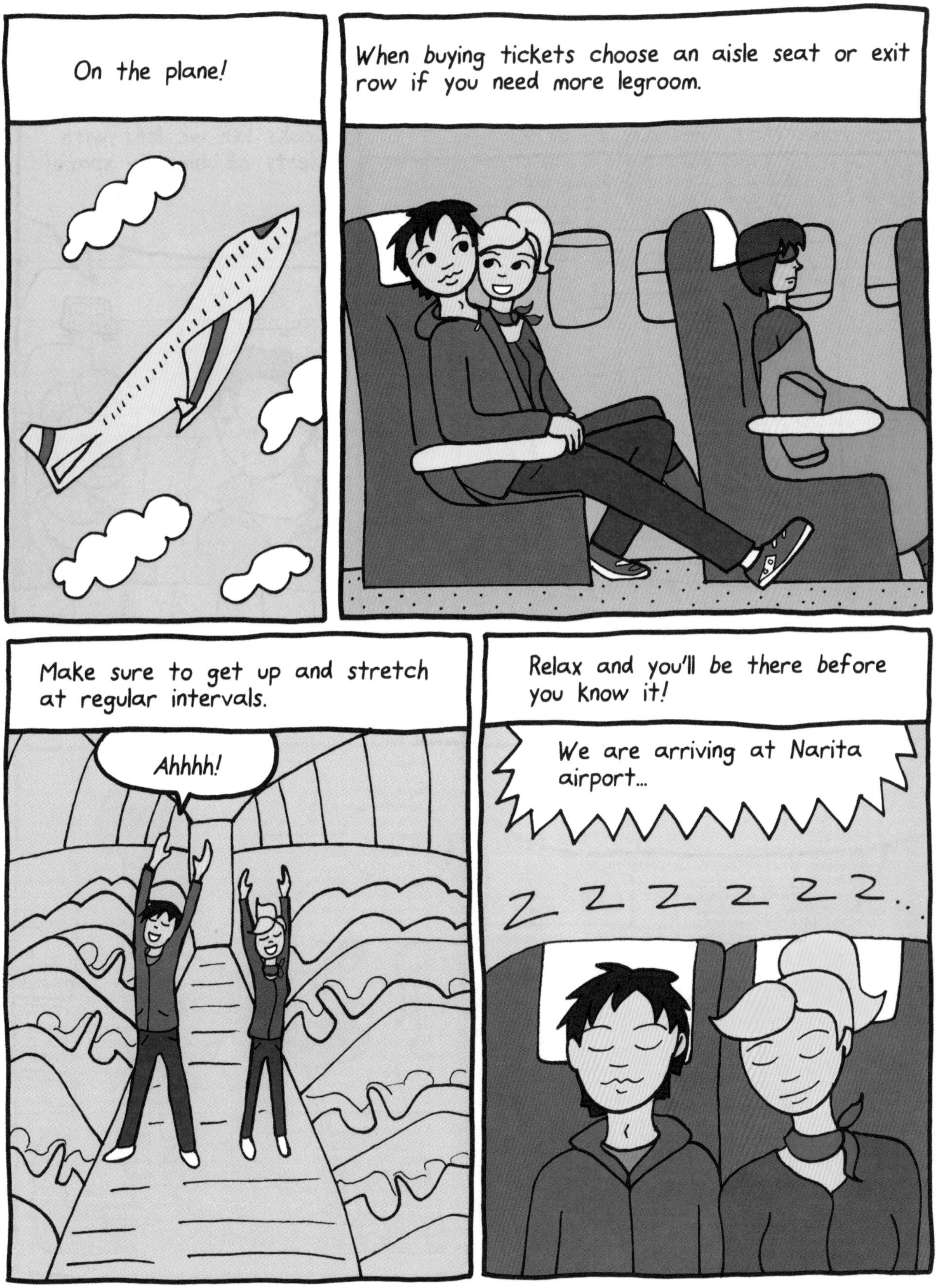
On the plane!
When buying tickets choose an aisle seat or exit row if you need more legroom.
Make sure to get up and stretch at regular intervals.
Ahhhh!
Relax and you'll be there before you know it!
We are arriving at Narita airport...
Z Z Z Z Z Z Z...

Let's learn new words with Kitty Sweet Tooth!

Chapter 2 introduces you to:

Sumimasen - Excuse me.

Arigatou gozaimasu - Thank you very much.

(your destination) wa nanban desu ka? -
What track number is (destination)?

Onigiri - rice ball

Bento - lunch box

Ekibento - train lunch box

Eki stampu - train stamp

Eki stampu wa doko desu ka? -
Where is the train stamp?

Chapter 2

We Have Arrived!

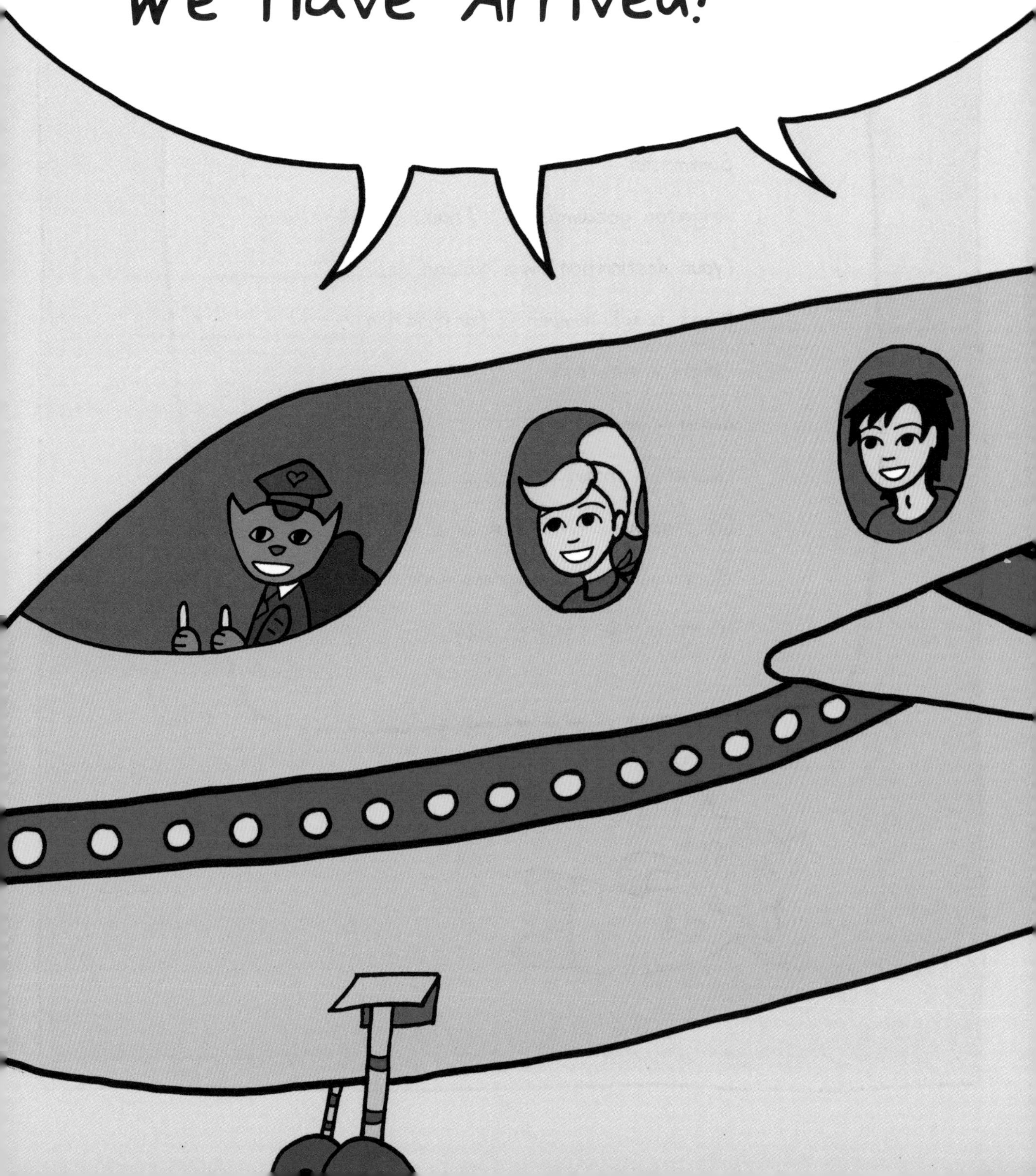

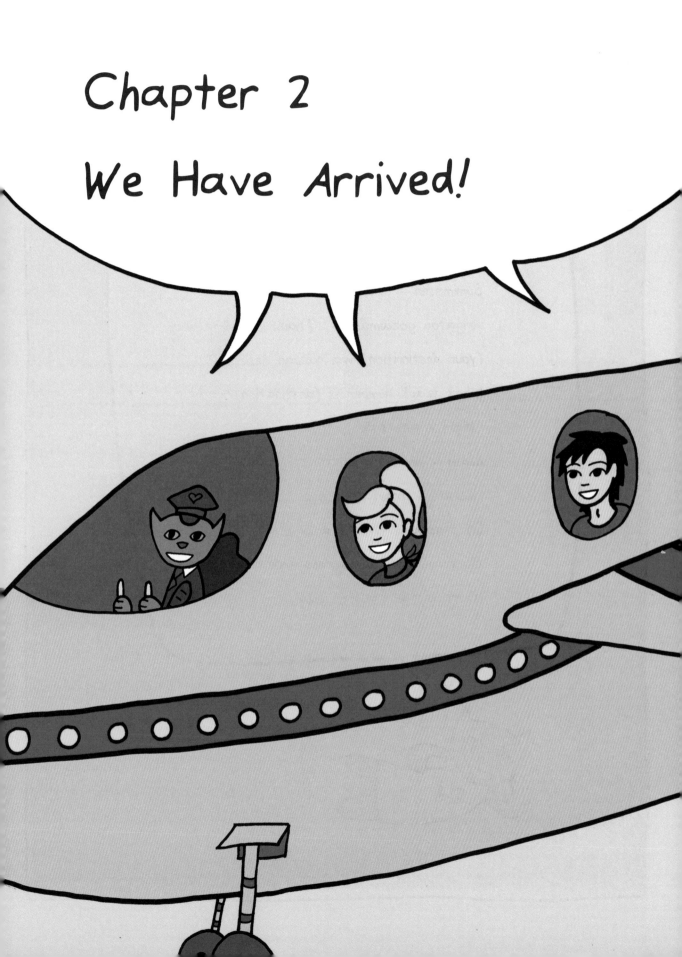

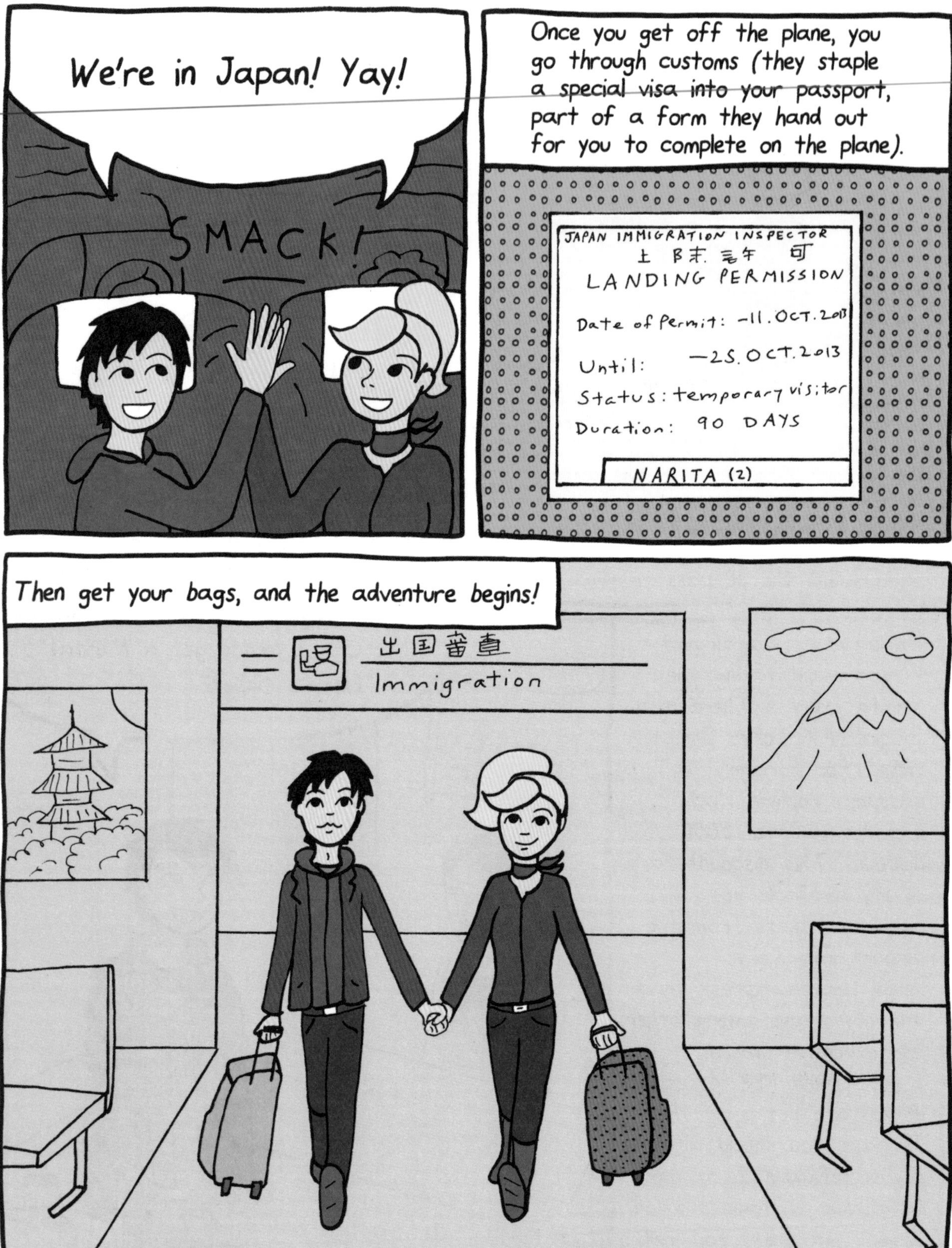
We're in Japan! Yay!
SMACK!
Once you get off the plane, you go through customs (they staple a special visa into your passport, part of a form they hand out for you to complete on the plane).
JAPAN IMMIGRATION INSPECTOR
上陸許可
LANDING PERMISSION
Date of Permit: -11. OCT. 2013
Until: -25. OCT. 2013
Status: temporary visitor
Duration: 90 DAYS
NARITA (2)
Then get your bags, and the adventure begins!
出国審査
Immigration

*At the airport you can find services to deliver the luggage to and from your hotel as well as cell phone rental services.

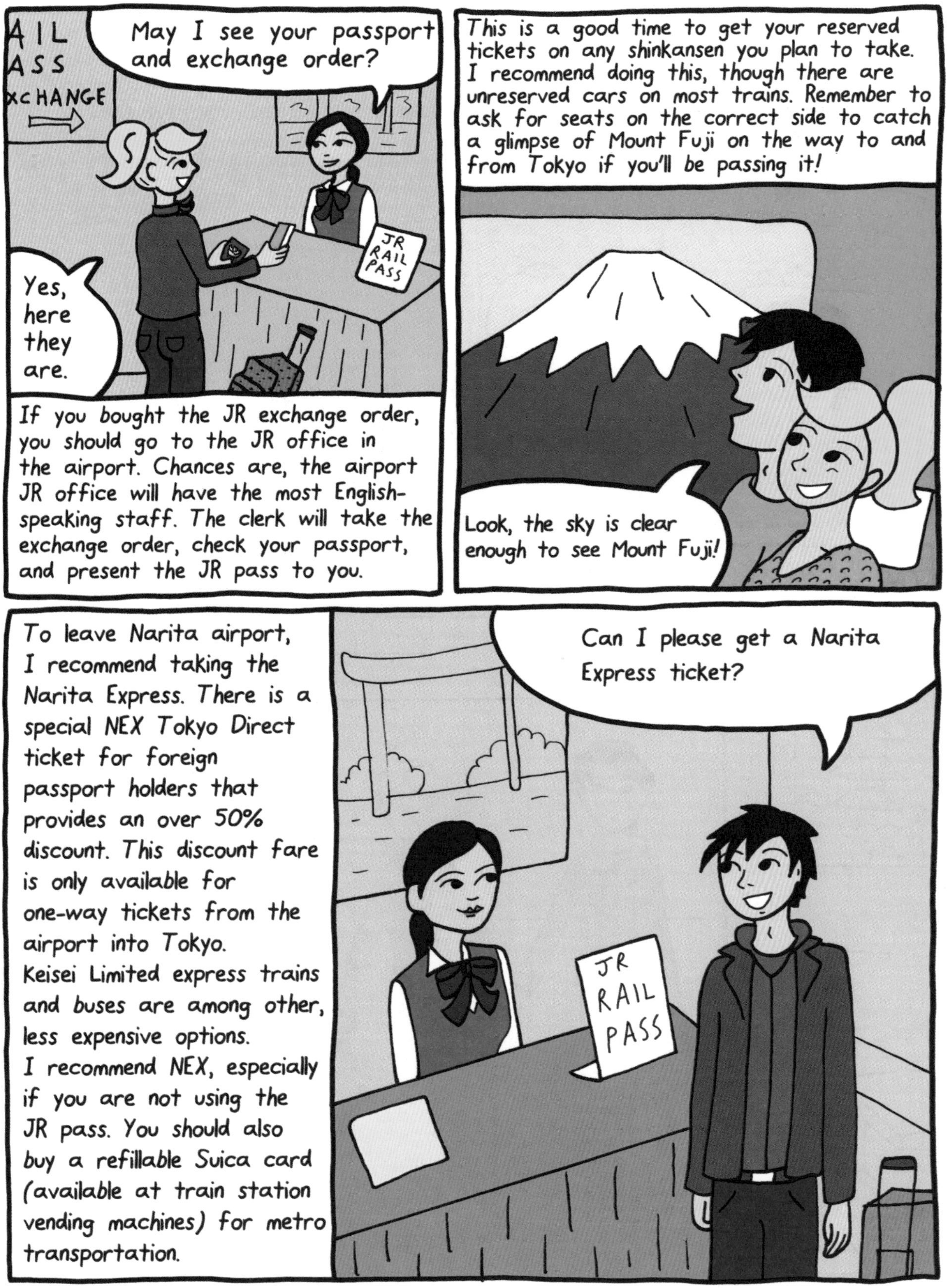
AIL
ASS
XCHANGE
May I see your passport and exchange order?
JR RAIL PASS
Yes, here they are.
If you bought the JR exchange order, you should go to the JR office in the airport. Chances are, the airport JR office will have the most English-speaking staff. The clerk will take the exchange order, check your passport, and present the JR pass to you.
This is a good time to get your reserved tickets on any shinkansen you plan to take. I recommend doing this, though there are unreserved cars on most trains. Remember to ask for seats on the correct side to catch a glimpse of Mount Fuji on the way to and from Tokyo if you'll be passing it!
Look, the sky is clear enough to see Mount Fuji!
To leave Narita airport, I recommend taking the Narita Express. There is a special NEX Tokyo Direct ticket for foreign passport holders that provides an over 50% discount. This discount fare is only available for one-way tickets from the airport into Tokyo. Keisei Limited express trains and buses are among other, less expensive options. I recommend NEX, especially if you are not using the JR pass. You should also buy a refillable Suica card (available at train station vending machines) for metro transportation.
Can I please get a Narita Express ticket?
JR RAIL PASS

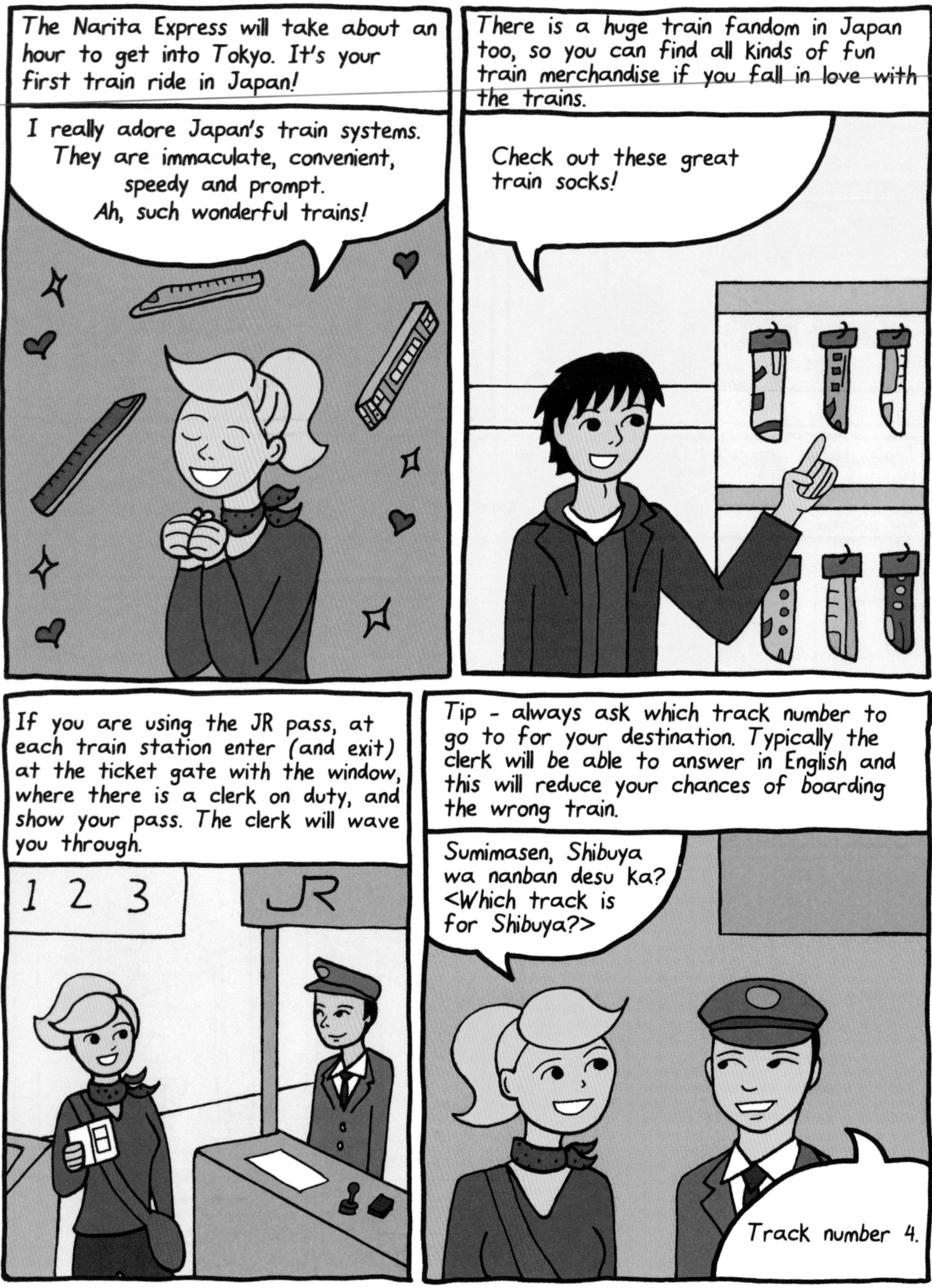
The Narita Express will take about an hour to get into Tokyo. It's your first train ride in Japan!
I really adore Japan's train systems. They are immaculate, convenient, speedy and prompt. Ah, such wonderful trains!
There is a huge train fandom in Japan too, so you can find all kinds of fun train merchandise if you fall in love with the trains.
Check out these great train socks!
If you are using the JR pass, at each train station enter (and exit) at the ticket gate with the window, where there is a clerk on duty, and show your pass. The clerk will wave you through.
1 2 3
JR
Tip - always ask which track number to go to for your destination. Typically the clerk will be able to answer in English and this will reduce your chances of boarding the wrong train.
Sumimasen, Shibuya wa nanban desu ka? <Which track is for Shibuya?>
Track number 4.

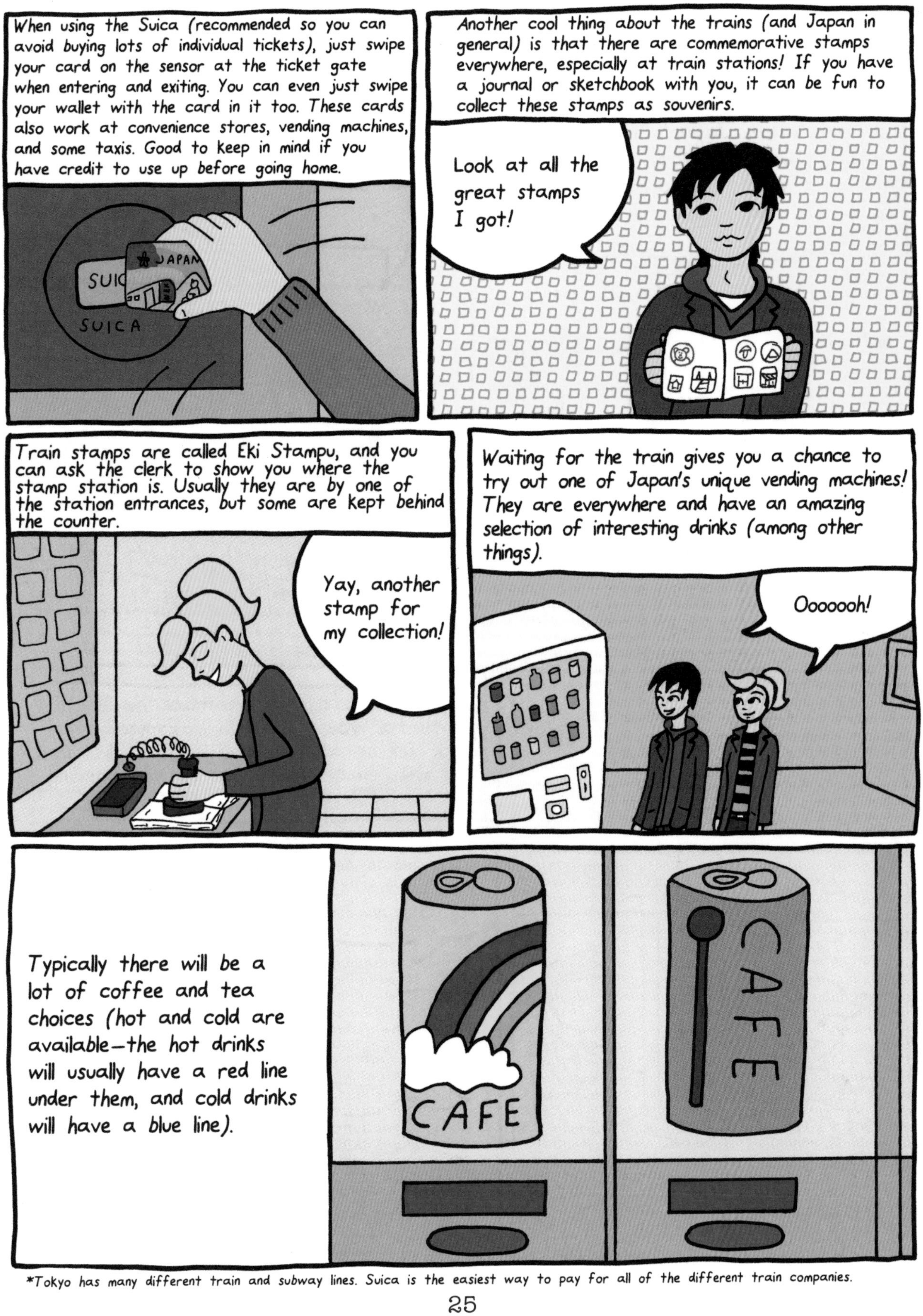
When using the Suica (recommended so you can avoid buying lots of individual tickets), just swipe your card on the sensor at the ticket gate when entering and exiting. You can even just swipe your wallet with the card in it too. These cards also work at convenience stores, vending machines, and some taxis. Good to keep in mind if you have credit to use up before going home.
SUICA
Another cool thing about the trains (and Japan in general) is that there are commemorative stamps everywhere, especially at train stations! If you have a journal or sketchbook with you, it can be fun to collect these stamps as souvenirs.
Look at all the great stamps I got!
Train stamps are called Eki Stampu, and you can ask the clerk to show you where the stamp station is. Usually they are by one of the station entrances, but some are kept behind the counter.
Yay, another stamp for my collection!
Waiting for the train gives you a chance to try out one of Japan's unique vending machines! They are everywhere and have an amazing selection of interesting drinks (among other things).
Oooooh!
Typically there will be a lot of coffee and tea choices (hot and cold are available—the hot drinks will usually have a red line under them, and cold drinks will have a blue line).
CAFE
CAFE

*Tokyo has many different train and subway lines. Suica is the easiest way to pay for all of the different train companies.

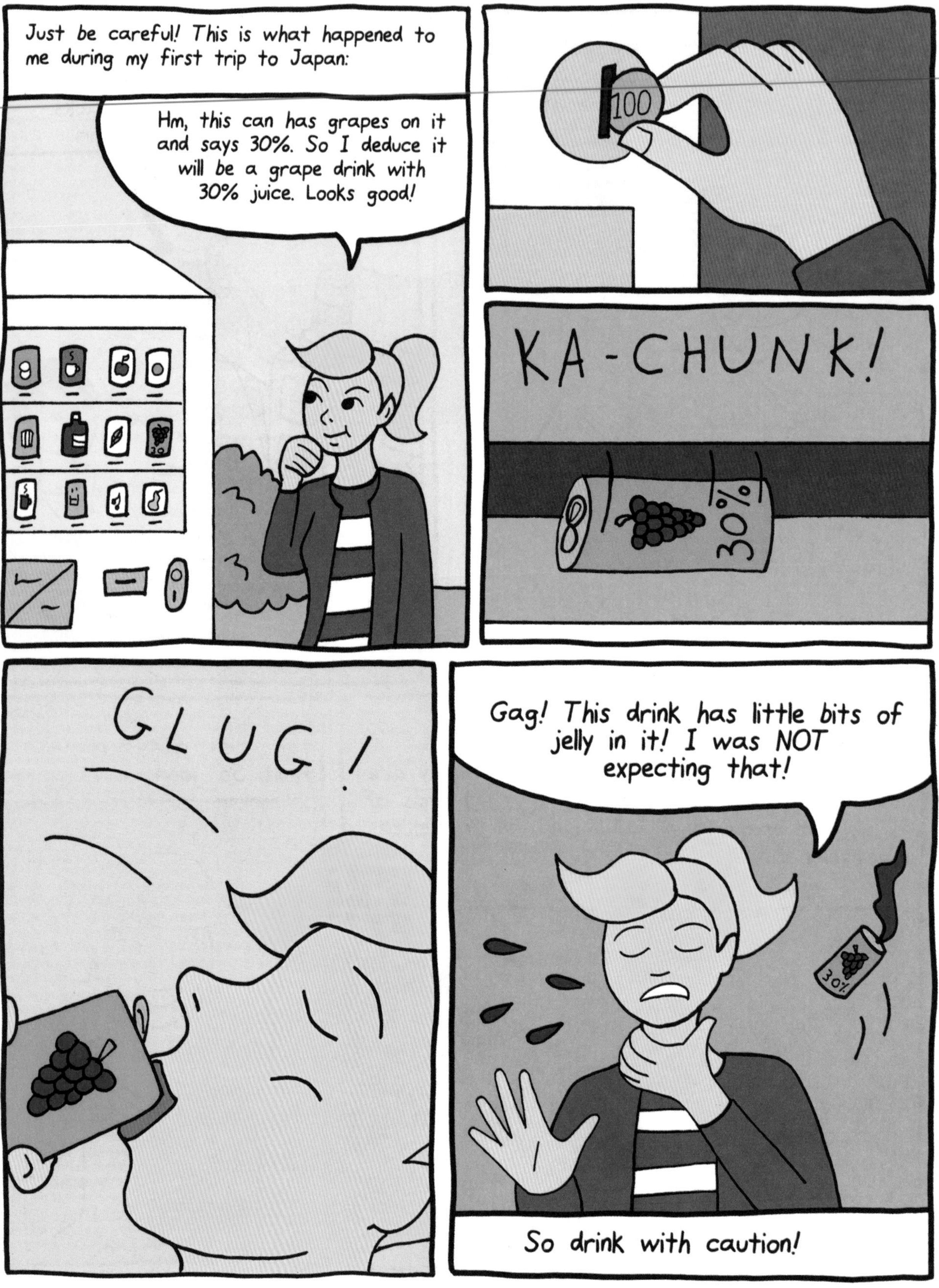
Just be careful! This is what happened to me during my first trip to Japan:
Hm, this can has grapes on it and says 30%. So I deduce it will be a grape drink with 30% juice. Looks good!
100
KA-CHUNK!
30%
GLUG!
Gag! This drink has little bits of jelly in it! I was NOT expecting that!
30%
So drink with caution!

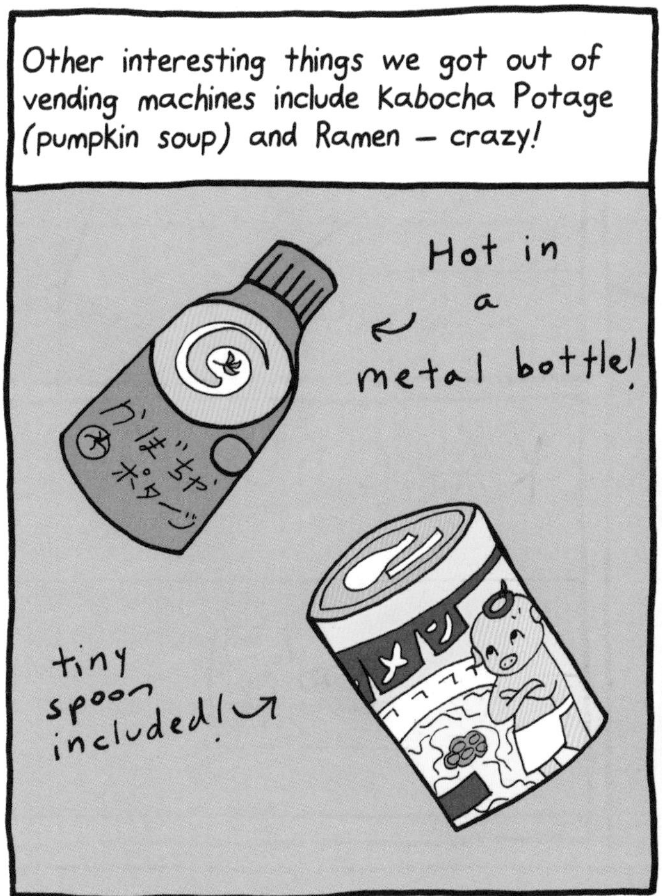
Other interesting things we got out of vending machines include Kabocha Potage (pumpkin soup) and Ramen – crazy!
Hot in a metal bottle!
tiny spoon included!

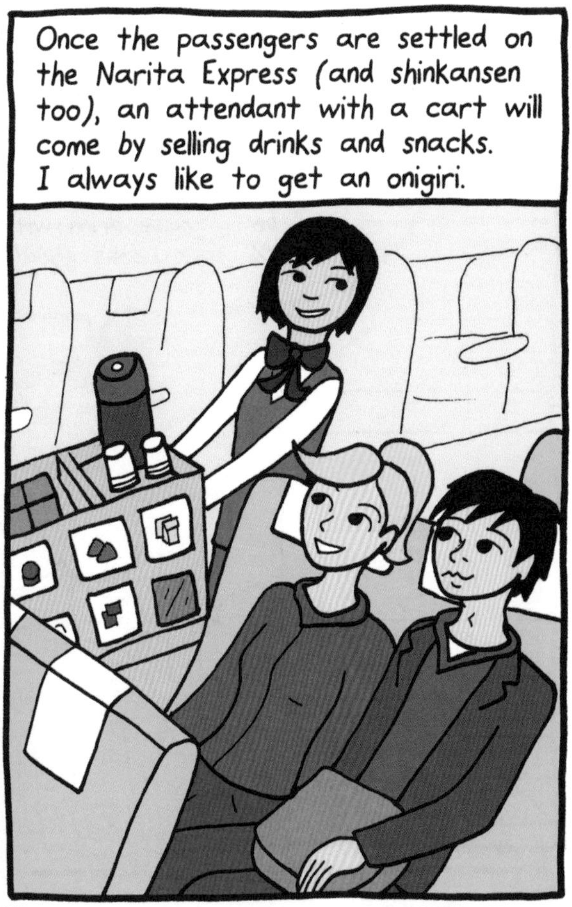
Once the passengers are settled on the Narita Express (and shinkansen too), an attendant with a cart will come by selling drinks and snacks. I always like to get an onigiri.

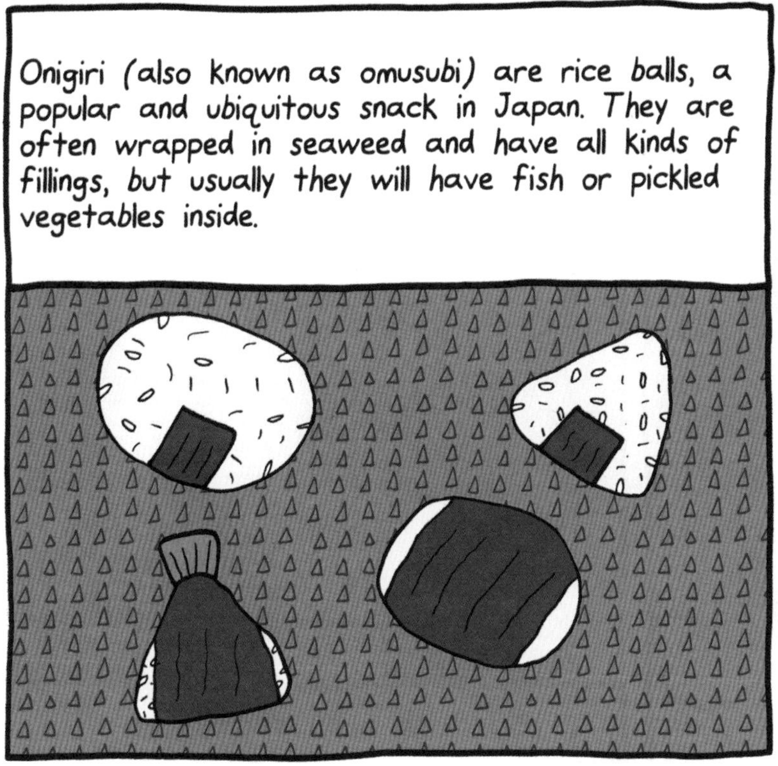
Onigiri (also known as omusubi) are rice balls, a popular and ubiquitous snack in Japan. They are often wrapped in seaweed and have all kinds of fillings, but usually they will have fish or pickled vegetables inside.

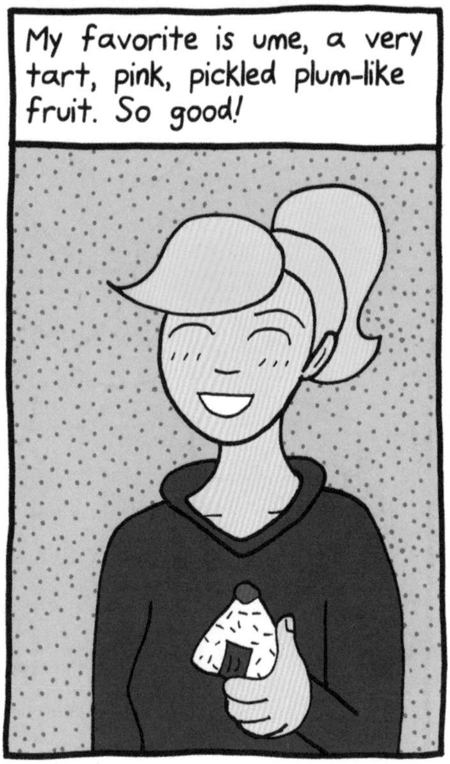
My favorite is ume, a very tart, pink, pickled plum-like fruit. So good!

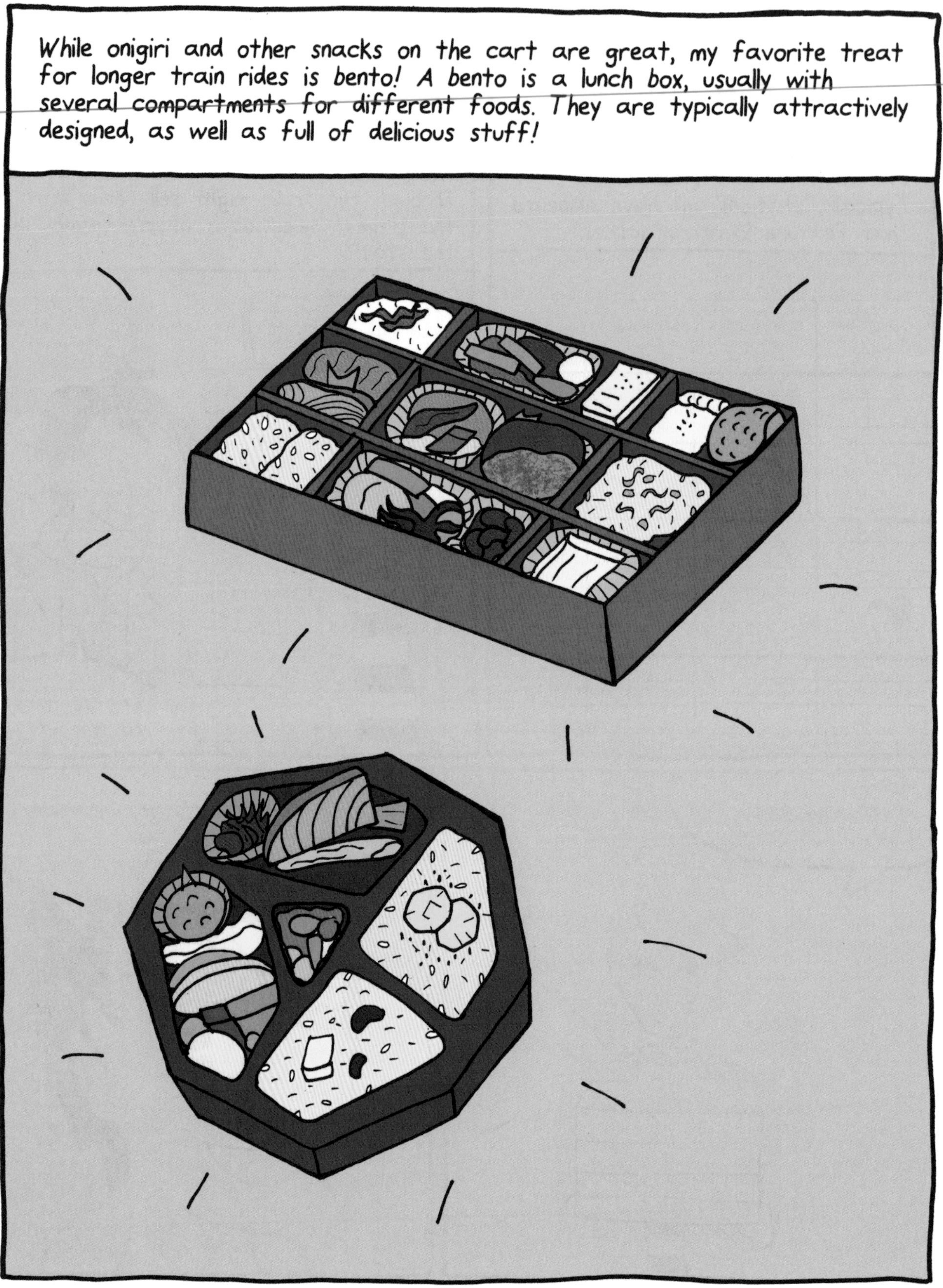
While onigiri and other snacks on the cart are great, my favorite treat for longer train rides is bento! A bento is a lunch box, usually with several compartments for different foods. They are typically attractively designed, as well as full of delicious stuff!

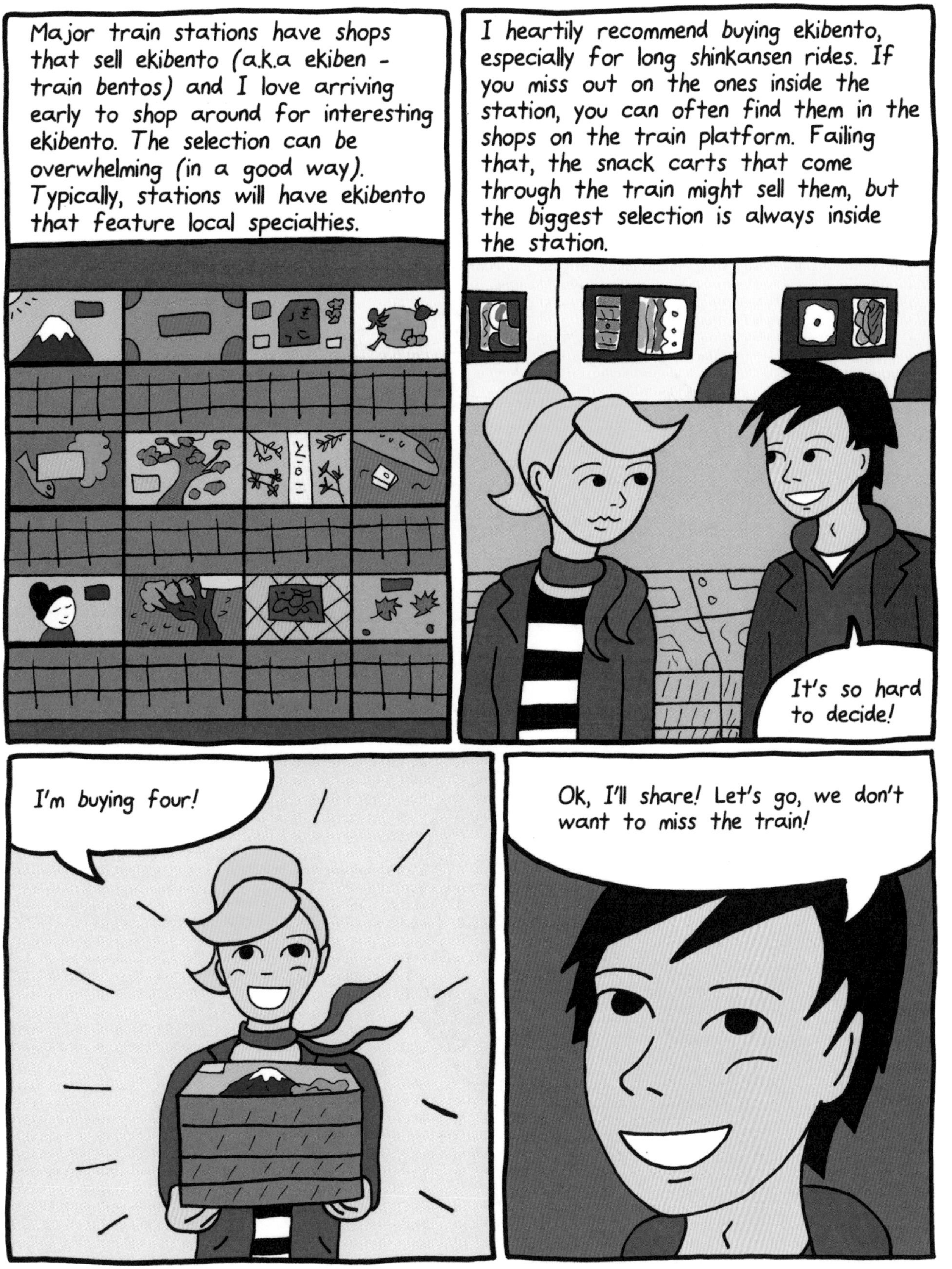
Major train stations have shops that sell ekibento (a.k.a ekiben - train bentos) and I love arriving early to shop around for interesting ekibento. The selection can be overwhelming (in a good way). Typically, stations will have ekibento that feature local specialties.
I heartily recommend buying ekibento, especially for long shinkansen rides. If you miss out on the ones inside the station, you can often find them in the shops on the train platform. Failing that, the snack carts that come through the train might sell them, but the biggest selection is always inside the station.
It's so hard to decide!
I'm buying four!
Ok, I'll share! Let's go, we don't want to miss the train!

Let's learn new words with Kitty Sweet Tooth!

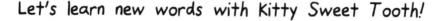

Chapter 3 introduces you to:

Depato - department store

Irasshaimase! - Welcome!

Taiyaki - fish-shaped cake filled with sweet bean

Combini - convenience store

Oishii - delicious

Omiyage - souvenir gifts (often food)

Kaitenzushi - conveyer belt sushi

Ramen - noodle soup

Okonomiyaki - savory pancake

Takoyaki - octopus balls

kaiseki ryori - traditional multi-course meal

Sofuto kureemu - soft-serve ice cream

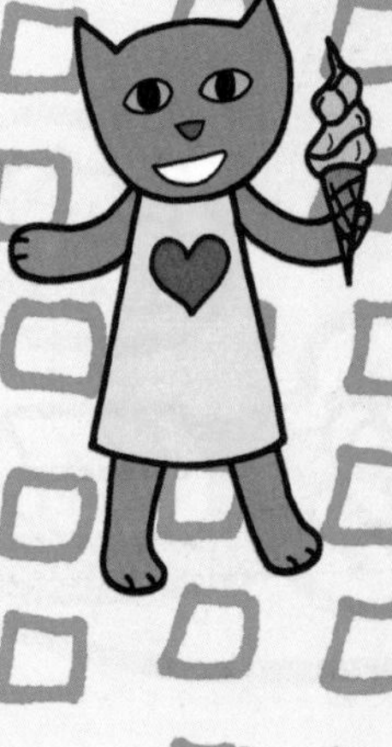

Chapter 3

What Will We Eat?

Food is a reason in itself to go to Japan. It's such a pleasure for me to try new foods when I travel, and Japan is a favorite food destination!

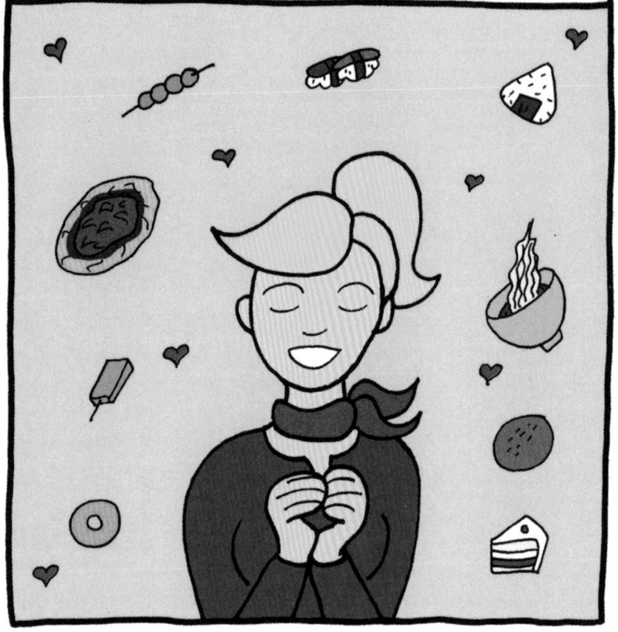

Every region has its specialties, and traditional foods are highly valued. At the same time, Japan's technology and innovations are very present in the food culture.

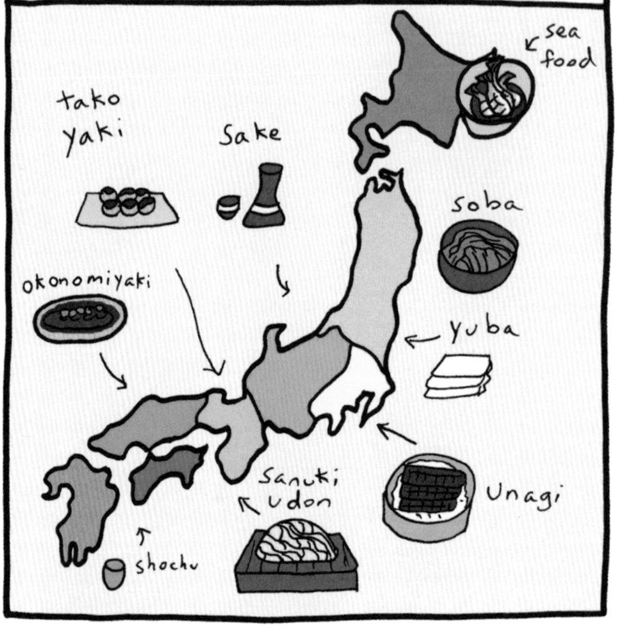
sea food
tako yaki
Sake
soba
okonomiyaki
yuba
Sanuki udon
Unagi
shochu

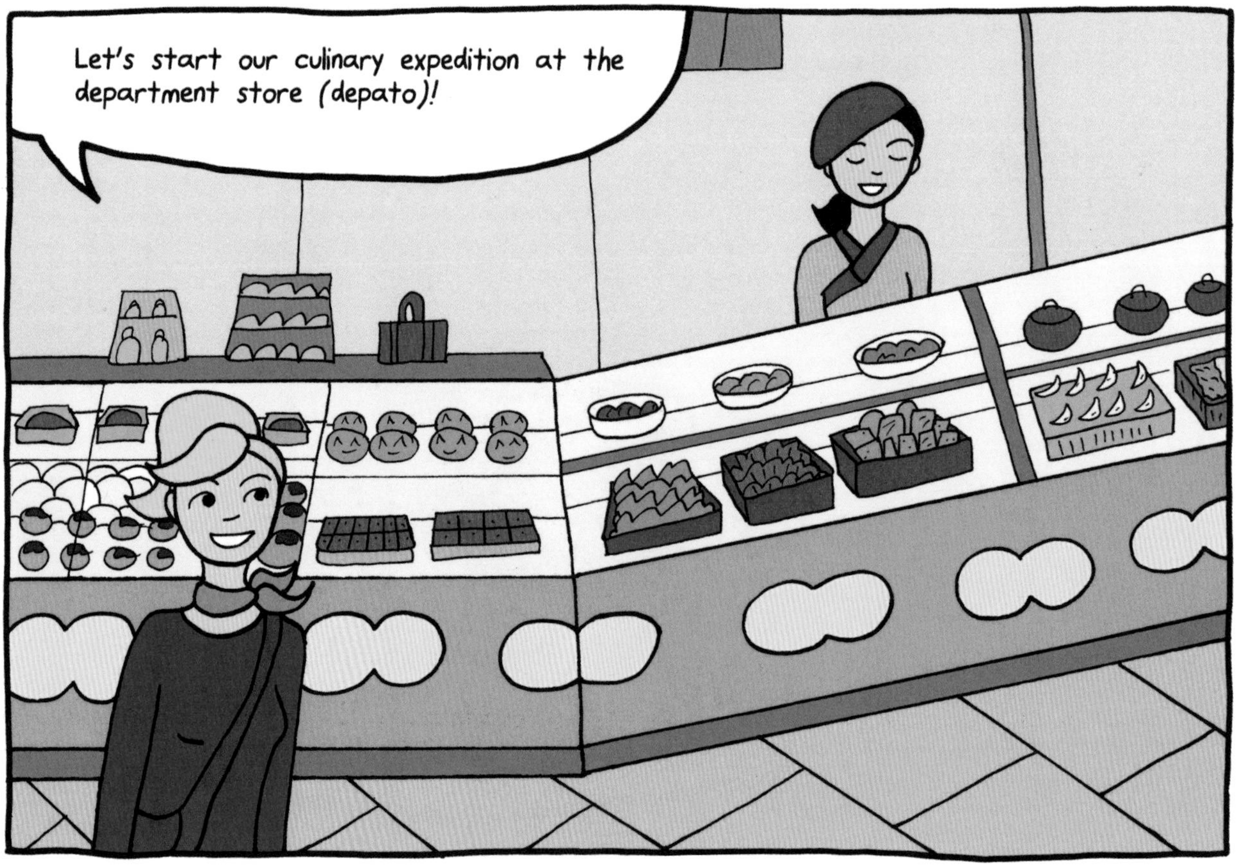
Let's start our culinary expedition at the department store (depato)!

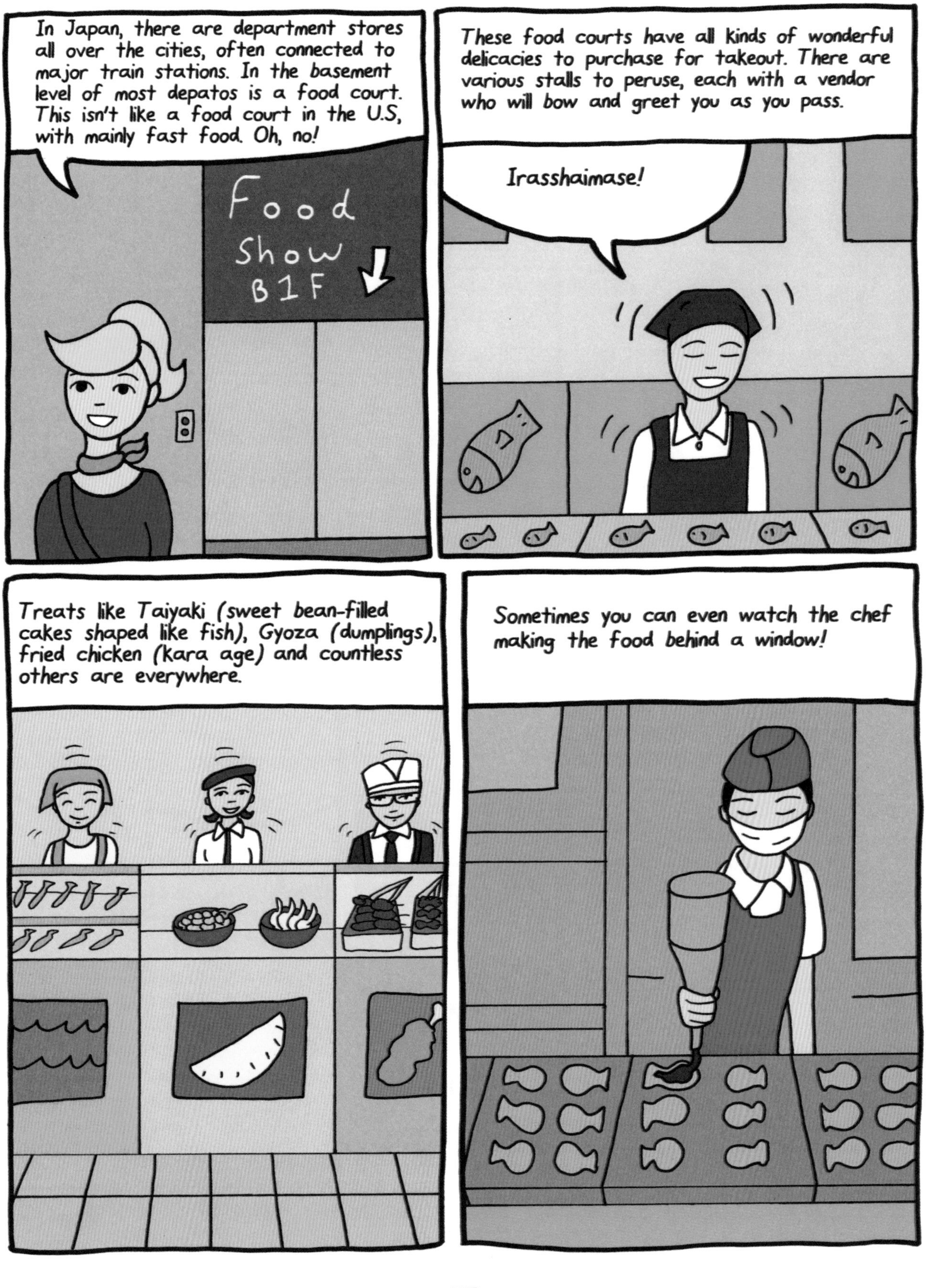
In Japan, there are department stores all over the cities, often connected to major train stations. In the basement level of most depatos is a food court. This isn't like a food court in the U.S, with mainly fast food. Oh, no!
Food Show B1F
These food courts have all kinds of wonderful delicacies to purchase for takeout. There are various stalls to peruse, each with a vendor who will bow and greet you as you pass.
Irasshaimase!
Treats like Taiyaki (sweet bean-filled cakes shaped like fish), Gyoza (dumplings), fried chicken (kara age) and countless others are everywhere.
Sometimes you can even watch the chef making the food behind a window!

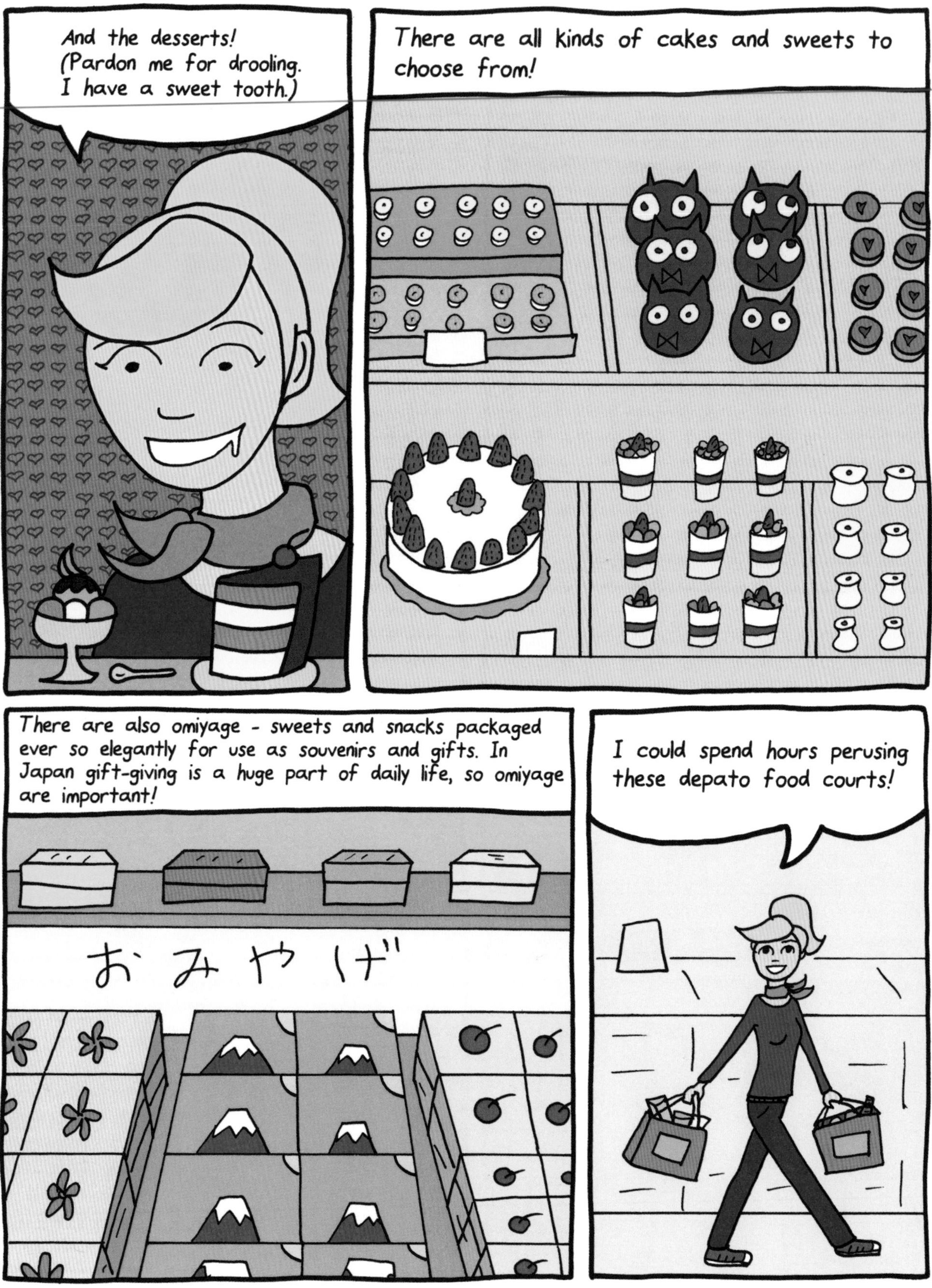

And the desserts! (Pardon me for drooling. I have a sweet tooth.)
There are all kinds of cakes and sweets to choose from!
There are also omiyage - sweets and snacks packaged ever so elegantly for use as souvenirs and gifts. In Japan gift-giving is a huge part of daily life, so omiyage are important!
おみやげ
I could spend hours perusing these depato food courts!

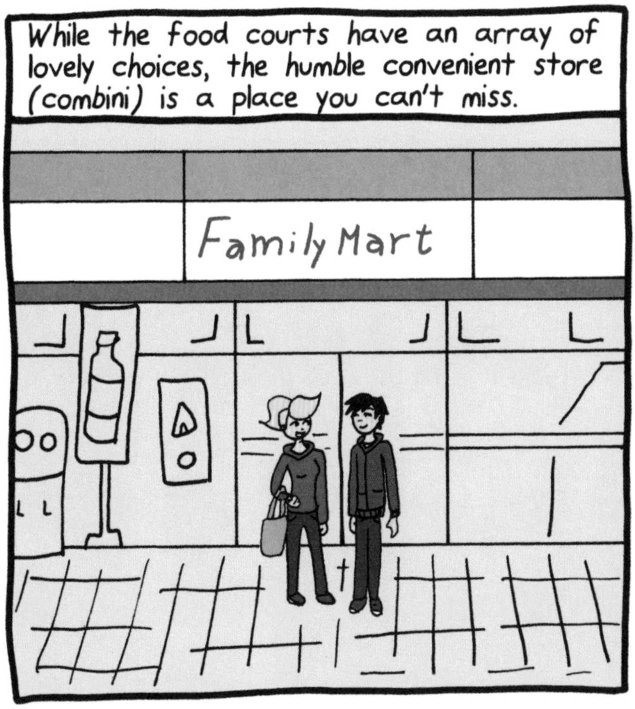
While the food courts have an array of lovely choices, the humble convenient store (combini) is a place you can't miss.
Family Mart

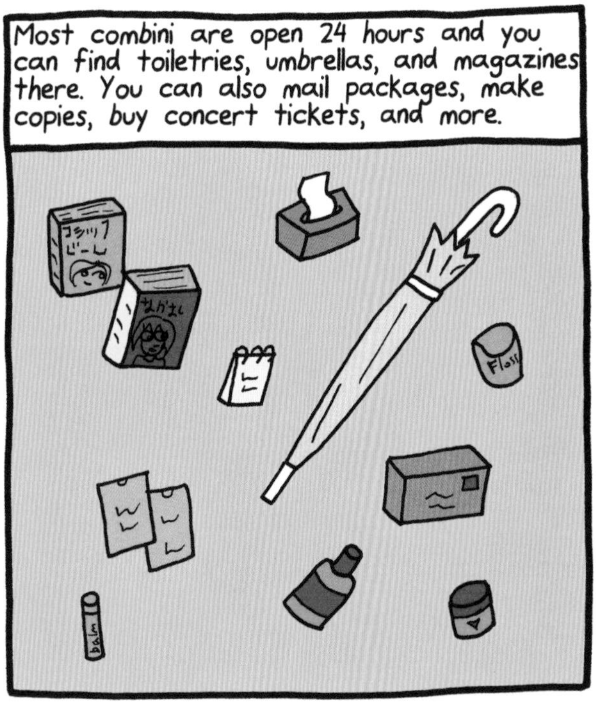
Most combini are open 24 hours and you can find toiletries, umbrellas, and magazines there. You can also mail packages, make copies, buy concert tickets, and more.
Floss
balm

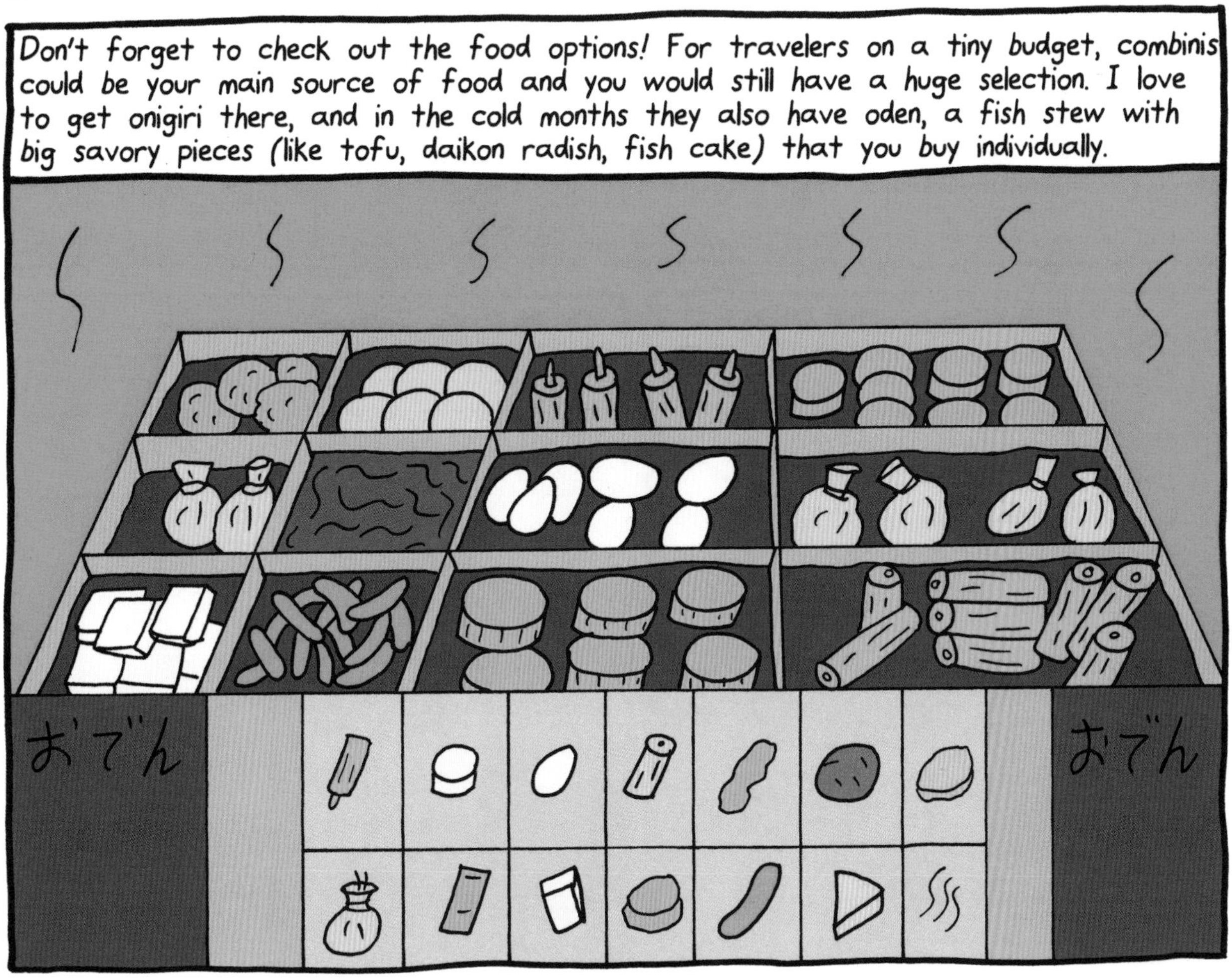
Don't forget to check out the food options! For travelers on a tiny budget, combinis could be your main source of food and you would still have a huge selection. I love to get onigiri there, and in the cold months they also have oden, a fish stew with big savory pieces (like tofu, daikon radish, fish cake) that you buy individually.
おでん
おでん

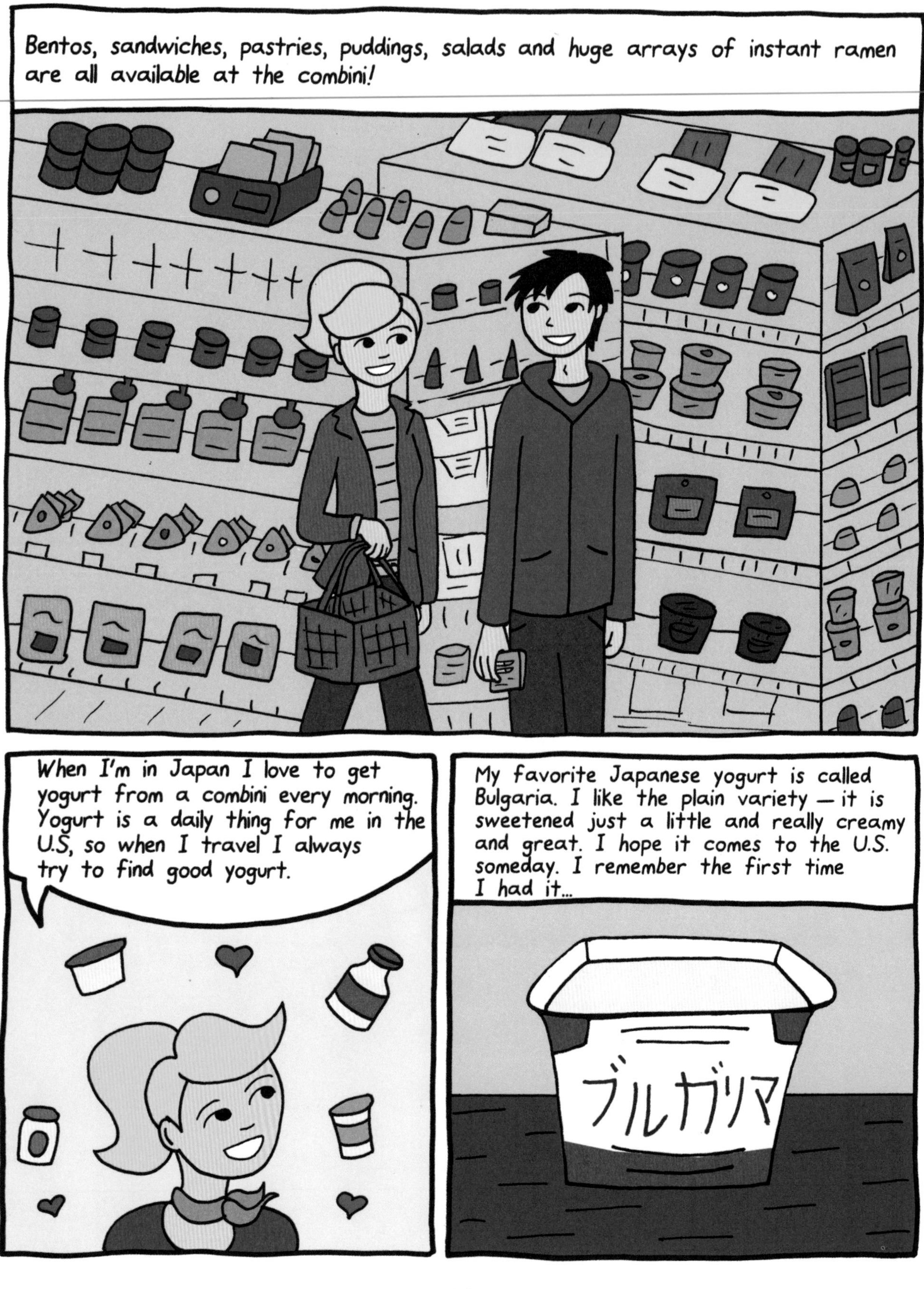
Bentos, sandwiches, pastries, puddings, salads and huge arrays of instant ramen are all available at the combini!
When I'm in Japan I love to get yogurt from a combini every morning. Yogurt is a daily thing for me in the U.S, so when I travel I always try to find good yogurt.
My favorite Japanese yogurt is called Bulgaria. I like the plain variety — it is sweetened just a little and really creamy and great. I hope it comes to the U.S. someday. I remember the first time I had it...
ブルガリア

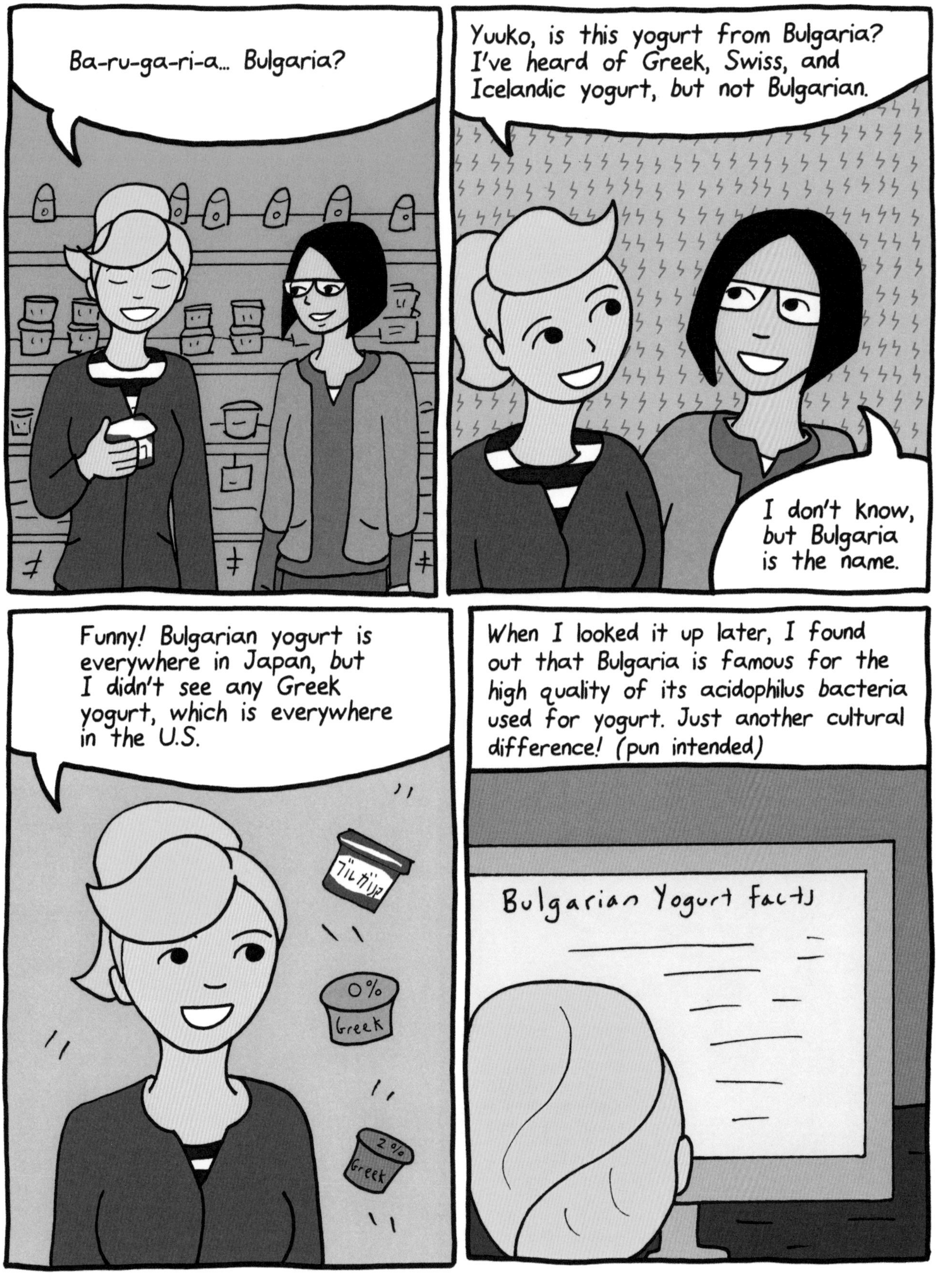
Ba-ru-ga-ri-a... Bulgaria?
Yuuko, is this yogurt from Bulgaria? I've heard of Greek, Swiss, and Icelandic yogurt, but not Bulgarian.
I don't know, but Bulgaria is the name.
Funny! Bulgarian yogurt is everywhere in Japan, but I didn't see any Greek yogurt, which is everywhere in the U.S.
ブルガリア
0%
Greek
2%
Greek
When I looked it up later, I found out that Bulgaria is famous for the high quality of its acidophilus bacteria used for yogurt. Just another cultural difference! (pun intended)
Bulgarian Yogurt facts

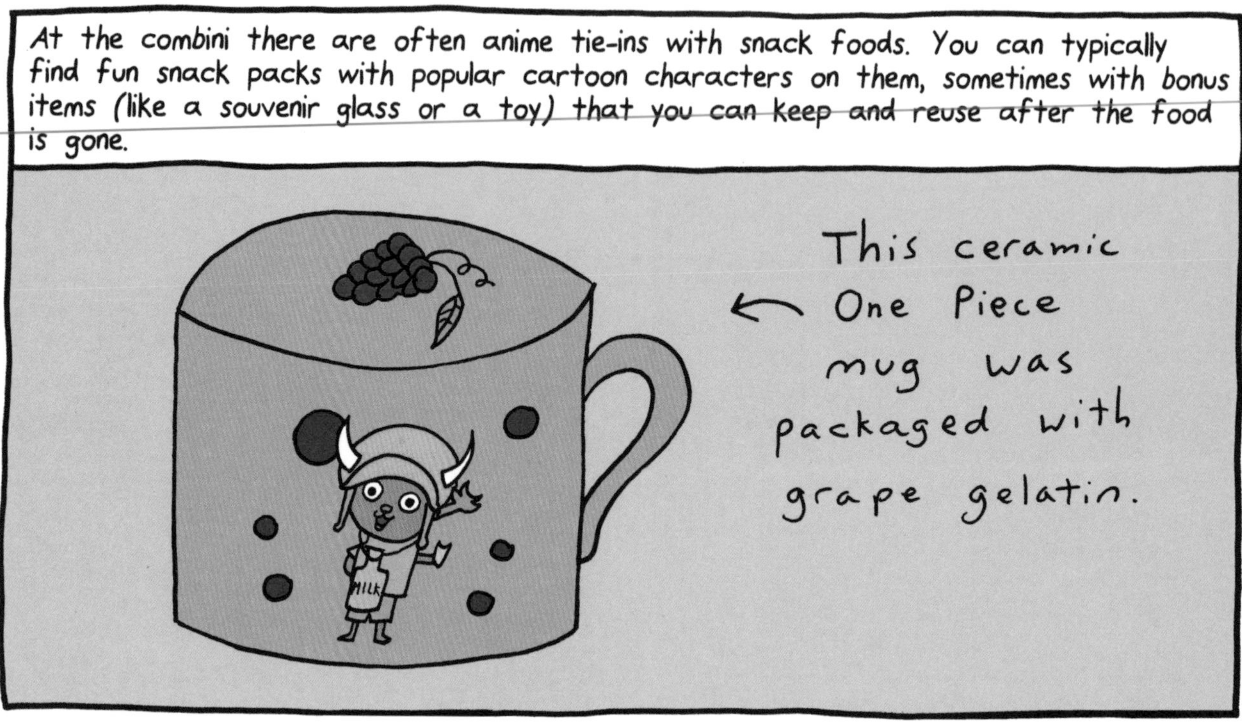
At the combini there are often anime tie-ins with snack foods. You can typically find fun snack packs with popular cartoon characters on them, sometimes with bonus items (like a souvenir glass or a toy) that you can keep and reuse after the food is gone.
This ceramic One Piece mug was packaged with grape gelatin.
MILK

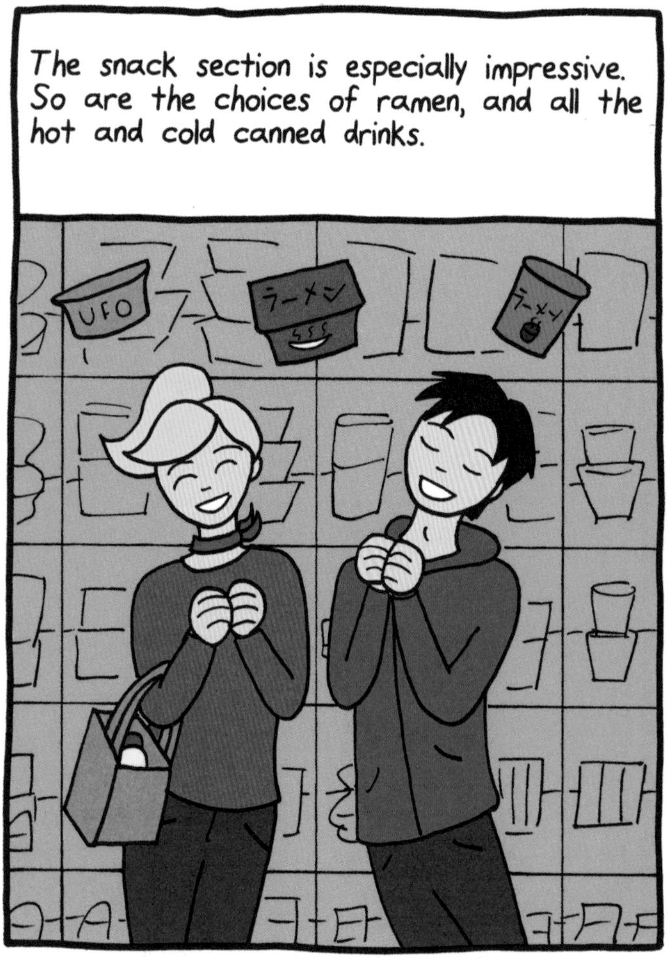
The snack section is especially impressive. So are the choices of ramen, and all the hot and cold canned drinks.
UFO
ラーメン

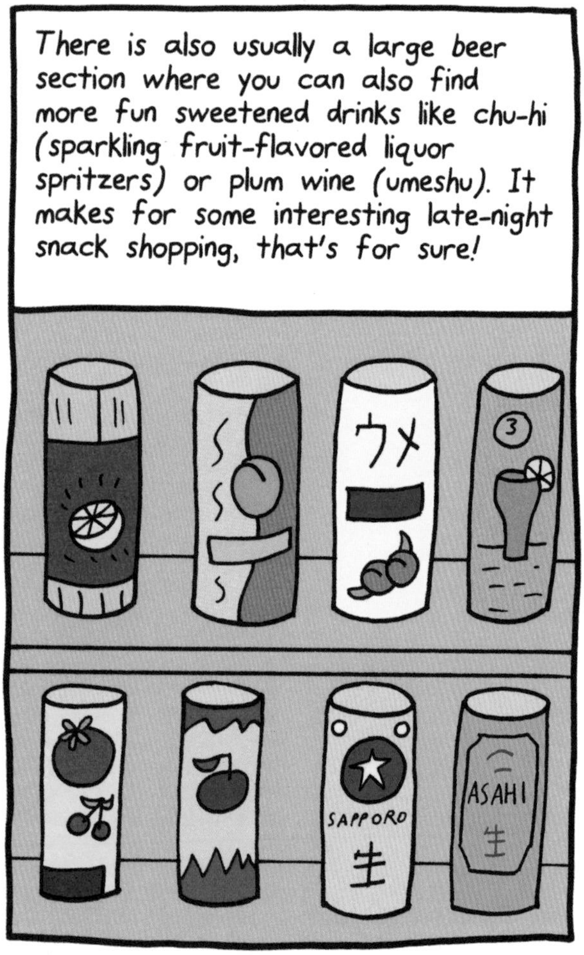
There is also usually a large beer section where you can also find more fun sweetened drinks like chu-hi (sparkling fruit-flavored liquor spritzers) or plum wine (umeshu). It makes for some interesting late-night snack shopping, that's for sure!
ウメ
SAPPORO
生
ASAHI
生

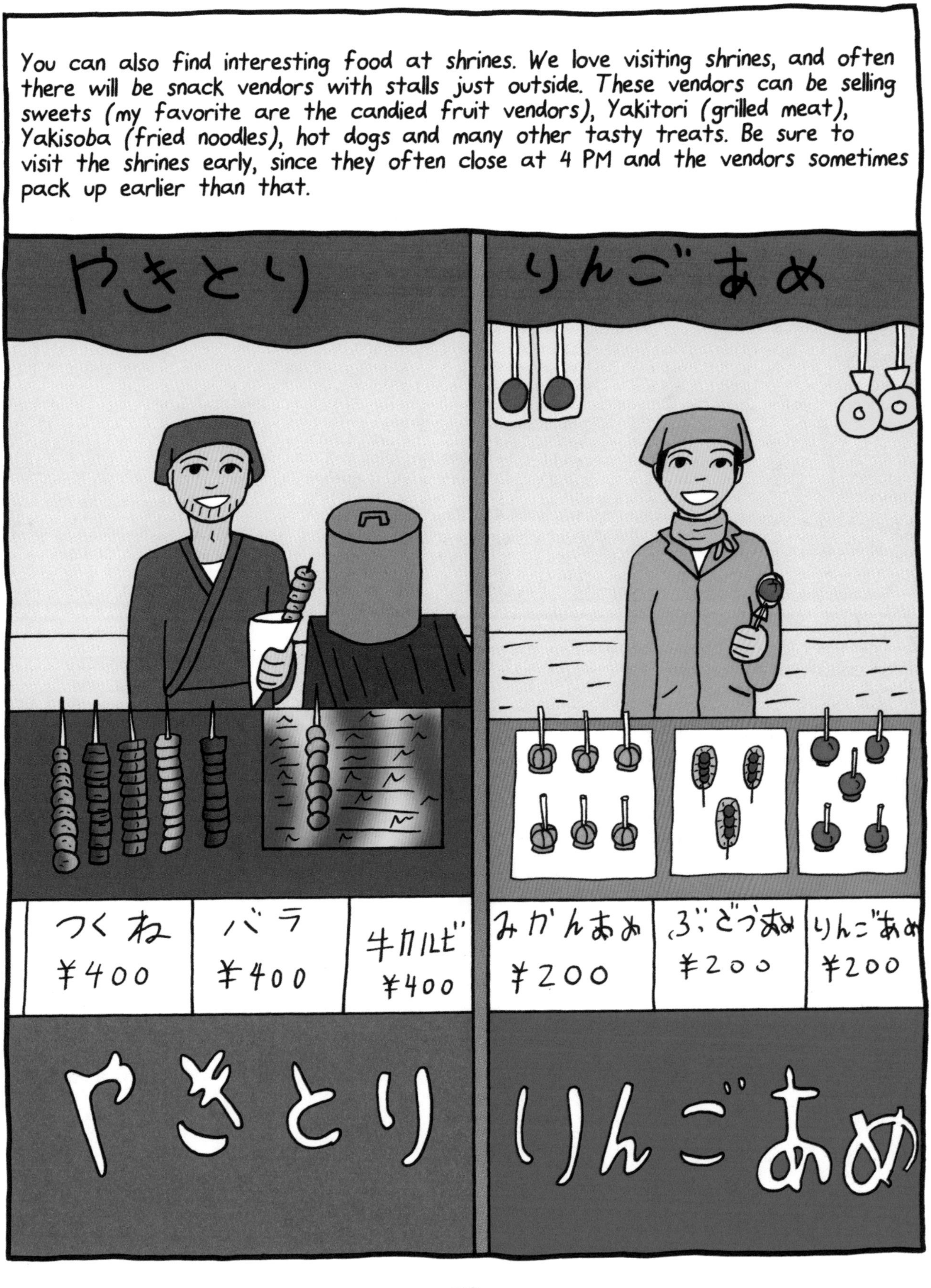
You can also find interesting food at shrines. We love visiting shrines, and often there will be snack vendors with stalls just outside. These vendors can be selling sweets (my favorite are the candied fruit vendors), Yakitori (grilled meat), Yakisoba (fried noodles), hot dogs and many other tasty treats. Be sure to visit the shrines early, since they often close at 4 PM and the vendors sometimes pack up earlier than that.
やきとり
りんごあめ
つくね ¥400
バラ ¥400
牛カルビ ¥400
みかんあめ ¥200
ぶどうあめ ¥200
りんごあめ ¥200
やきとり
りんごあめ

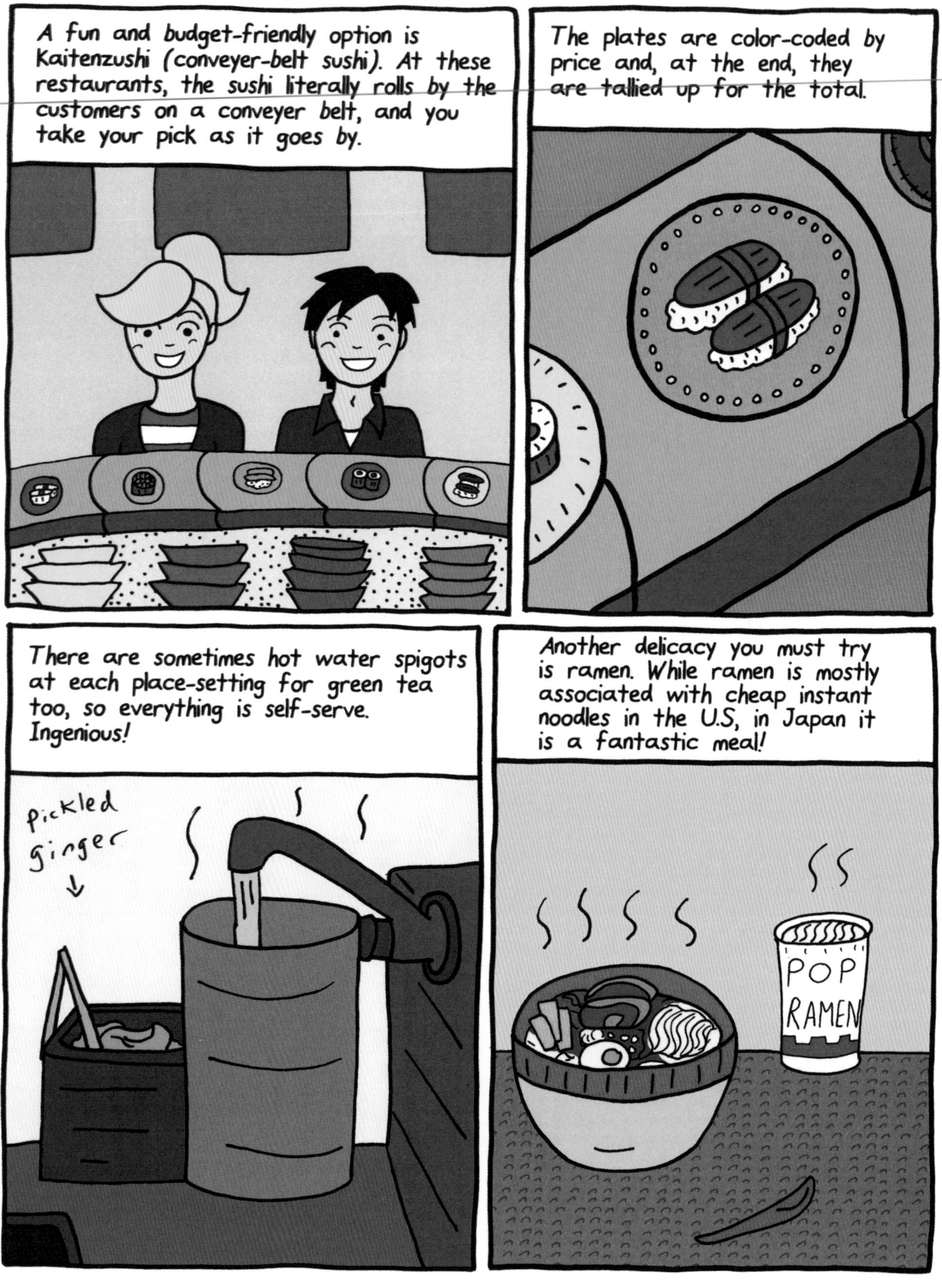
A fun and budget-friendly option is Kaitenzushi (conveyer-belt sushi). At these restaurants, the sushi literally rolls by the customers on a conveyer belt, and you take your pick as it goes by.
The plates are color-coded by price and, at the end, they are tallied up for the total.
There are sometimes hot water spigots at each place-setting for green tea too, so everything is self-serve. Ingenious!
pickled ginger
Another delicacy you must try is ramen. While ramen is mostly associated with cheap instant noodles in the U.S, in Japan it is a fantastic meal!
POP RAMEN

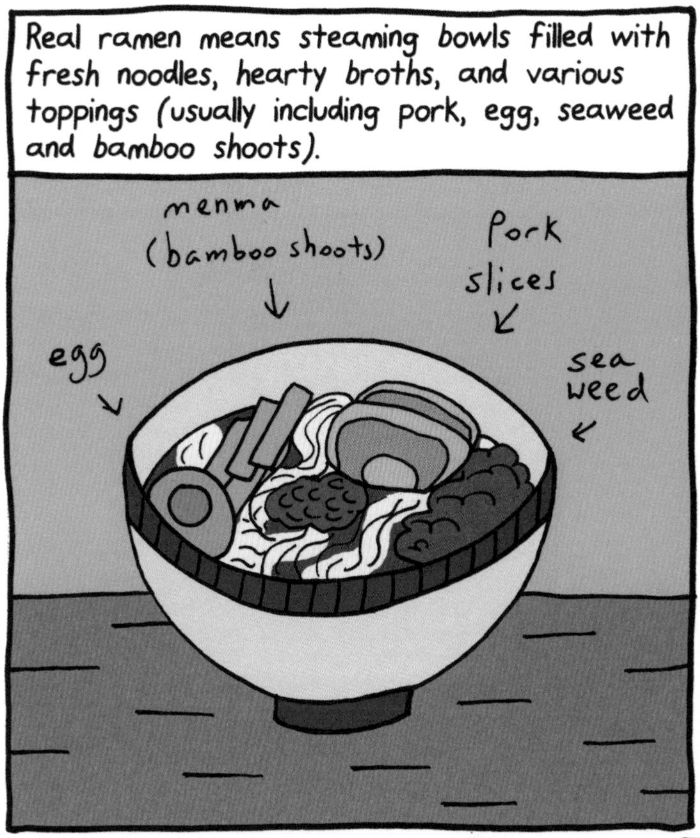
Real ramen means steaming bowls filled with fresh noodles, hearty broths, and various toppings (usually including pork, egg, seaweed and bamboo shoots).
menma (bamboo shoots)
pork slices
egg
sea weed

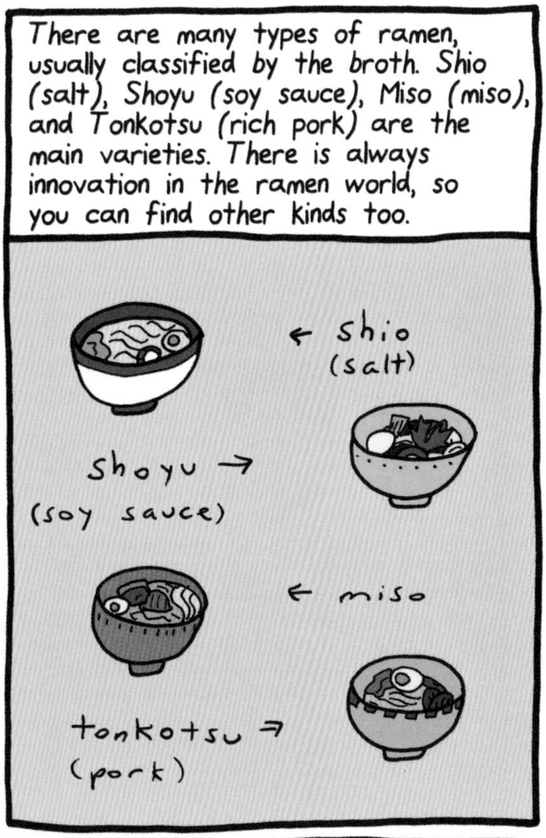
There are many types of ramen, usually classified by the broth. Shio (salt), Shoyu (soy sauce), Miso (miso), and Tonkotsu (rich pork) are the main varieties. There is always innovation in the ramen world, so you can find other kinds too.
shio (salt)
shoyu (soy sauce)
miso
tonkotsu (pork)

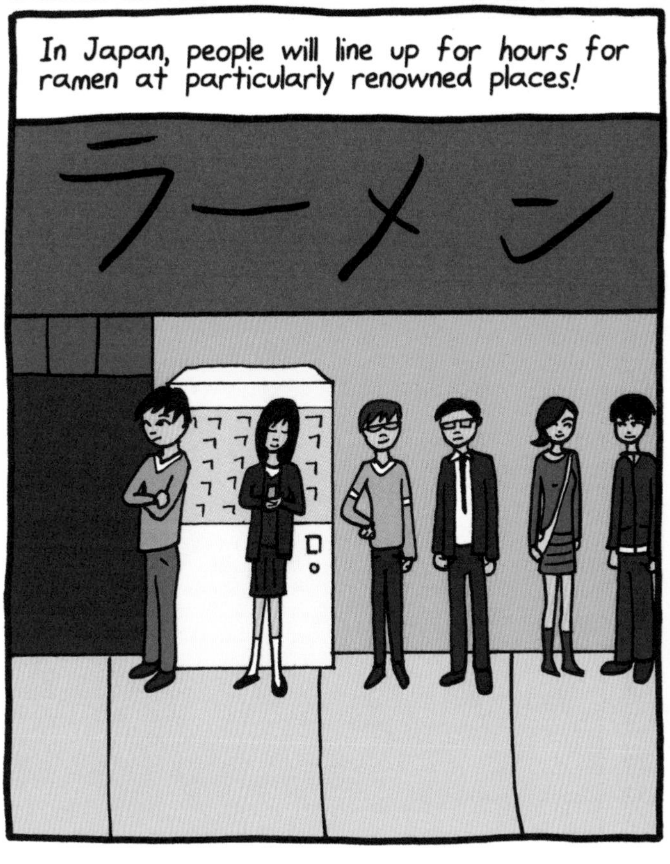
In Japan, people will line up for hours for ramen at particularly renowned places!
ラーメン

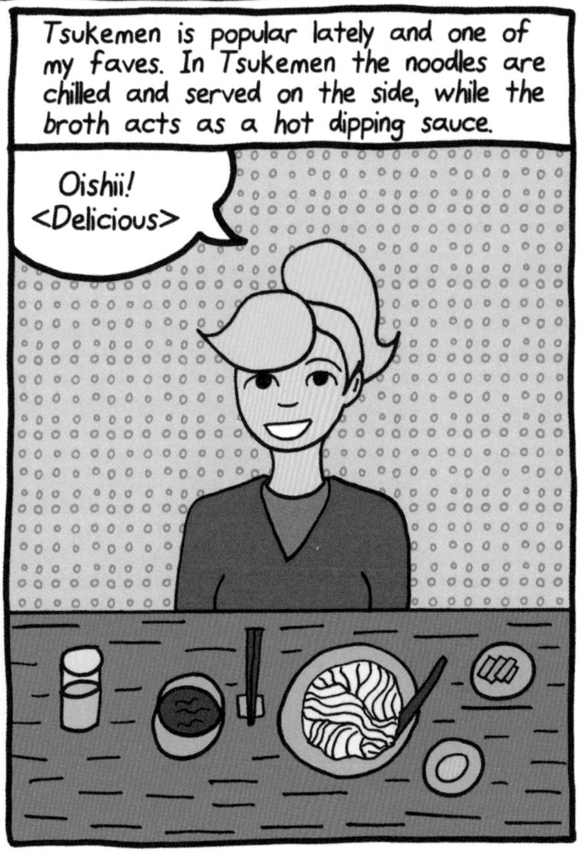
Tsukemen is popular lately and one of my faves. In Tsukemen the noodles are chilled and served on the side, while the broth acts as a hot dipping sauce.
Oishii! <Delicious>

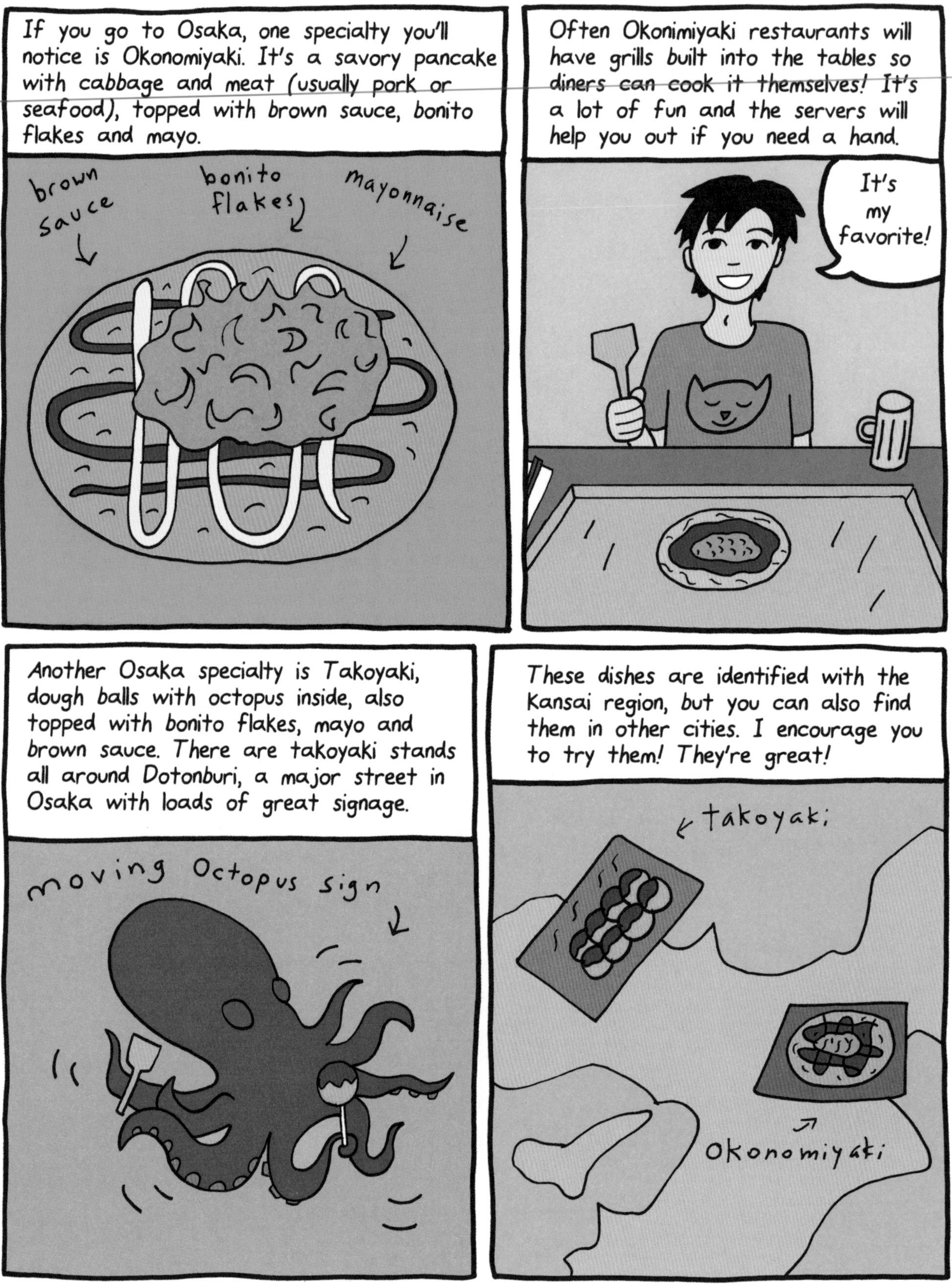
If you go to Osaka, one specialty you'll notice is Okonomiyaki. It's a savory pancake with cabbage and meat (usually pork or seafood), topped with brown sauce, bonito flakes and mayo.
brown sauce
bonito flakes
mayonnaise
Often Okonimiyaki restaurants will have grills built into the tables so diners can cook it themselves! It's a lot of fun and the servers will help you out if you need a hand.
It's my favorite!
Another Osaka specialty is Takoyaki, dough balls with octopus inside, also topped with bonito flakes, mayo and brown sauce. There are takoyaki stands all around Dotonburi, a major street in Osaka with loads of great signage.
moving Octopus sign
These dishes are identified with the Kansai region, but you can also find them in other cities. I encourage you to try them! They're great!
takoyaki
Okonomiyaki

For a more elegant experience you should try kaiseki, a traditional multi-course dinner. It's an elaborate feast that is often served at ryokan (traditional hotels) or kaiseki restaurants. It's not cheap, but this is a whole other level of dining. This classic style of cuisine is associated with Kyoto. It truly is a work of art!

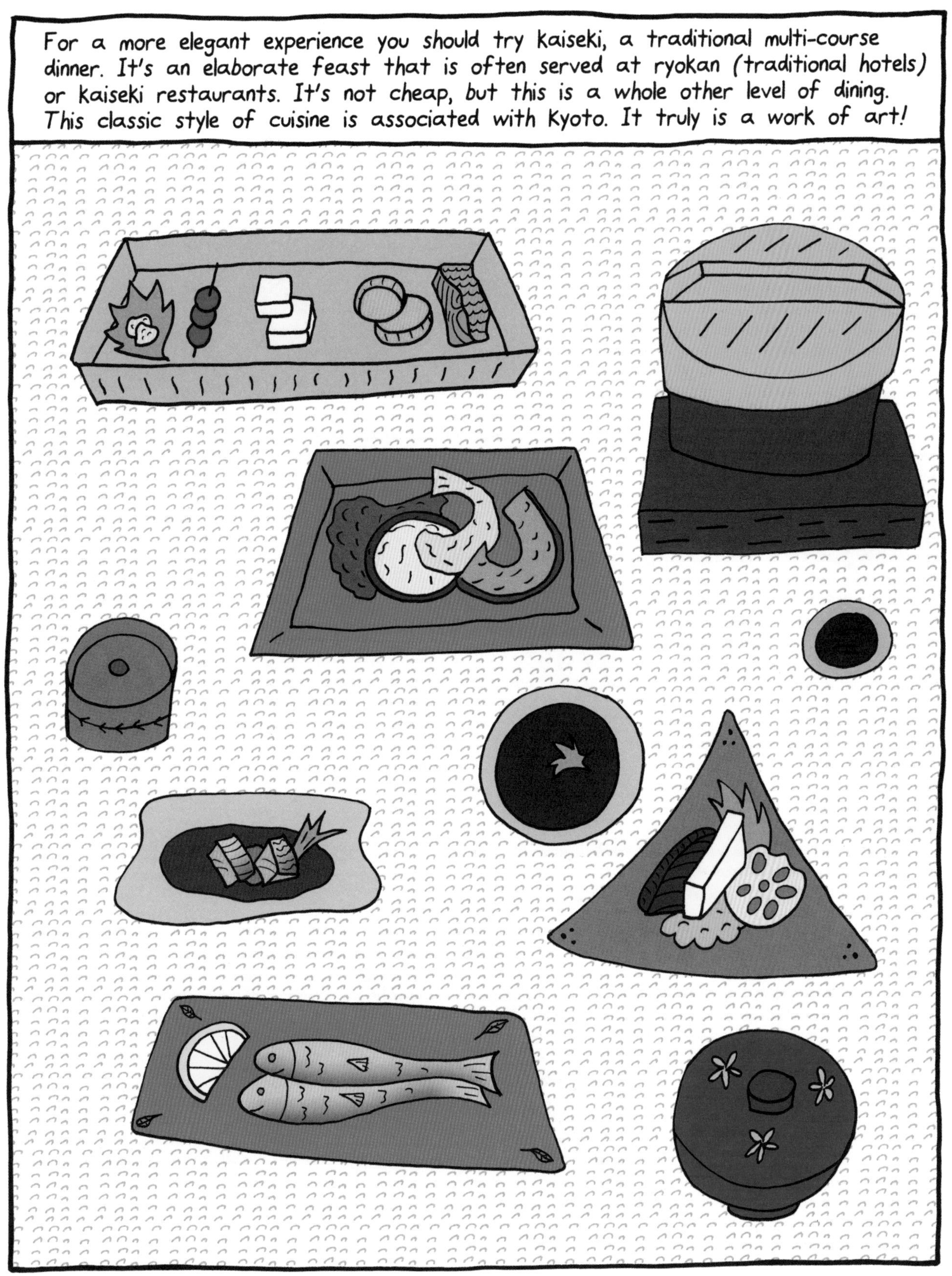

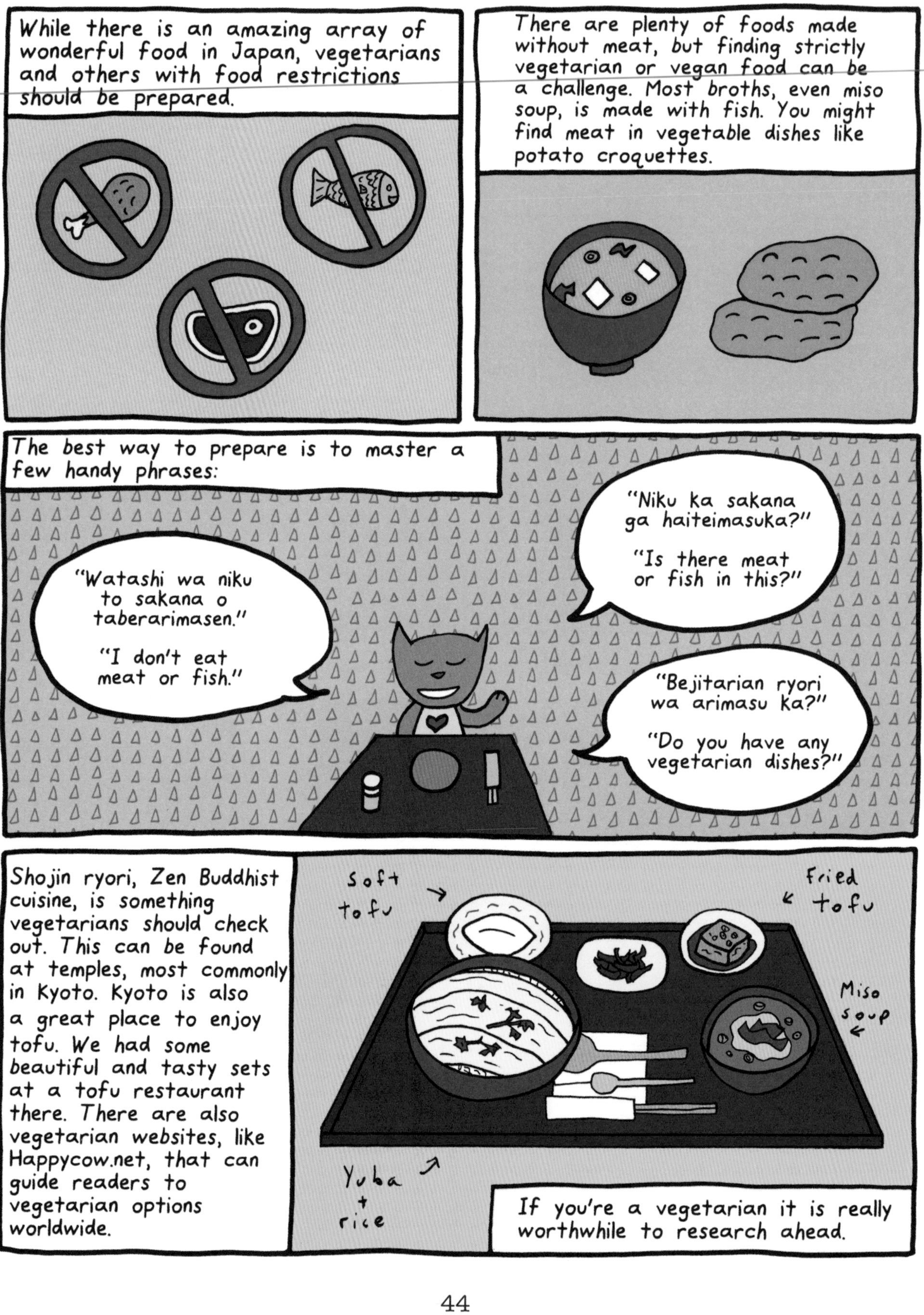
While there is an amazing array of wonderful food in Japan, vegetarians and others with food restrictions should be prepared.
There are plenty of foods made without meat, but finding strictly vegetarian or vegan food can be a challenge. Most broths, even miso soup, is made with fish. You might find meat in vegetable dishes like potato croquettes.
The best way to prepare is to master a few handy phrases:
"Watashi wa niku to sakana o taberarimasen." "I don't eat meat or fish."
"Niku ka sakana ga haiteimasuka?" "Is there meat or fish in this?"
"Bejitarian ryori wa arimasu ka?" "Do you have any vegetarian dishes?"
Shojin ryori, Zen Buddhist cuisine, is something vegetarians should check out. This can be found at temples, most commonly in Kyoto. Kyoto is also a great place to enjoy tofu. We had some beautiful and tasty sets at a tofu restaurant there. There are also vegetarian websites, like Happycow.net, that can guide readers to vegetarian options worldwide.
Soft tofu
Fried tofu
Miso soup
Yuba + rice
If you're a vegetarian it is really worthwhile to research ahead.

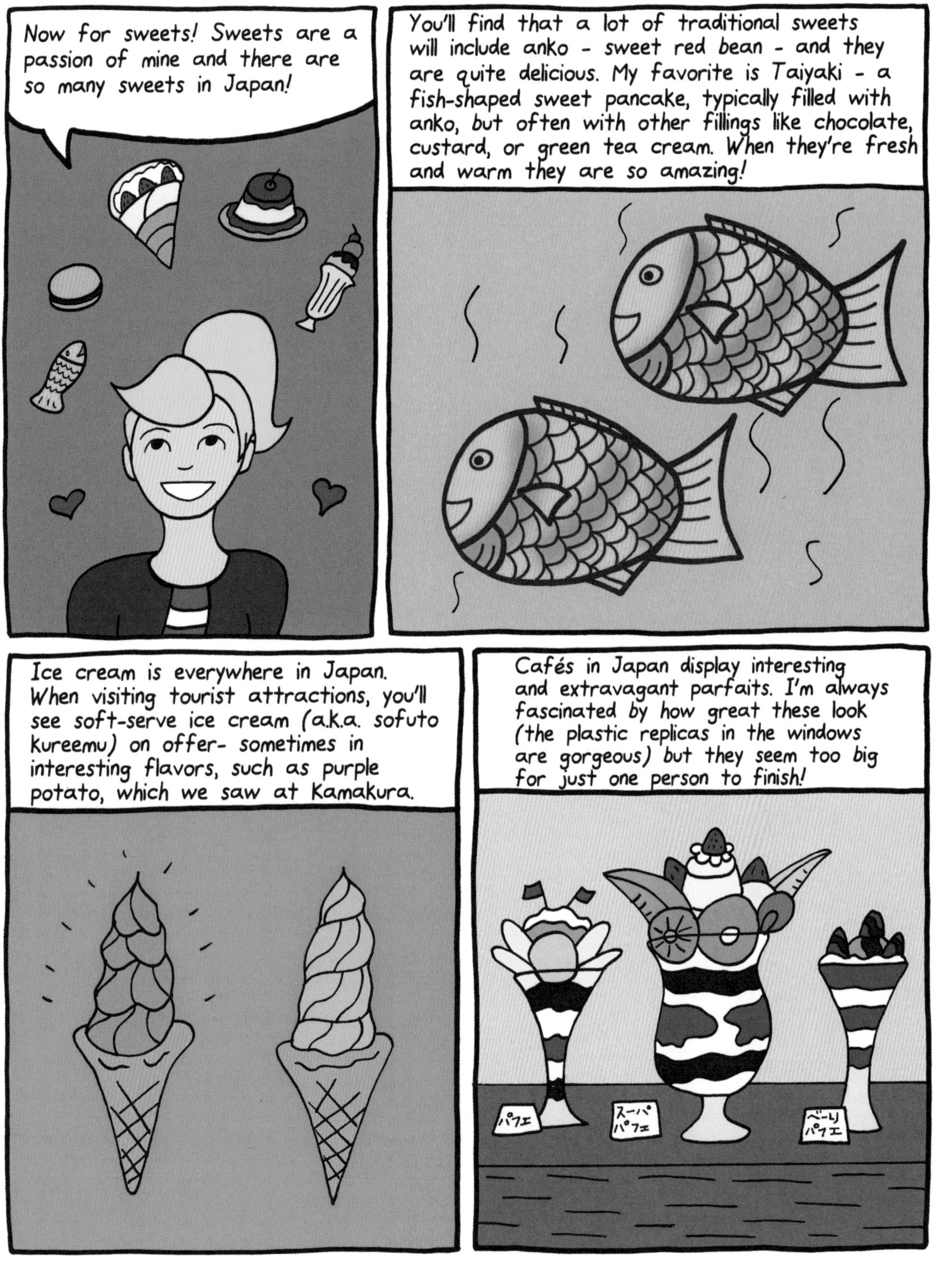

Now for sweets! Sweets are a passion of mine and there are so many sweets in Japan!
You'll find that a lot of traditional sweets will include anko - sweet red bean - and they are quite delicious. My favorite is Taiyaki - a fish-shaped sweet pancake, typically filled with anko, but often with other fillings like chocolate, custard, or green tea cream. When they're fresh and warm they are so amazing!
Ice cream is everywhere in Japan. When visiting tourist attractions, you'll see soft-serve ice cream (a.k.a. sofuto kureemu) on offer- sometimes in interesting flavors, such as purple potato, which we saw at Kamakura.
Cafés in Japan display interesting and extravagant parfaits. I'm always fascinated by how great these look (the plastic replicas in the windows are gorgeous) but they seem too big for just one person to finish!
パフェ
スーパ
パフェ
ベーリ
パフェ

French-style bakeries have proliferated in Japan and you can usually find some with interesting breads and sweets, often with Japanese fillings like curry, or even yakisoba inside a roll! Thick white bread toast is popular too. Really, you can find so many great baked goods in Japan, everywhere you go!

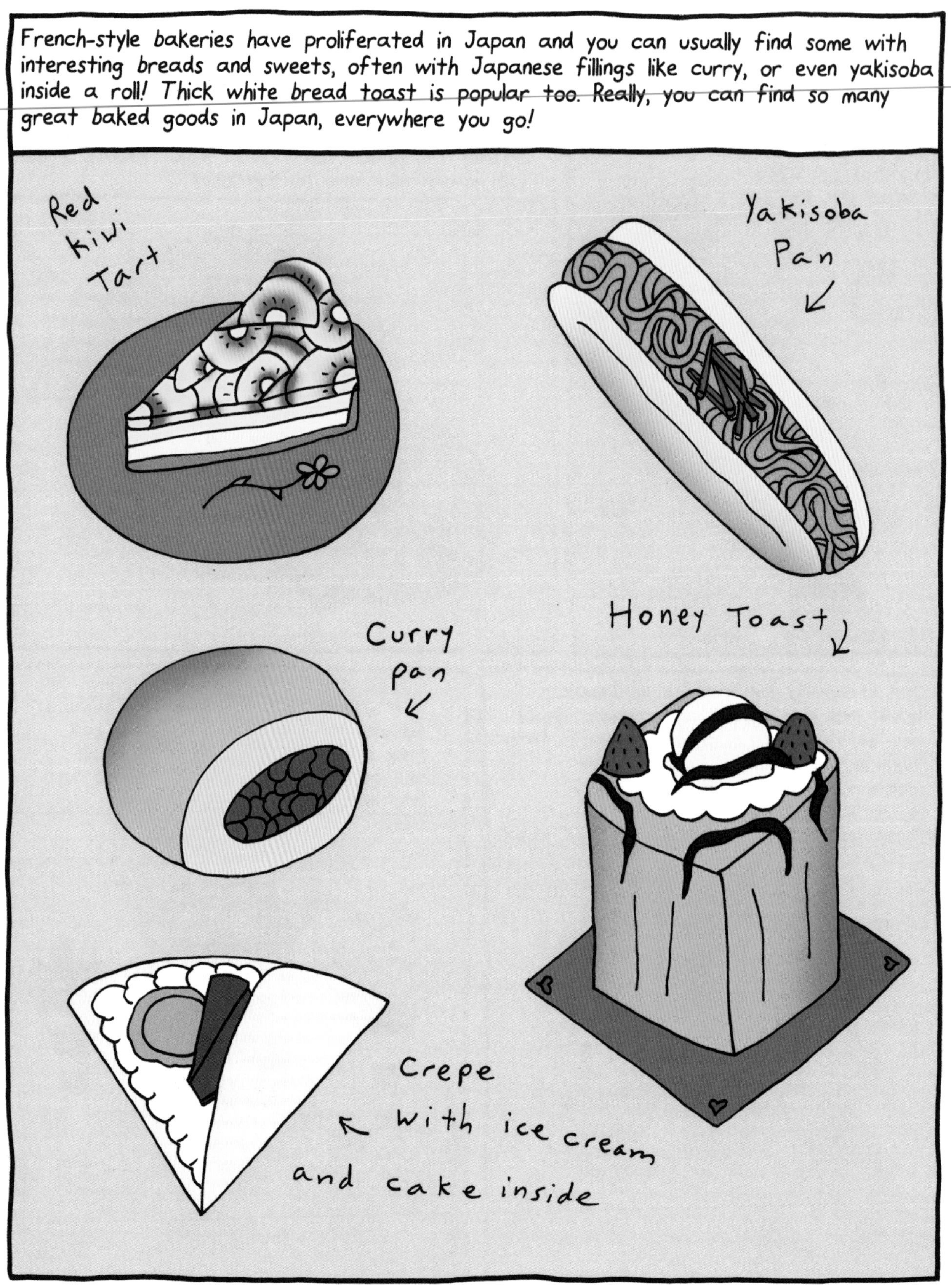
Red kiwi Tart
Yakisoba Pan
Curry pan
Honey Toast
Crepe with ice cream and cake inside

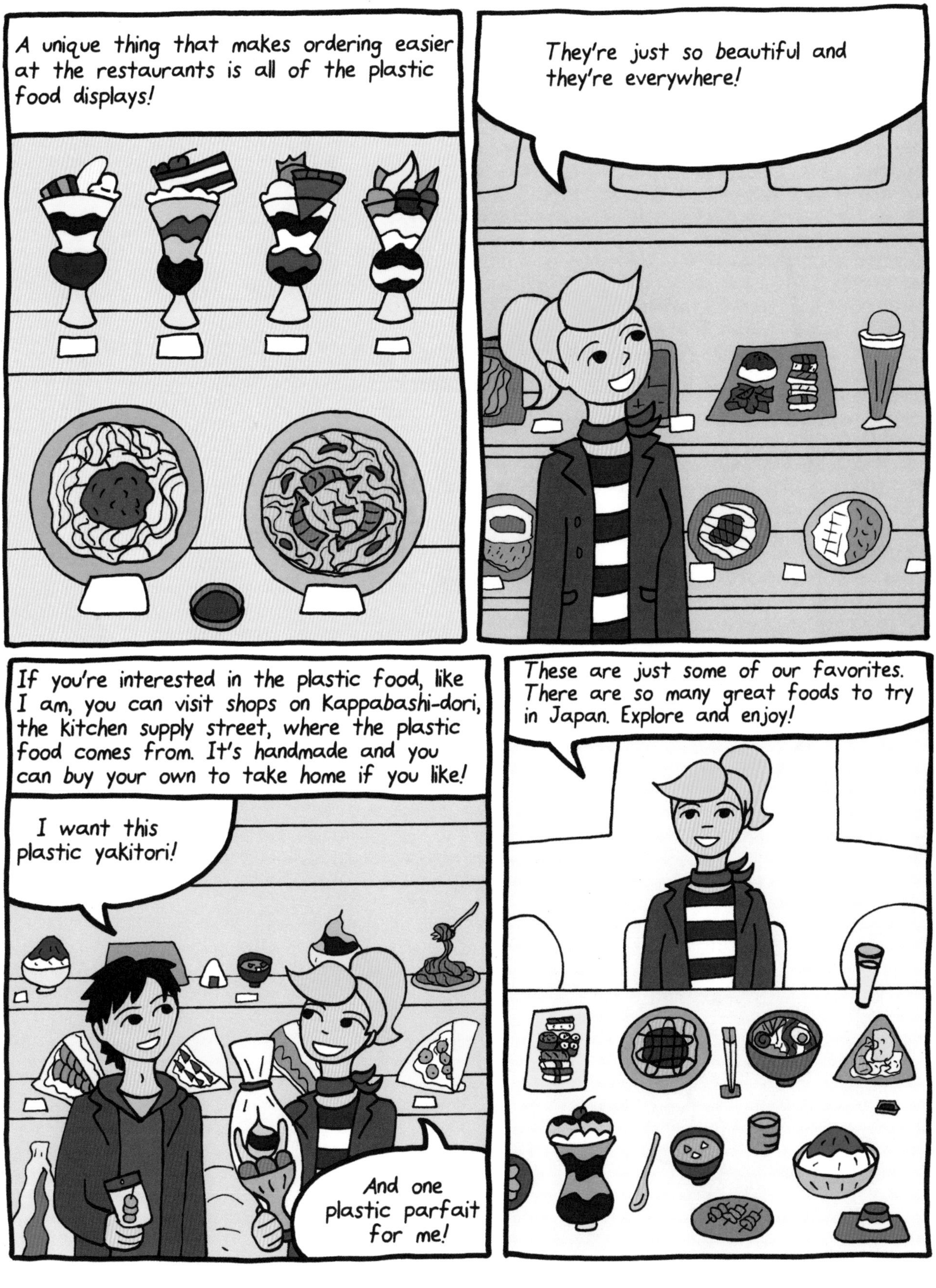
A unique thing that makes ordering easier at the restaurants is all of the plastic food displays!
They're just so beautiful and they're everywhere!
If you're interested in the plastic food, like I am, you can visit shops on Kappabashi-dori, the kitchen supply street, where the plastic food comes from. It's handmade and you can buy your own to take home if you like!
I want this plastic yakitori!
And one plastic parfait for me!
These are just some of our favorites. There are so many great foods to try in Japan. Explore and enjoy!

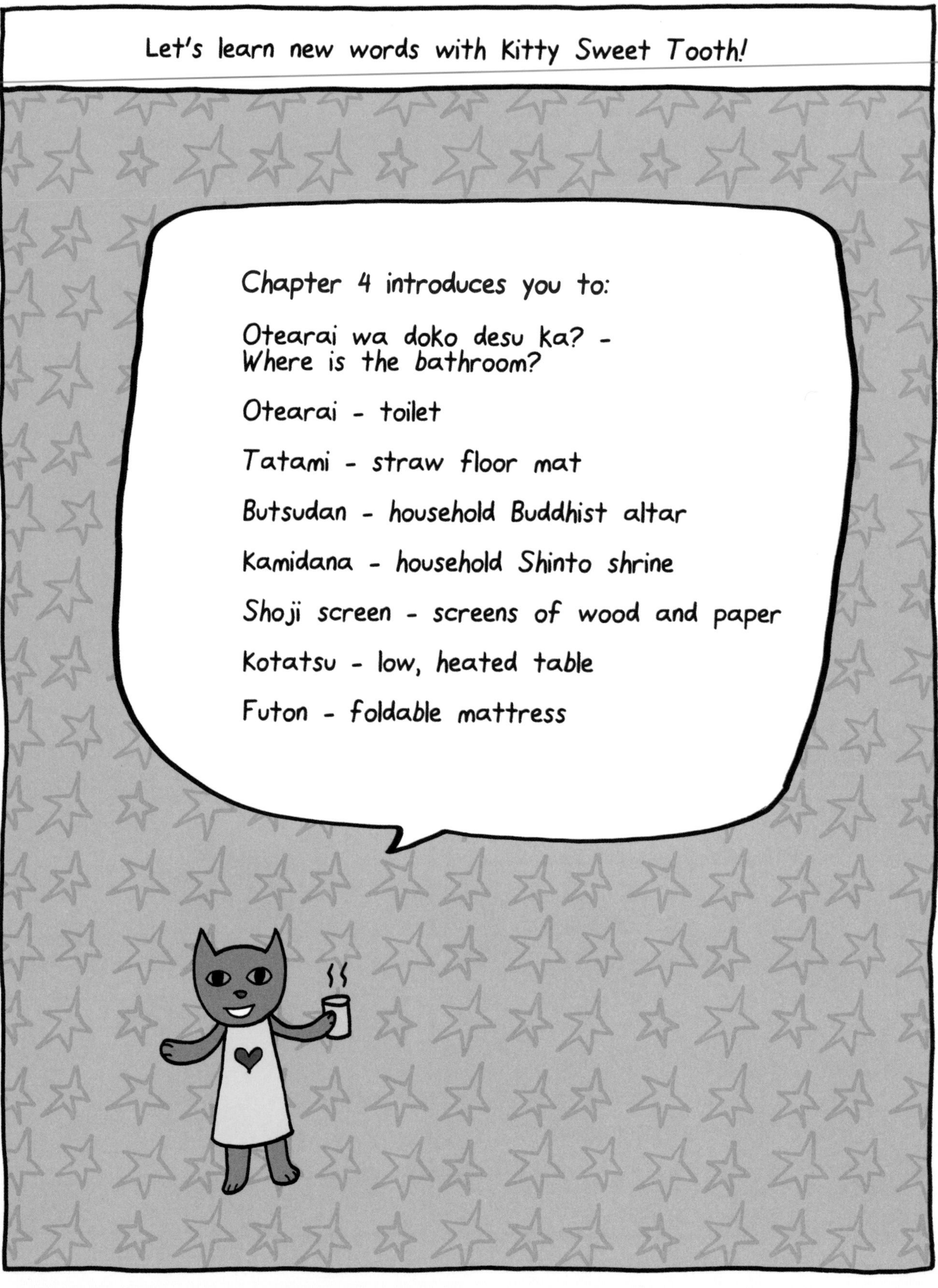
Let's learn new words with Kitty Sweet Tooth!
Chapter 4 introduces you to:
Otearai wa doko desu ka? - Where is the bathroom?
Otearai - toilet
Tatami - straw floor mat
Butsudan - household Buddhist altar
Kamidana - household Shinto shrine
Shoji screen - screens of wood and paper
Kotatsu - low, heated table
Futon - foldable mattress

Chapter 4

Home, Sweet Homestay!

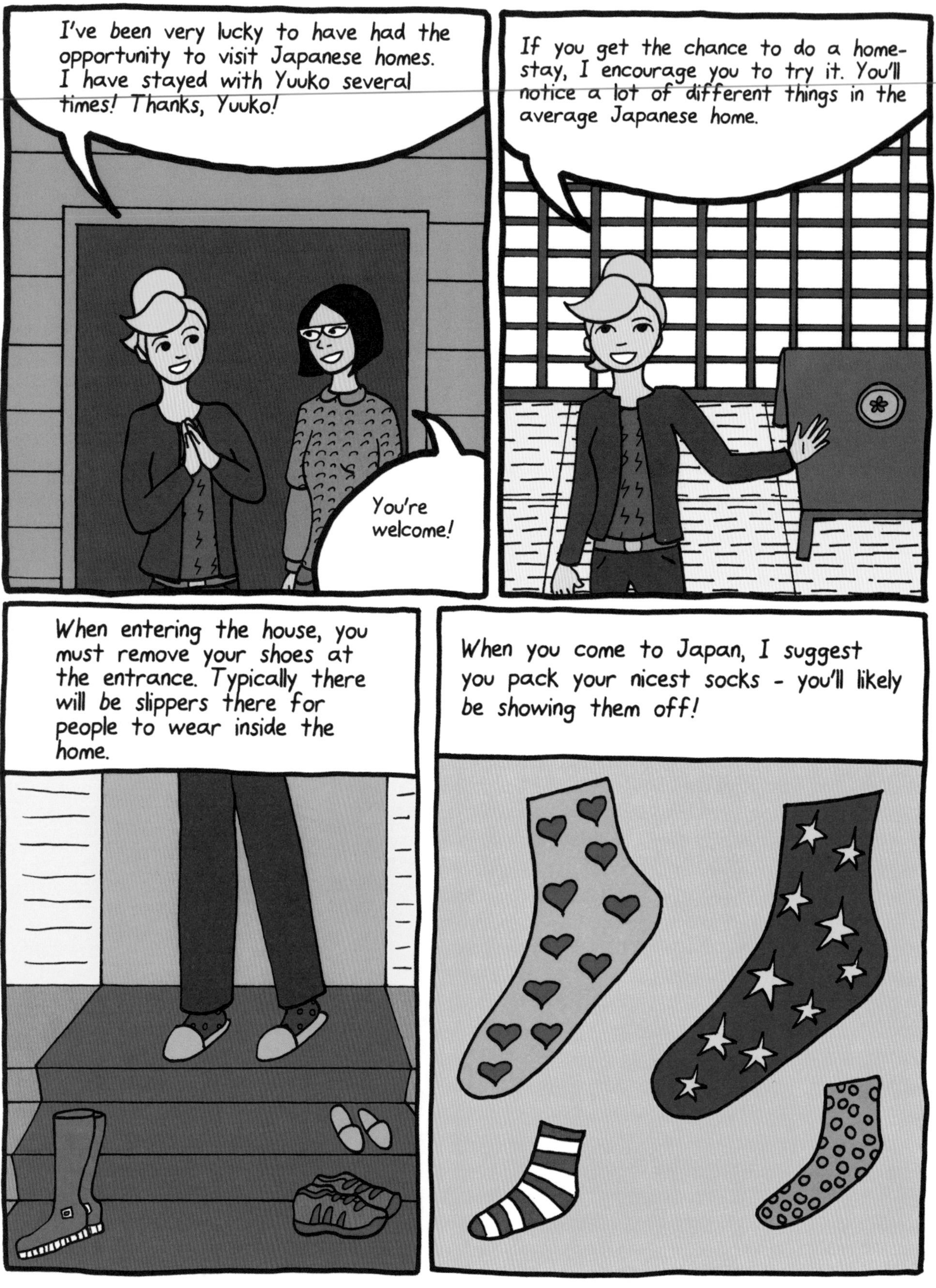
I've been very lucky to have had the opportunity to visit Japanese homes. I have stayed with Yuuko several times! Thanks, Yuuko!
You're welcome!
If you get the chance to do a home-stay, I encourage you to try it. You'll notice a lot of different things in the average Japanese home.
When entering the house, you must remove your shoes at the entrance. Typically there will be slippers there for people to wear inside the home.
When you come to Japan, I suggest you pack your nicest socks - you'll likely be showing them off!

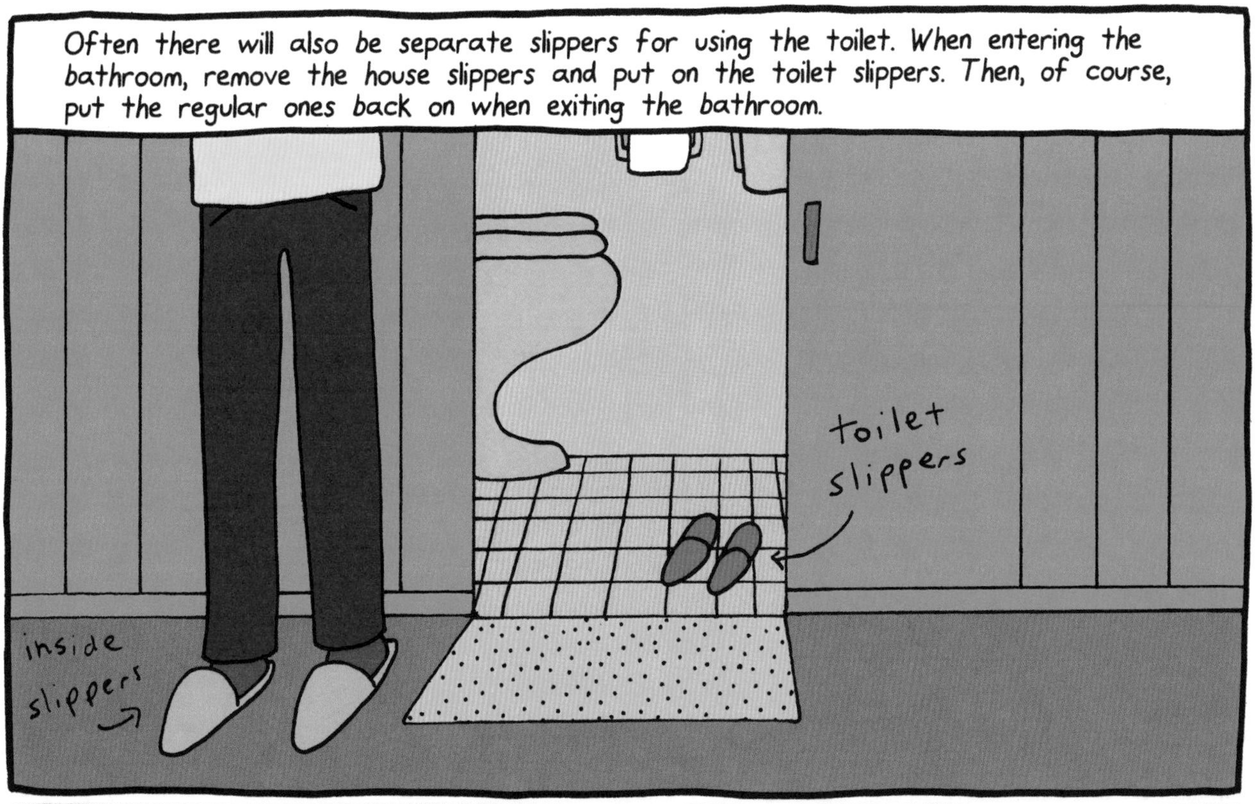
Often there will also be separate slippers for using the toilet. When entering the bathroom, remove the house slippers and put on the toilet slippers. Then, of course, put the regular ones back on when exiting the bathroom.
toilet slippers
inside slippers

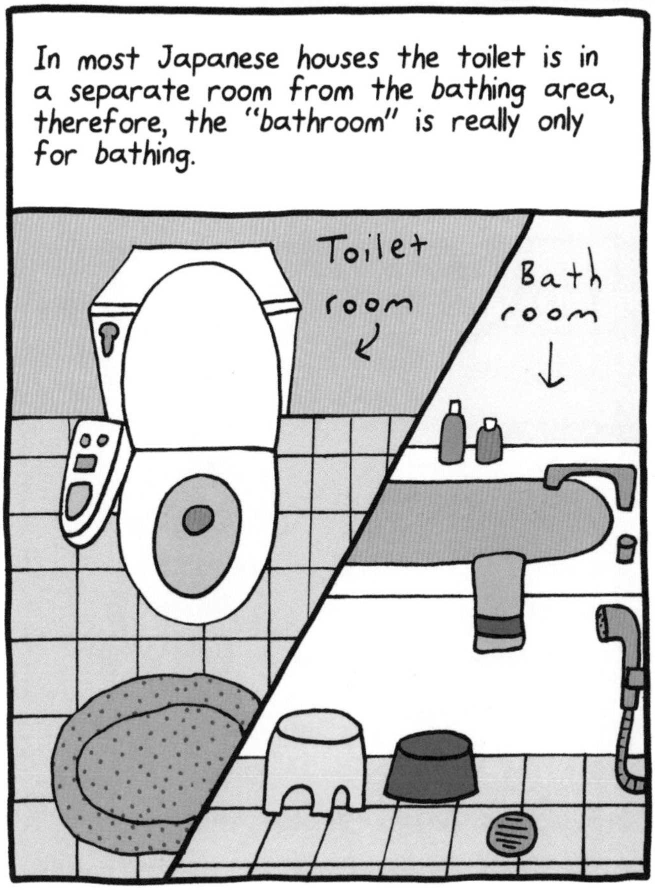
In most Japanese houses the toilet is in a separate room from the bathing area, therefore, the "bathroom" is really only for bathing.
Toilet room
Bath room

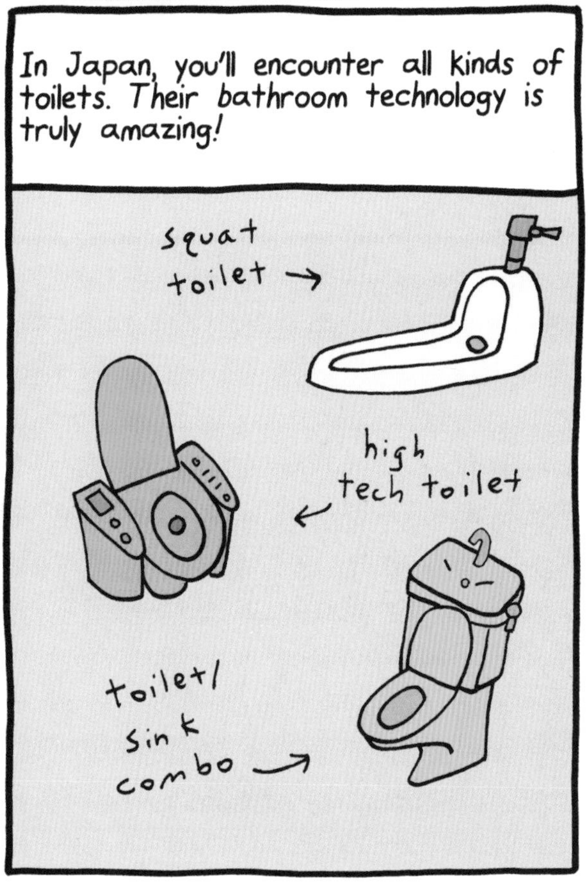
In Japan, you'll encounter all kinds of toilets. Their bathroom technology is truly amazing!
squat toilet
high tech toilet
toilet/ sink combo

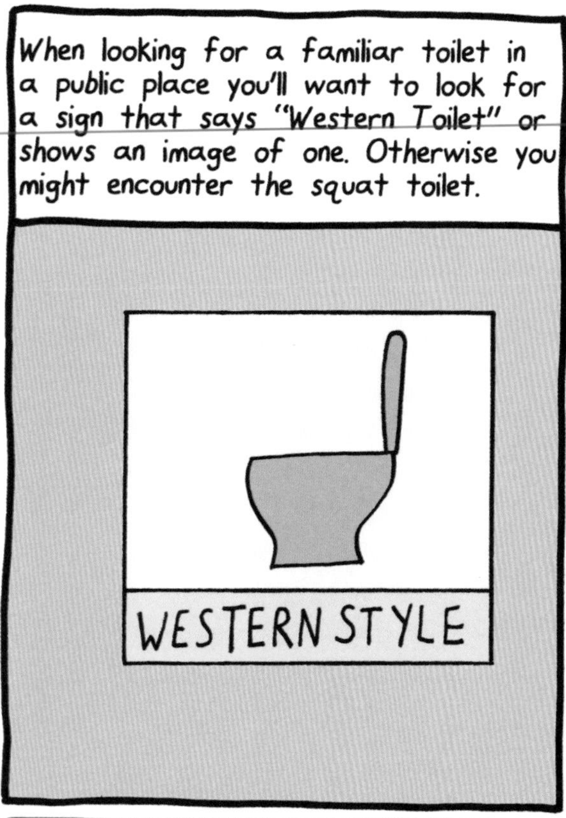
When looking for a familiar toilet in a public place you'll want to look for a sign that says "Western Toilet" or shows an image of one. Otherwise you might encounter the squat toilet.
WESTERN STYLE

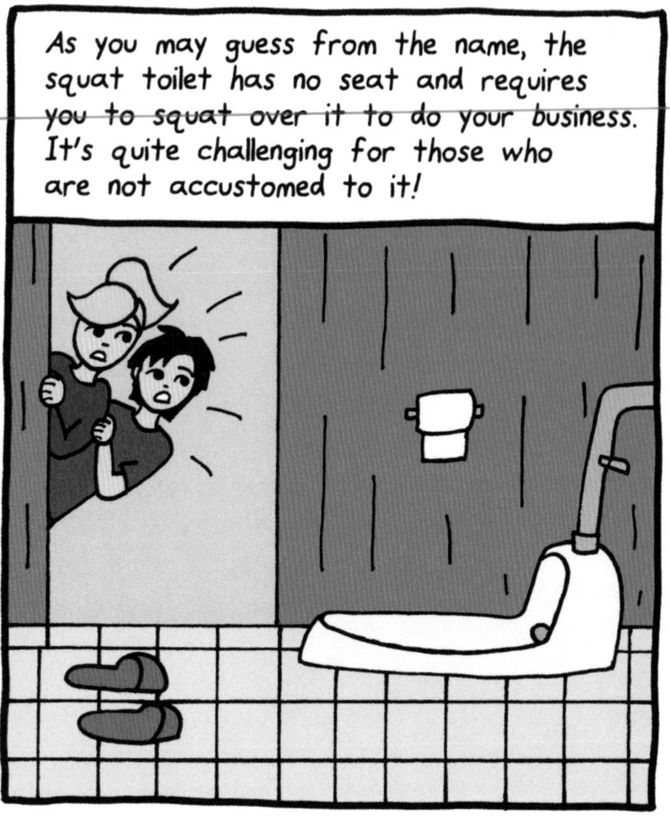
As you may guess from the name, the squat toilet has no seat and requires you to squat over it to do your business. It's quite challenging for those who are not accustomed to it!

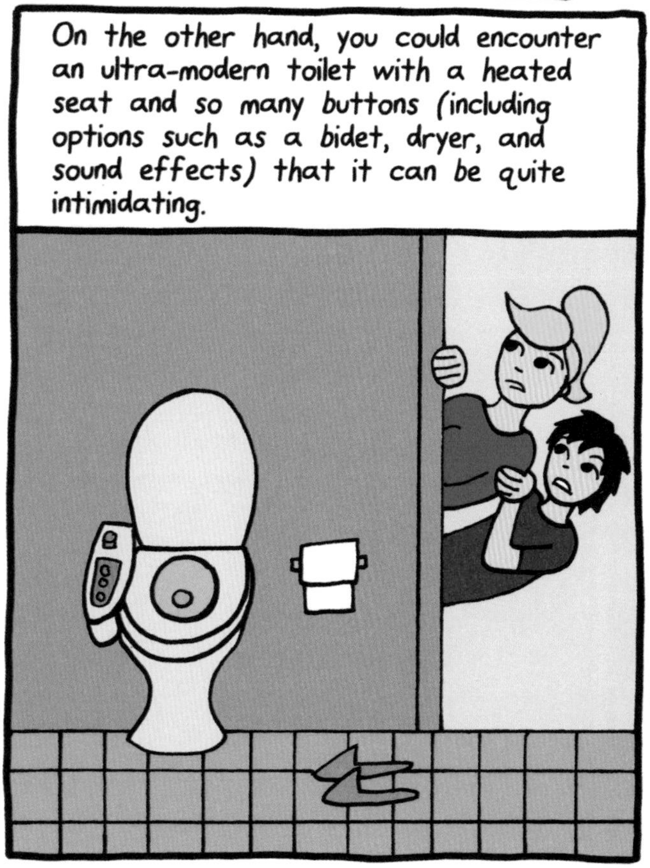
On the other hand, you could encounter an ultra-modern toilet with a heated seat and so many buttons (including options such as a bidet, dryer, and sound effects) that it can be quite intimidating.

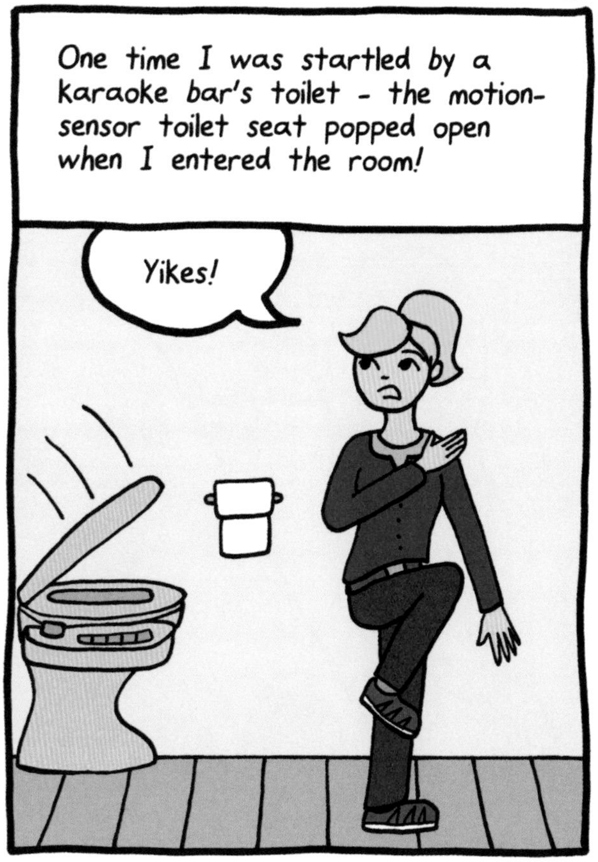
One time I was startled by a karaoke bar's toilet - the motion-sensor toilet seat popped open when I entered the room!
Yikes!

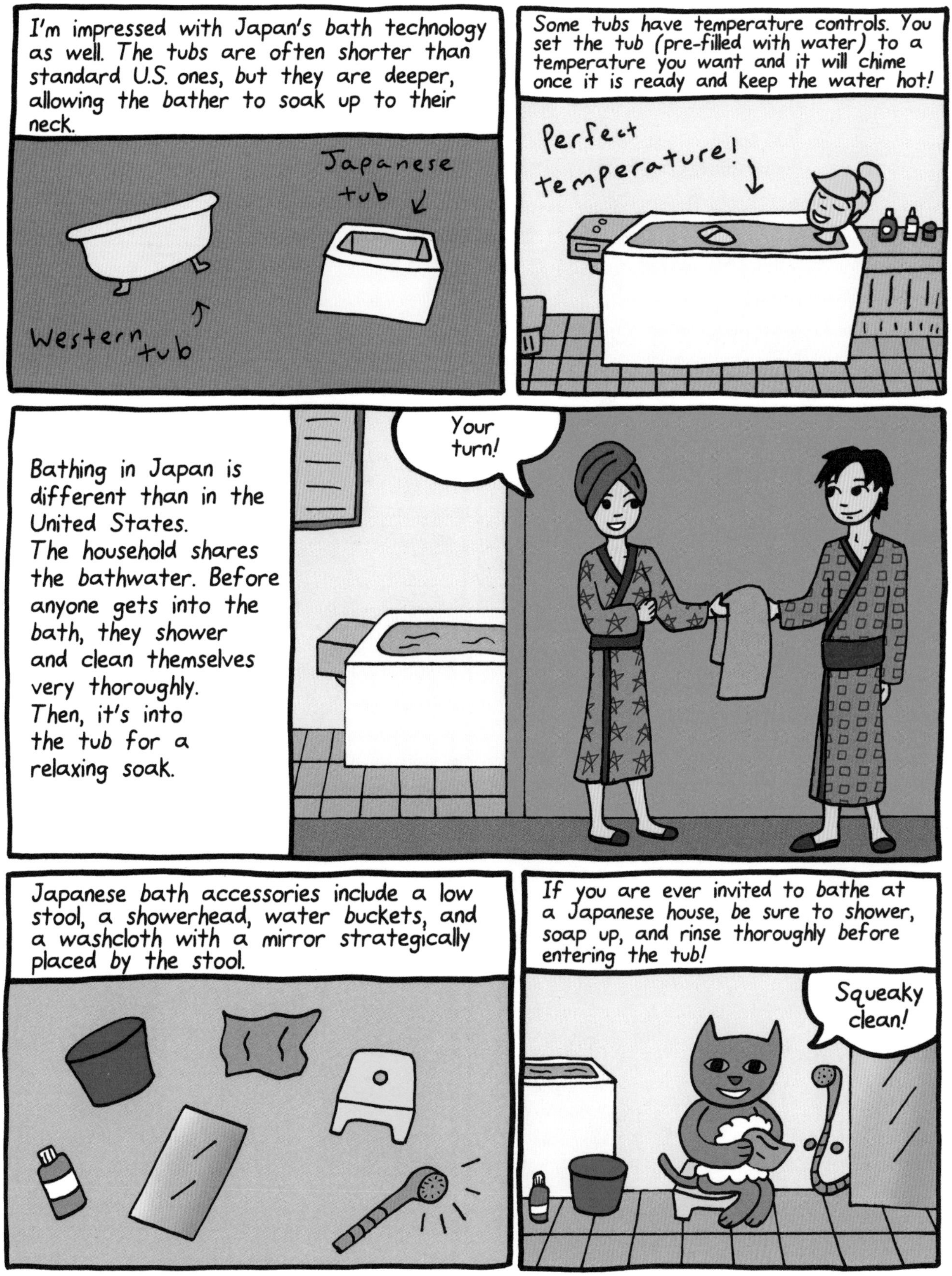
I'm impressed with Japan's bath technology as well. The tubs are often shorter than standard U.S. ones, but they are deeper, allowing the bather to soak up to their neck.
Japanese tub
Western tub
Some tubs have temperature controls. You set the tub (pre-filled with water) to a temperature you want and it will chime once it is ready and keep the water hot!
Perfect temperature!
Bathing in Japan is different than in the United States. The household shares the bathwater. Before anyone gets into the bath, they shower and clean themselves very thoroughly. Then, it's into the tub for a relaxing soak.
Your turn!
Japanese bath accessories include a low stool, a showerhead, water buckets, and a washcloth with a mirror strategically placed by the stool.
If you are ever invited to bathe at a Japanese house, be sure to shower, soap up, and rinse thoroughly before entering the tub!
Squeaky clean!

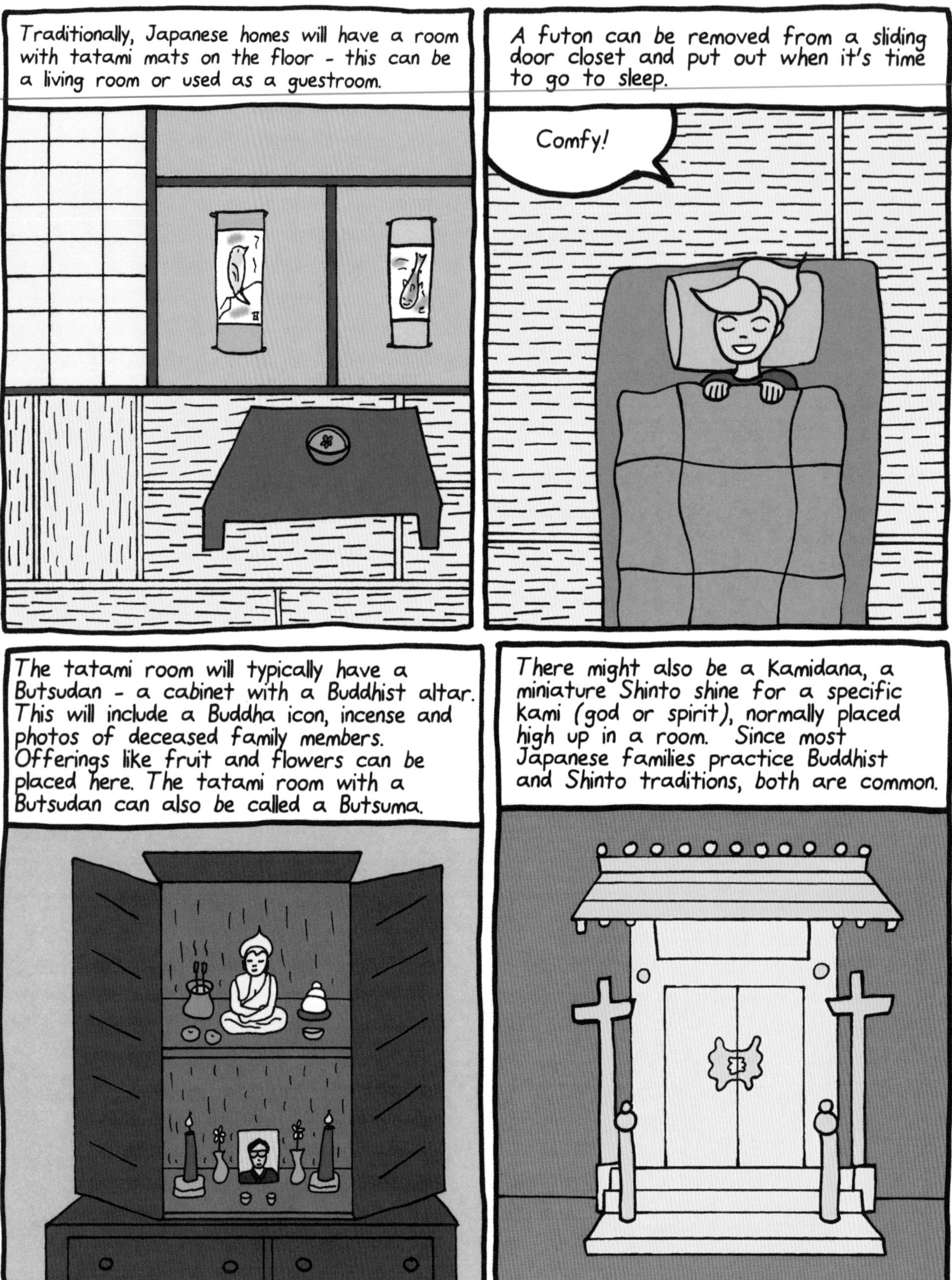
Traditionally, Japanese homes will have a room with tatami mats on the floor - this can be a living room or used as a guestroom.
A futon can be removed from a sliding door closet and put out when it's time to go to sleep.
Comfy!
The tatami room will typically have a Butsudan - a cabinet with a Buddhist altar. This will include a Buddha icon, incense and photos of deceased family members. Offerings like fruit and flowers can be placed here. The tatami room with a Butsudan can also be called a Butsuma.
There might also be a Kamidana, a miniature Shinto shine for a specific kami (god or spirit), normally placed high up in a room. Since most Japanese families practice Buddhist and Shinto traditions, both are common.

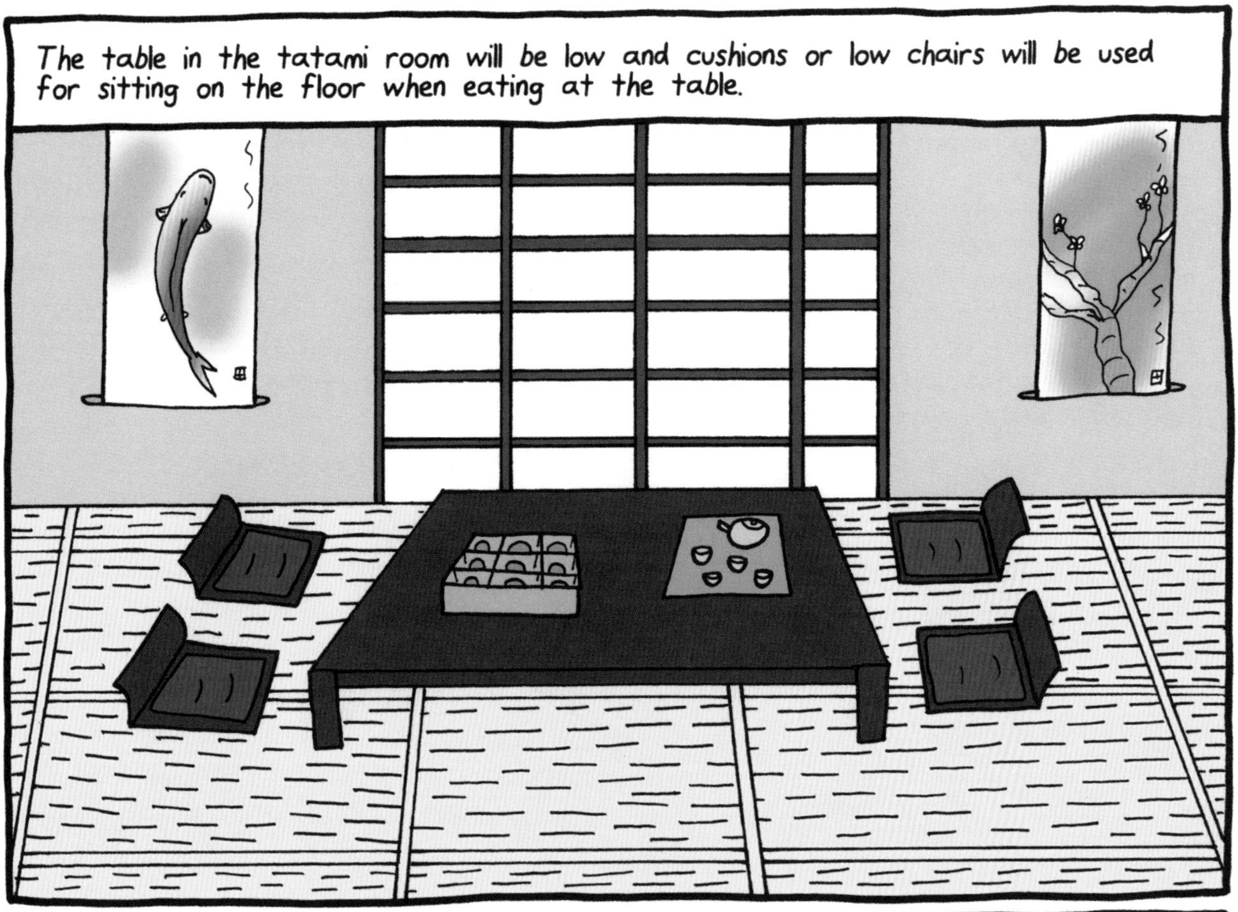
The table in the tatami room will be low and cushions or low chairs will be used for sitting on the floor when eating at the table.

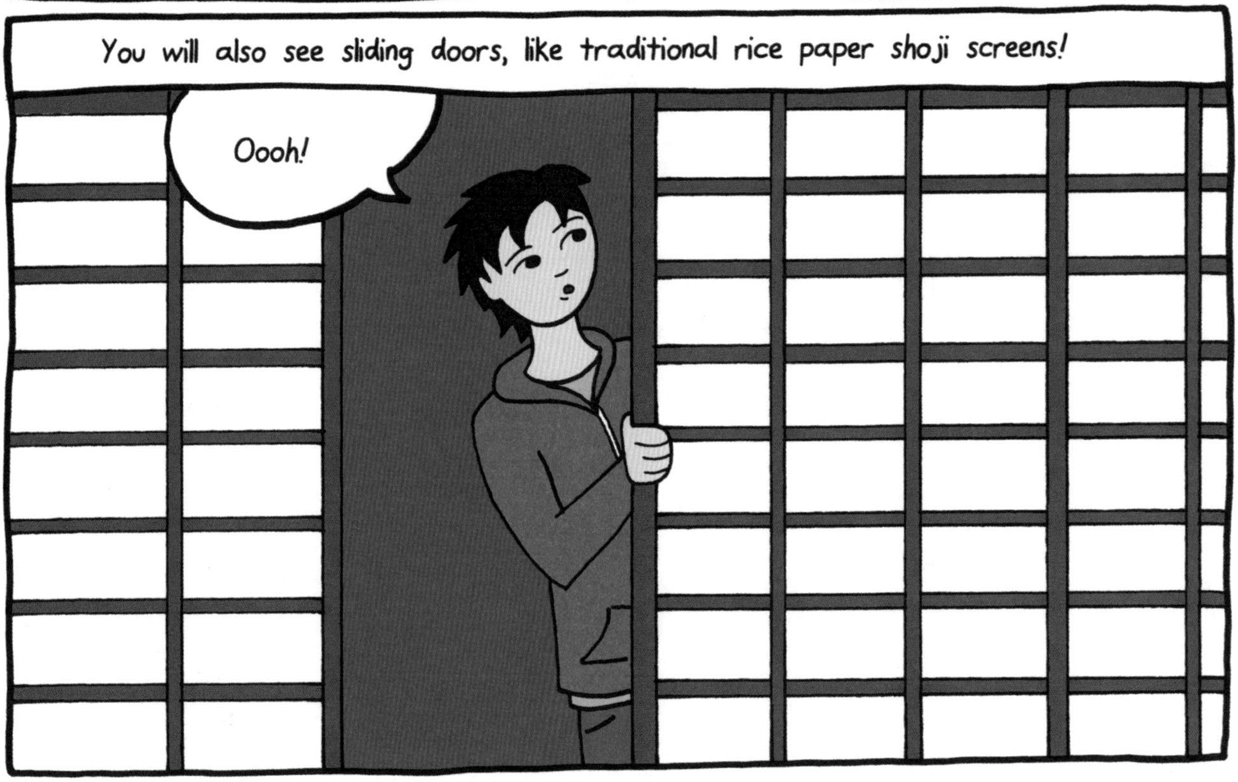
You will also see sliding doors, like traditional rice paper shoji screens!
Oooh!

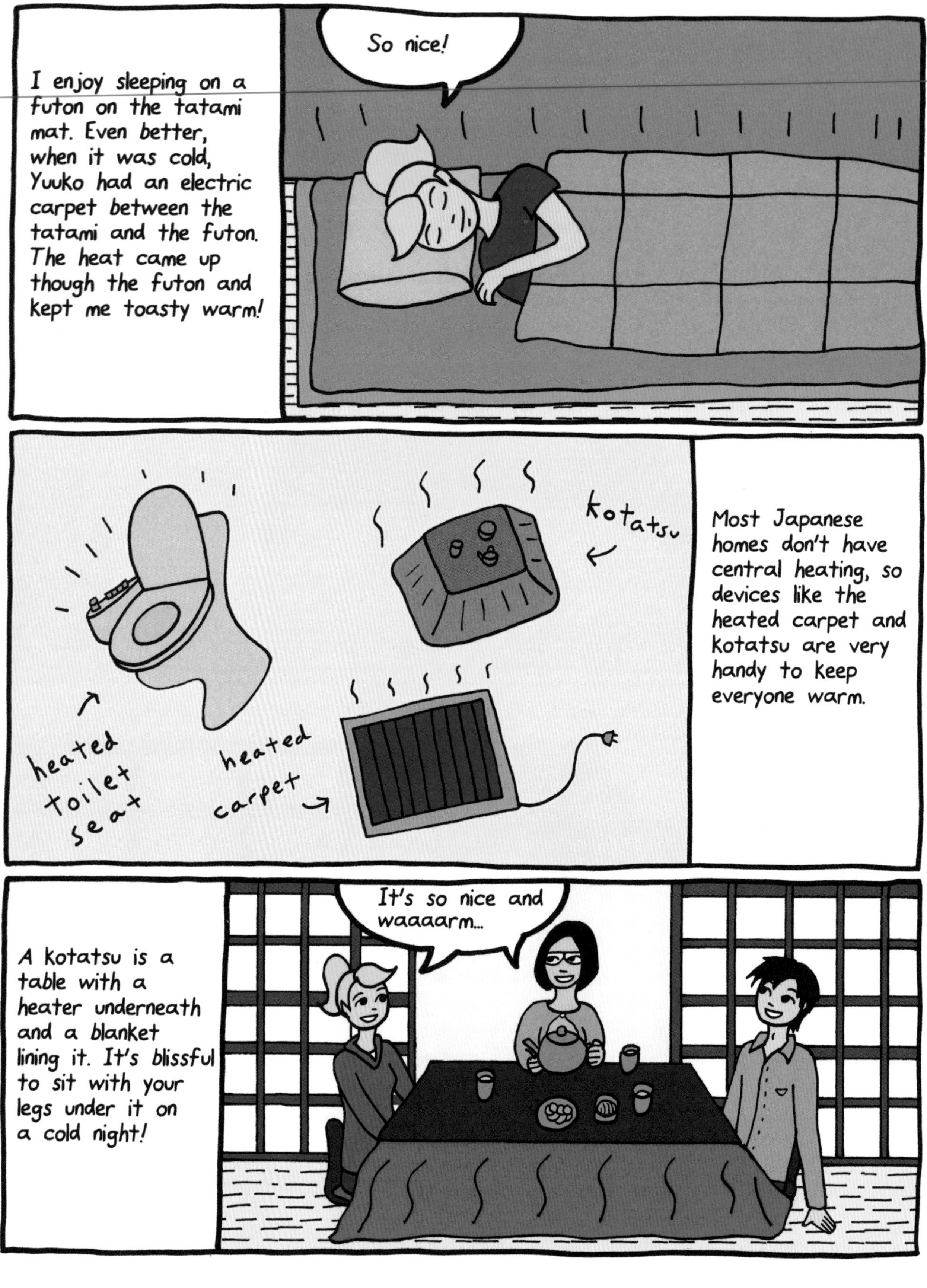
I enjoy sleeping on a futon on the tatami mat. Even better, when it was cold, Yuuko had an electric carpet between the tatami and the futon. The heat came up though the futon and kept me toasty warm!
So nice!
heated toilet seat
kotatsu
heated carpet
Most Japanese homes don't have central heating, so devices like the heated carpet and kotatsu are very handy to keep everyone warm.
A kotatsu is a table with a heater underneath and a blanket lining it. It's blissful to sit with your legs under it on a cold night!
It's so nice and waaaarm...

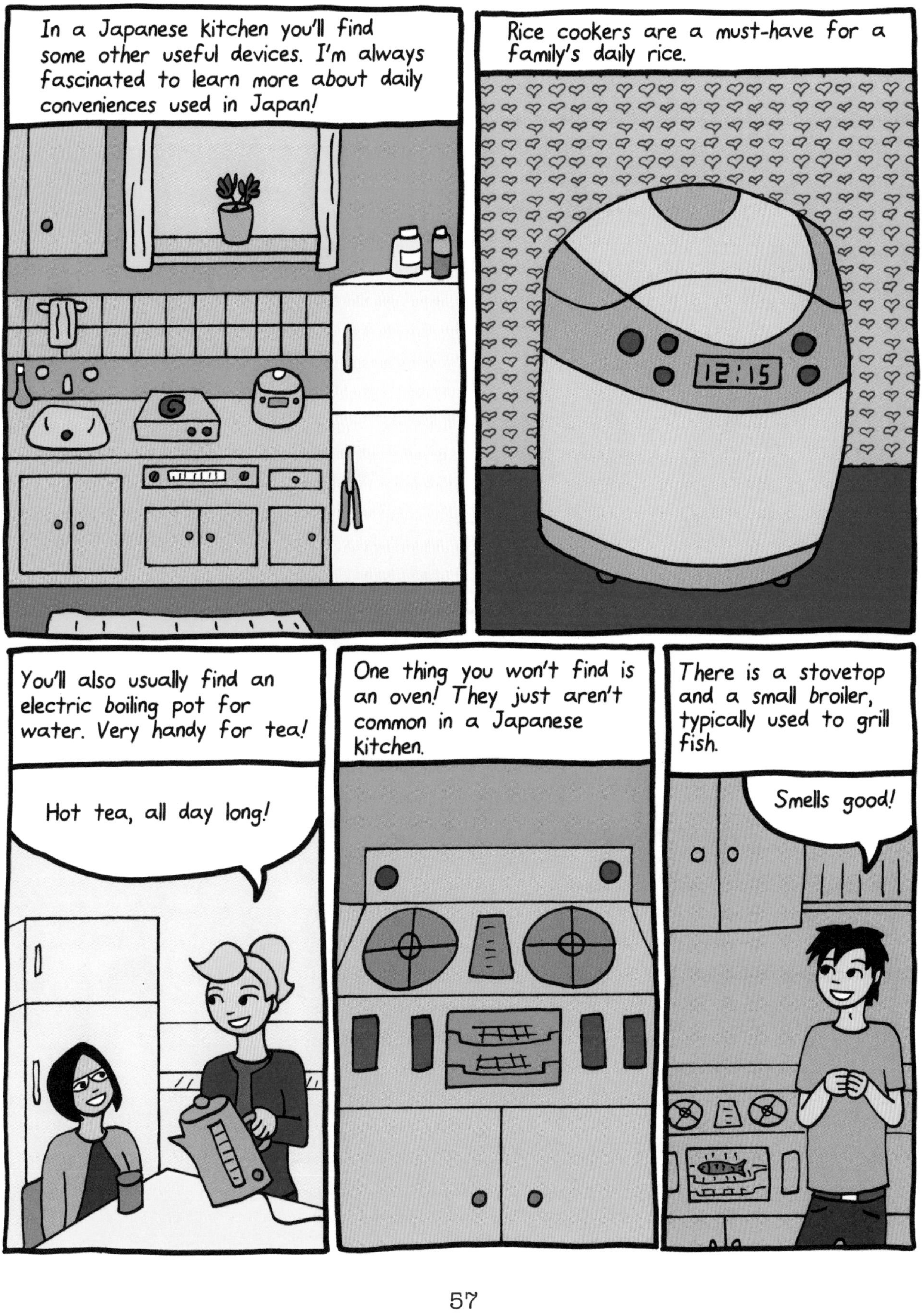
In a Japanese kitchen you'll find some other useful devices. I'm always fascinated to learn more about daily conveniences used in Japan!
Rice cookers are a must-have for a family's daily rice.
12:15
You'll also usually find an electric boiling pot for water. Very handy for tea!
Hot tea, all day long!
One thing you won't find is an oven! They just aren't common in a Japanese kitchen.
There is a stovetop and a small broiler, typically used to grill fish.
Smells good!

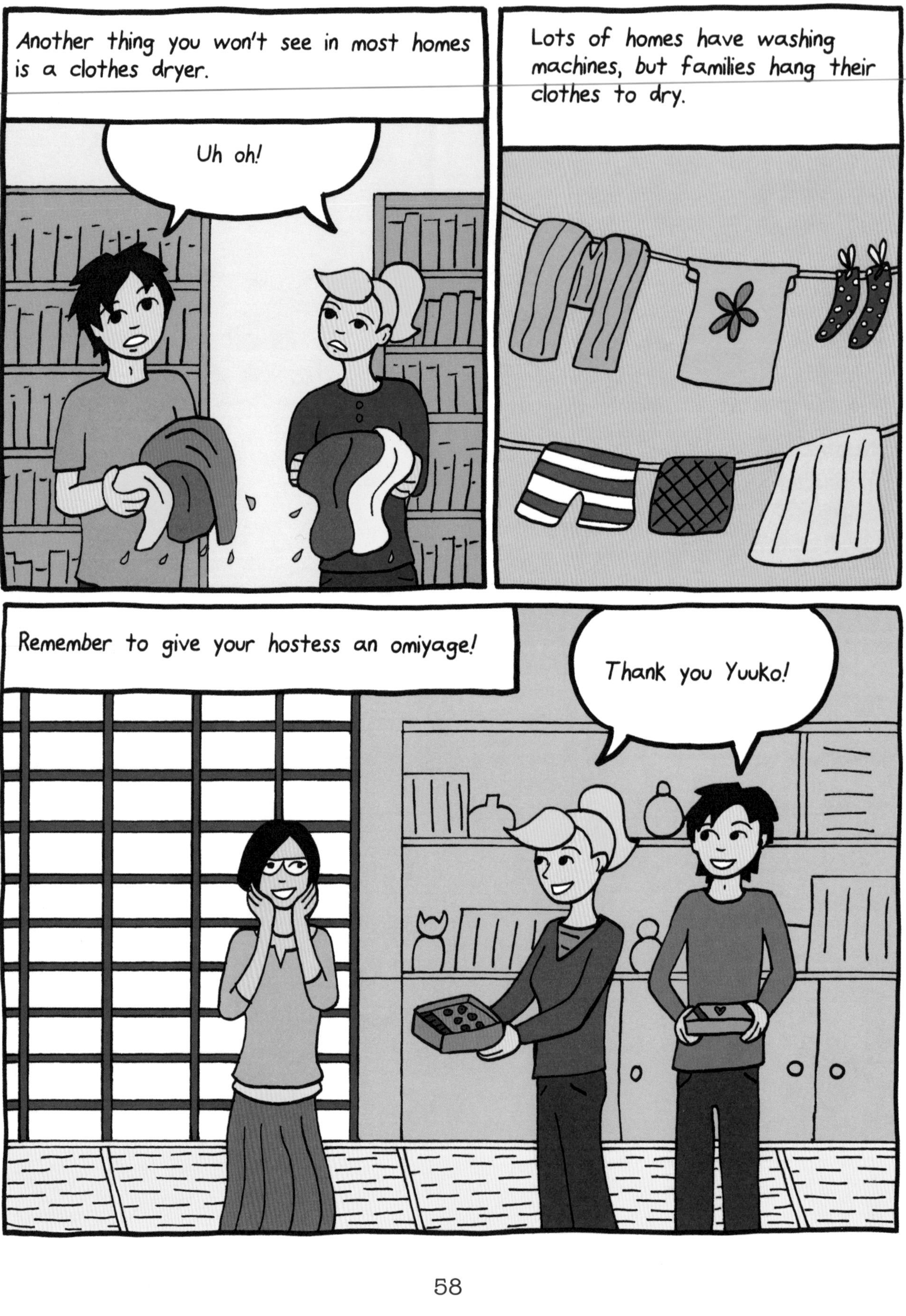
Another thing you won't see in most homes is a clothes dryer.
Uh oh!
Lots of homes have washing machines, but families hang their clothes to dry.
Remember to give your hostess an omiyage!
Thank you Yuuko!

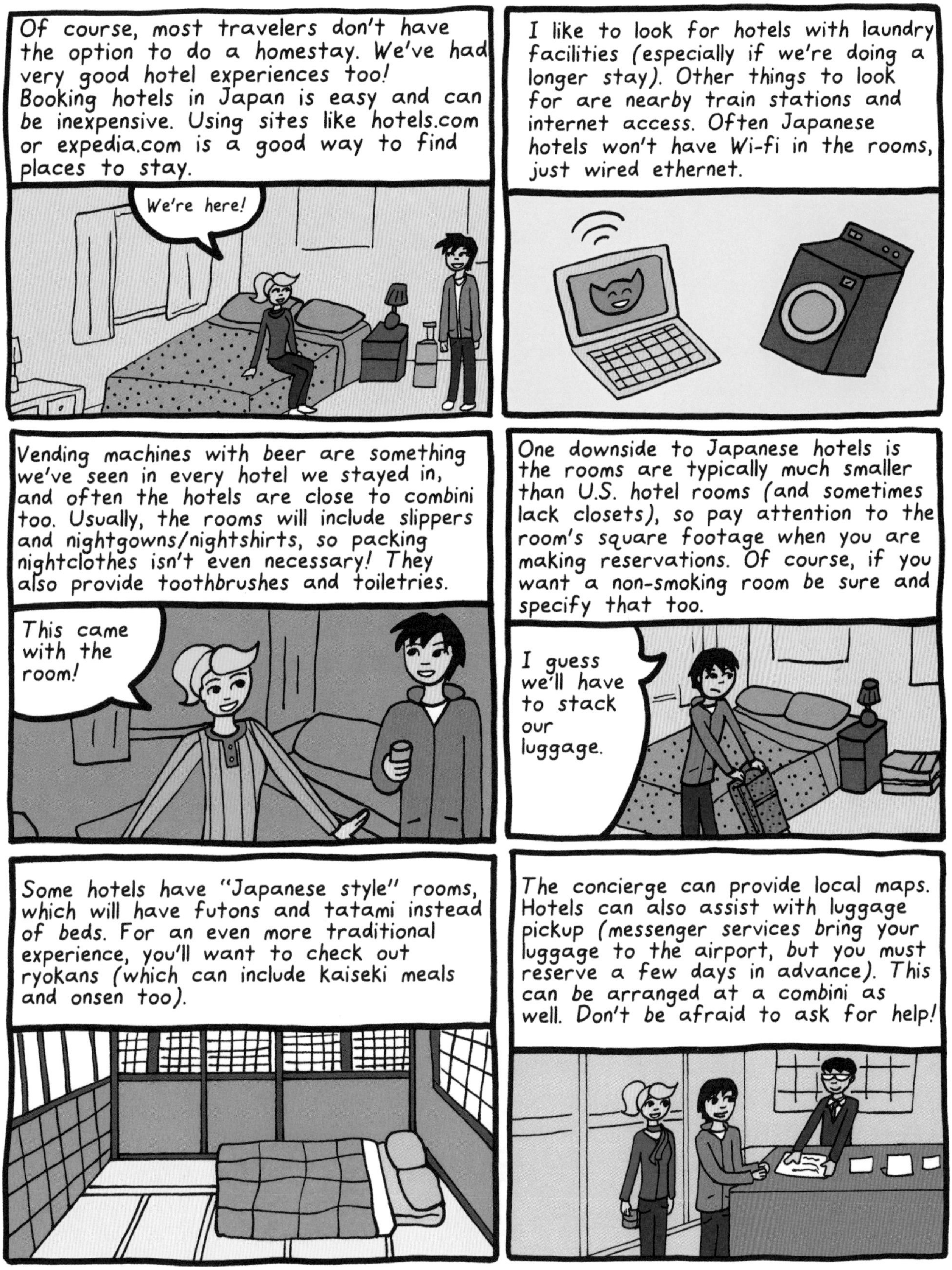
Of course, most travelers don't have the option to do a homestay. We've had very good hotel experiences too! Booking hotels in Japan is easy and can be inexpensive. Using sites like hotels.com or expedia.com is a good way to find places to stay.
We're here!
I like to look for hotels with laundry facilities (especially if we're doing a longer stay). Other things to look for are nearby train stations and internet access. Often Japanese hotels won't have Wi-fi in the rooms, just wired ethernet.
Vending machines with beer are something we've seen in every hotel we stayed in, and often the hotels are close to combini too. Usually, the rooms will include slippers and nightgowns/nightshirts, so packing nightclothes isn't even necessary! They also provide toothbrushes and toiletries.
This came with the room!
One downside to Japanese hotels is the rooms are typically much smaller than U.S. hotel rooms (and sometimes lack closets), so pay attention to the room's square footage when you are making reservations. Of course, if you want a non-smoking room be sure and specify that too.
I guess we'll have to stack our luggage.
Some hotels have "Japanese style" rooms, which will have futons and tatami instead of beds. For an even more traditional experience, you'll want to check out ryokans (which can include kaiseki meals and onsen too).
The concierge can provide local maps. Hotels can also assist with luggage pickup (messenger services bring your luggage to the airport, but you must reserve a few days in advance). This can be arranged at a combini as well. Don't be afraid to ask for help!

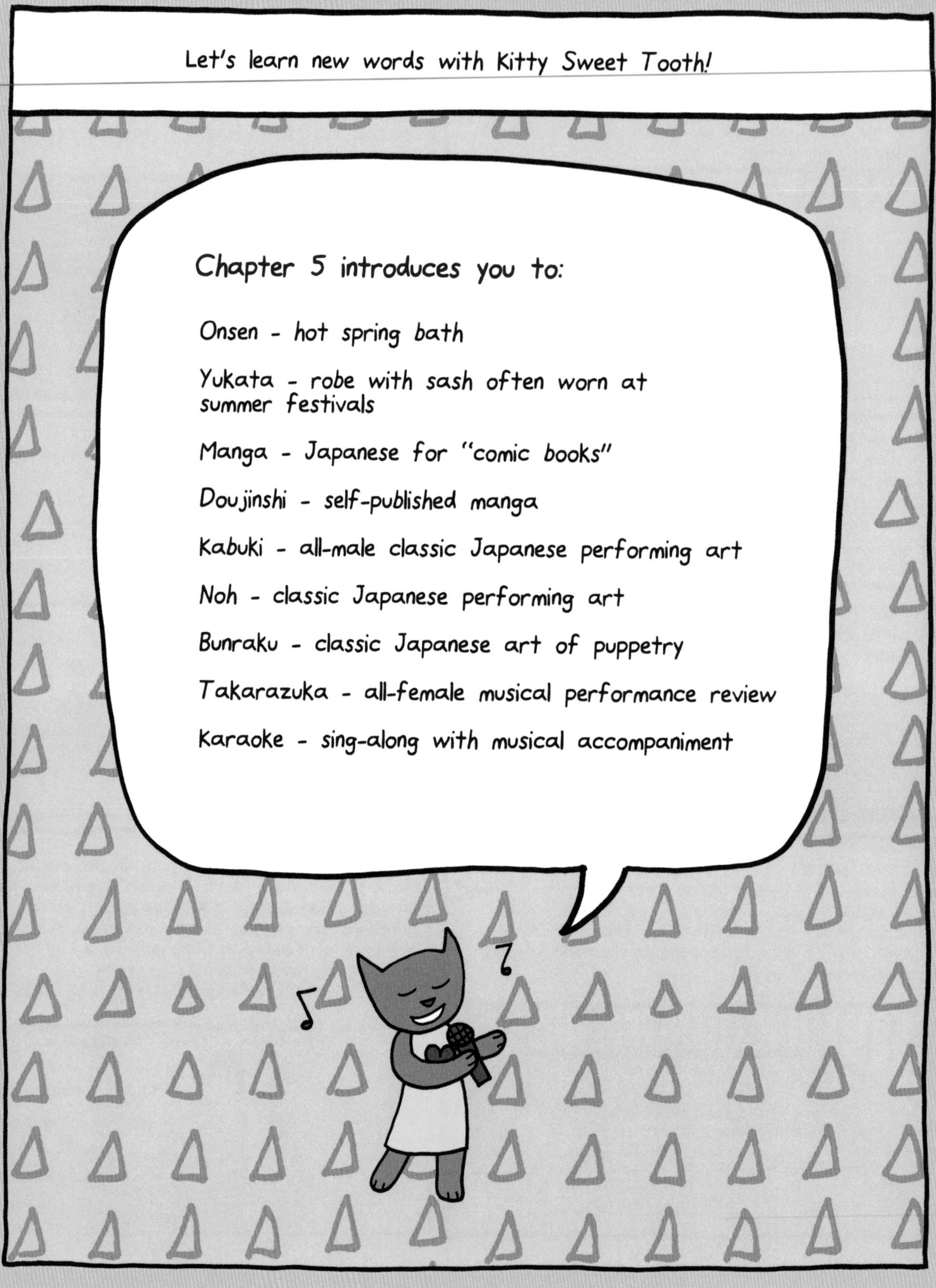
Let's learn new words with Kitty Sweet Tooth!
Chapter 5 introduces you to:
Onsen - hot spring bath
Yukata - robe with sash often worn at summer festivals
Manga - Japanese for "comic books"
Doujinshi - self-published manga
Kabuki - all-male classic Japanese performing art
Noh - classic Japanese performing art
Bunraku - classic Japanese art of puppetry
Takarazuka - all-female musical performance review
Karaoke - sing-along with musical accompaniment

Chapter 5

Let's Have Some Fun!

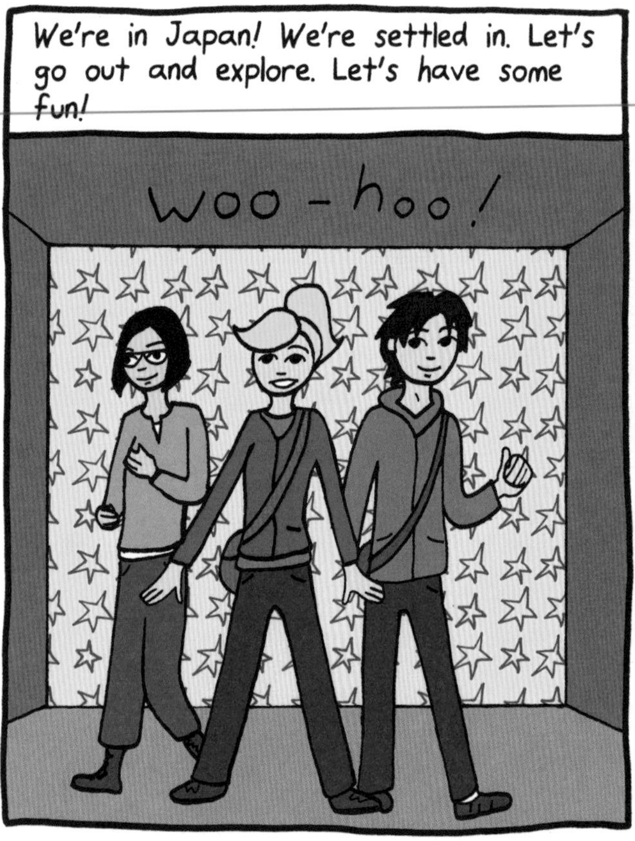
We're in Japan! We're settled in. Let's go out and explore. Let's have some fun!
woo-hoo!

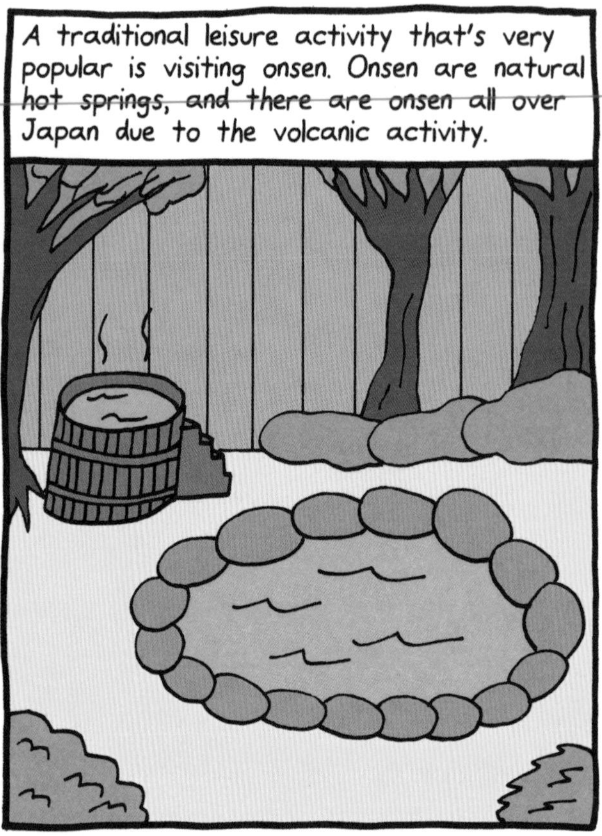
A traditional leisure activity that's very popular is visiting onsen. Onsen are natural hot springs, and there are onsen all over Japan due to the volcanic activity.

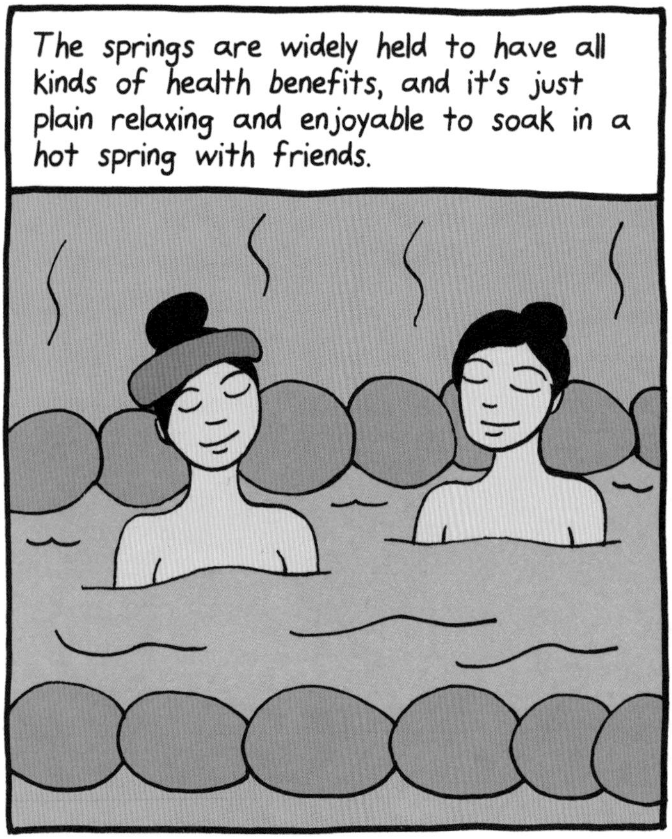
The springs are widely held to have all kinds of health benefits, and it's just plain relaxing and enjoyable to soak in a hot spring with friends.

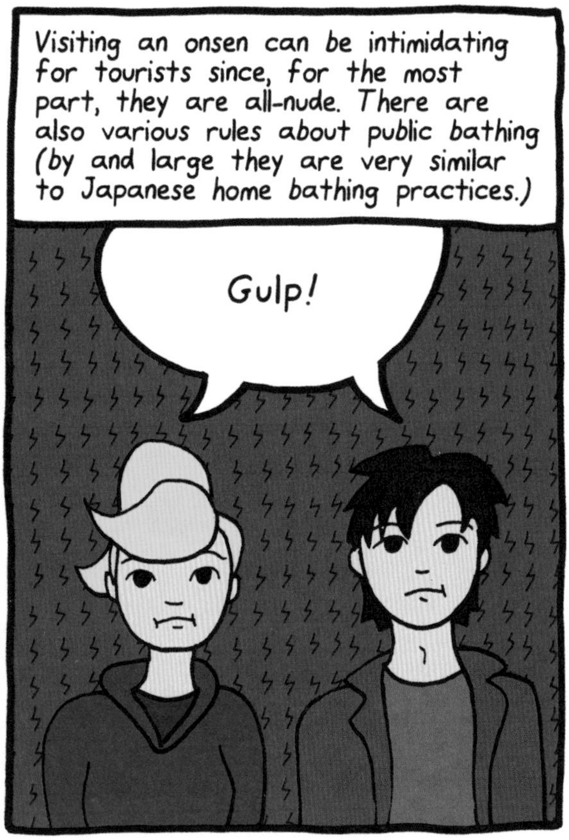
Visiting an onsen can be intimidating for tourists since, for the most part, they are all-nude. There are also various rules about public bathing (by and large they are very similar to Japanese home bathing practices.)
Gulp!

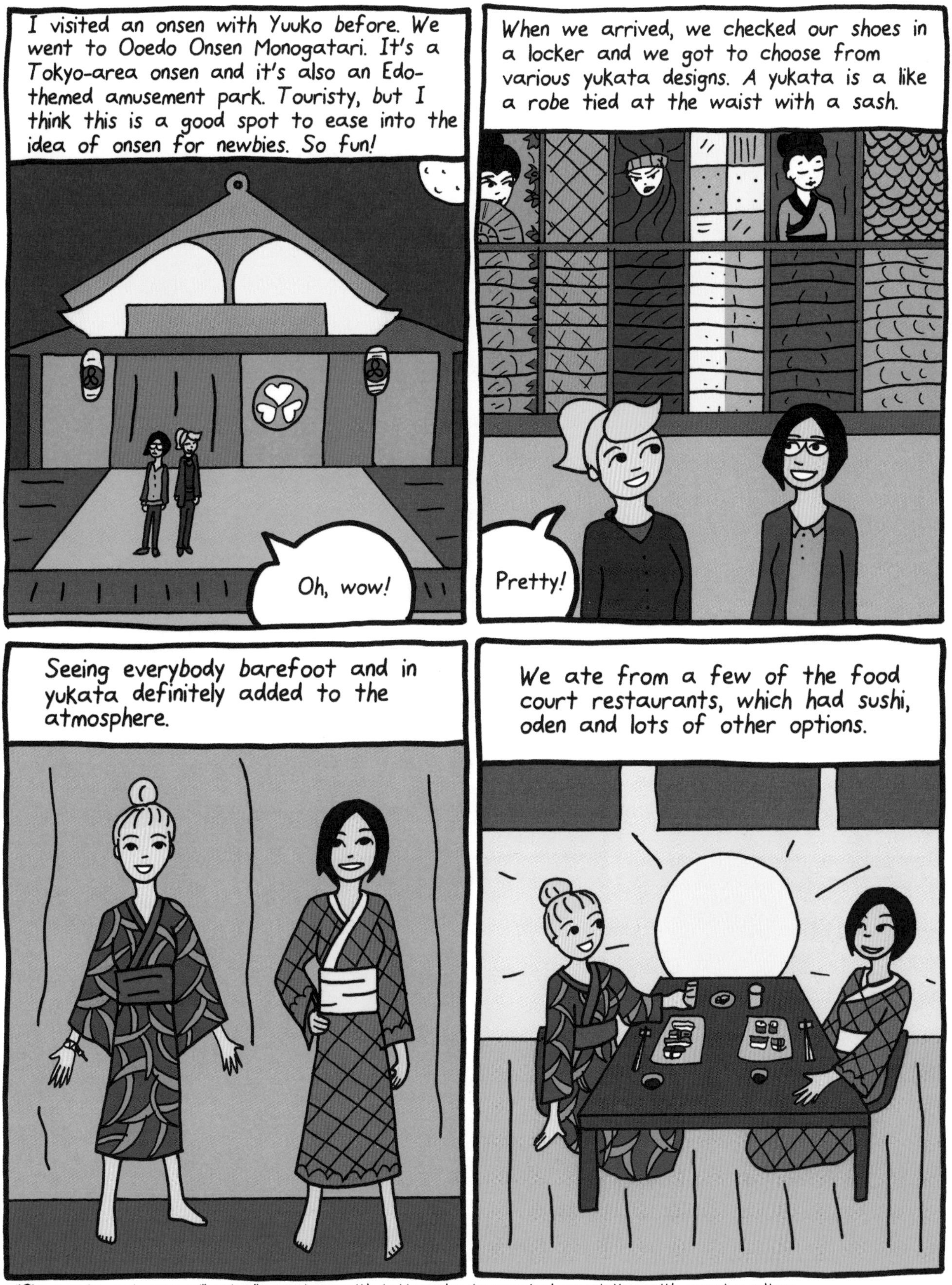
I visited an onsen with Yuuko before. We went to Ooedo Onsen Monogatari. It's a Tokyo-area onsen and it's also an Edo-themed amusement park. Touristy, but I think this is a good spot to ease into the idea of onsen for newbies. So fun!
Oh, wow!
When we arrived, we checked our shoes in a locker and we got to choose from various yukata designs. A yukata is a like a robe tied at the waist with a sash.
Pretty!
Seeing everybody barefoot and in yukata definitely added to the atmosphere.
We ate from a few of the food court restaurants, which had sushi, oden and lots of other options.

*Please note most onsen will not allow patrons with tattoos due to perceived associations with gangster culture.

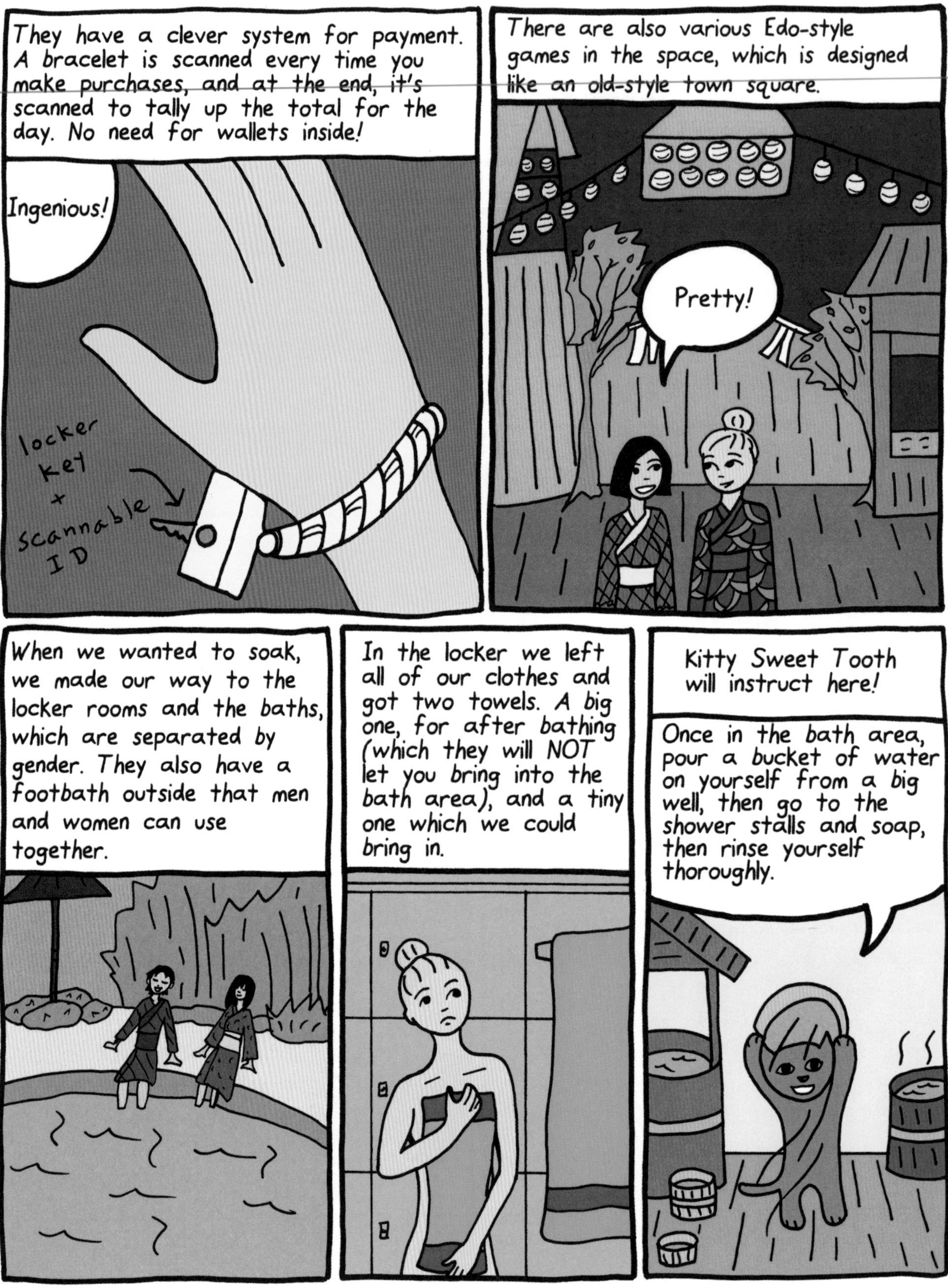
They have a clever system for payment. A bracelet is scanned every time you make purchases, and at the end, it's scanned to tally up the total for the day. No need for wallets inside!
Ingenious!
locker key + scannable ID
There are also various Edo-style games in the space, which is designed like an old-style town square.
Pretty!
When we wanted to soak, we made our way to the locker rooms and the baths, which are separated by gender. They also have a footbath outside that men and women can use together.
In the locker we left all of our clothes and got two towels. A big one, for after bathing (which they will NOT let you bring into the bath area), and a tiny one which we could bring in.
Kitty Sweet Tooth will instruct here!
Once in the bath area, pour a bucket of water on yourself from a big well, then go to the shower stalls and soap, then rinse yourself thoroughly.

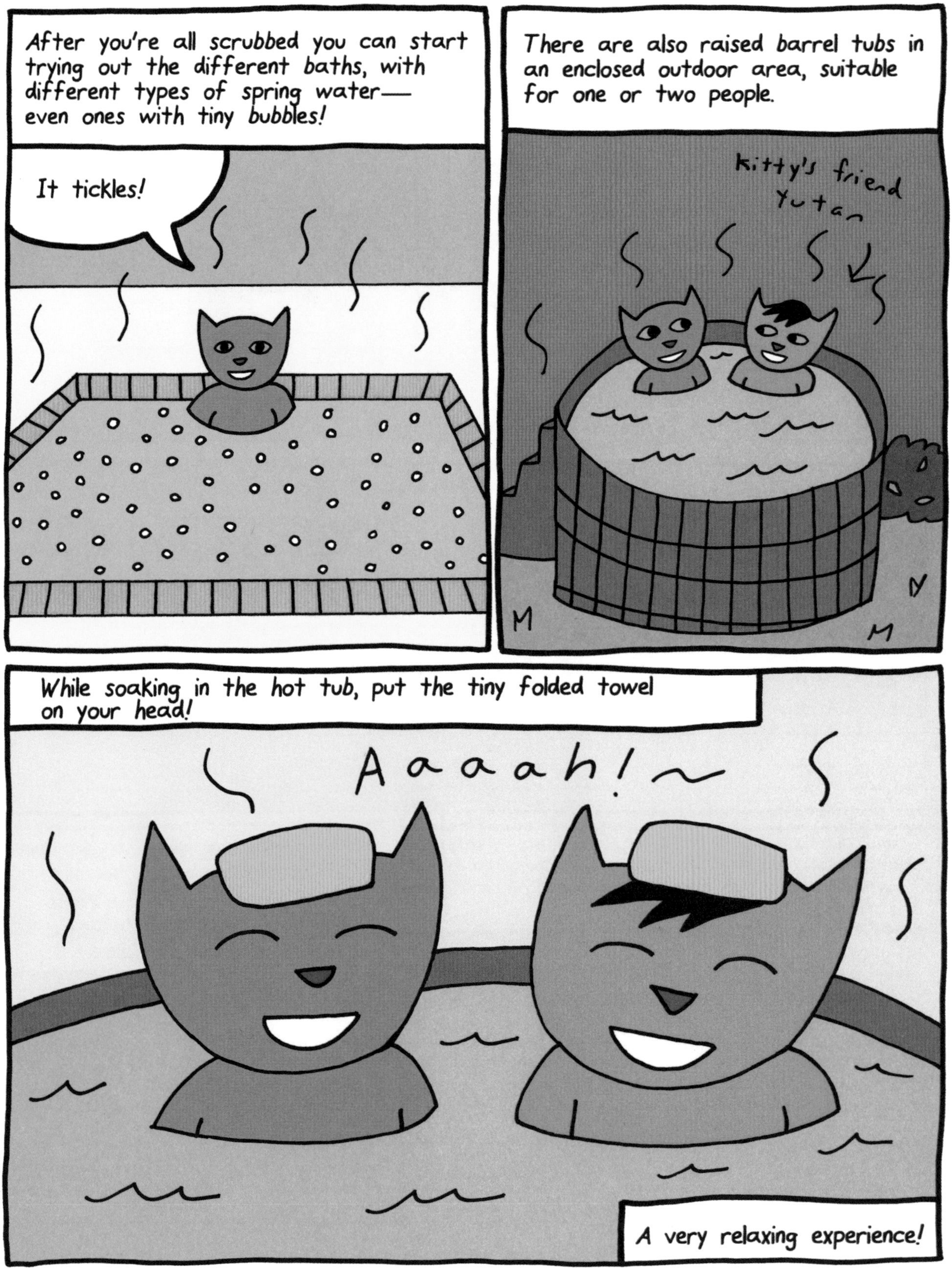
After you're all scrubbed you can start trying out the different baths, with different types of spring water—even ones with tiny bubbles!
It tickles!
There are also raised barrel tubs in an enclosed outdoor area, suitable for one or two people.
Kitty's friend Yutan
While soaking in the hot tub, put the tiny folded towel on your head!
Aaaah!~
A very relaxing experience!

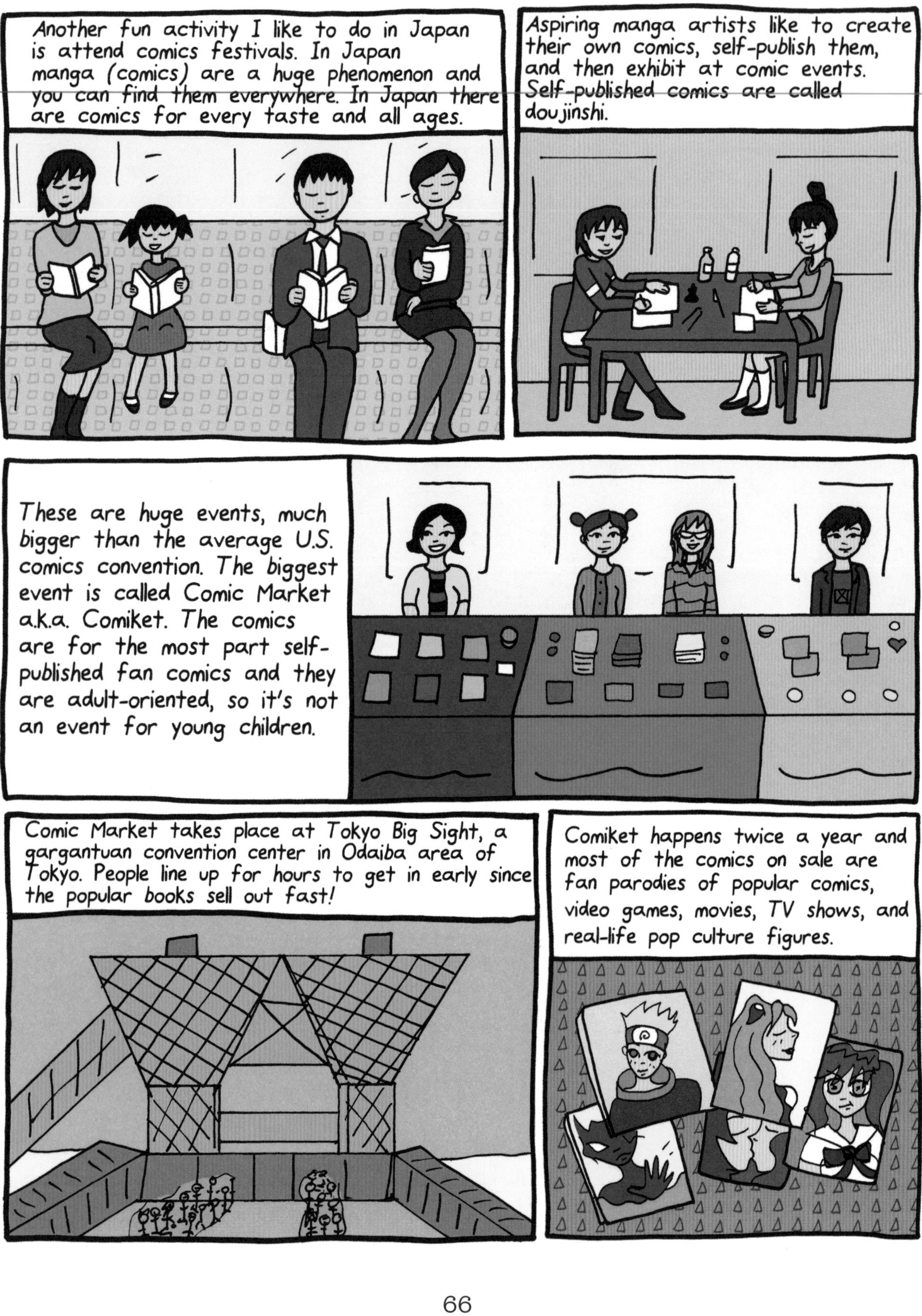
Another fun activity I like to do in Japan is attend comics festivals. In Japan manga (comics) are a huge phenomenon and you can find them everywhere. In Japan there are comics for every taste and all ages.
Aspiring manga artists like to create their own comics, self-publish them, and then exhibit at comic events. Self-published comics are called doujinshi.
These are huge events, much bigger than the average U.S. comics convention. The biggest event is called Comic Market a.k.a. Comiket. The comics are for the most part self-published fan comics and they are adult-oriented, so it's not an event for young children.
Comic Market takes place at Tokyo Big Sight, a gargantuan convention center in Odaiba area of Tokyo. People line up for hours to get in early since the popular books sell out fast!
Comiket happens twice a year and most of the comics on sale are fan parodies of popular comics, video games, movies, TV shows, and real-life pop culture figures.

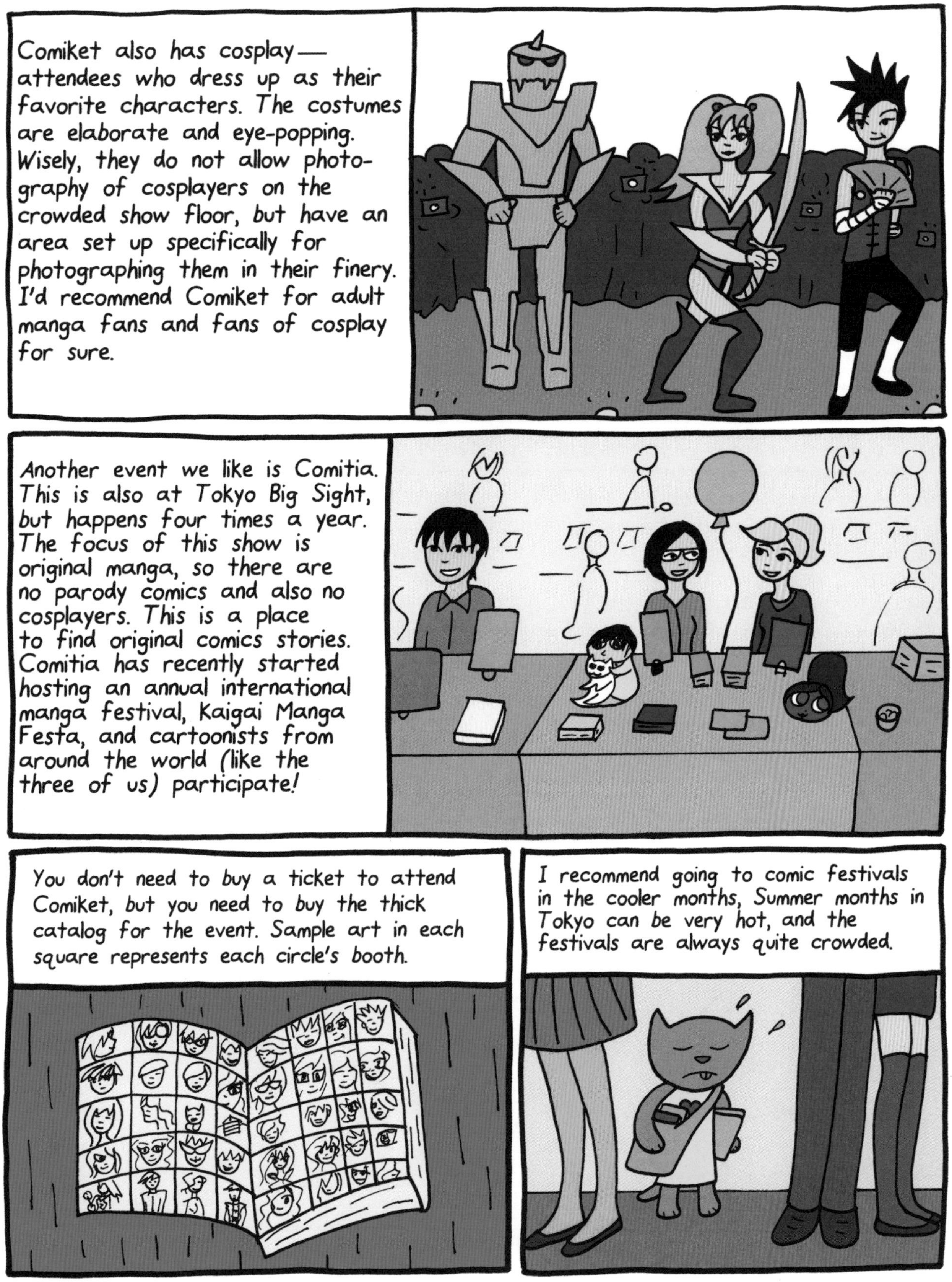
Comiket also has cosplay—attendees who dress up as their favorite characters. The costumes are elaborate and eye-popping. Wisely, they do not allow photography of cosplayers on the crowded show floor, but have an area set up specifically for photographing them in their finery. I'd recommend Comiket for adult manga fans and fans of cosplay for sure.
Another event we like is Comitia. This is also at Tokyo Big Sight, but happens four times a year. The focus of this show is original manga, so there are no parody comics and also no cosplayers. This is a place to find original comics stories. Comitia has recently started hosting an annual international manga festival, Kaigai Manga Festa, and cartoonists from around the world (like the three of us) participate!
You don't need to buy a ticket to attend Comiket, but you need to buy the thick catalog for the event. Sample art in each square represents each circle's booth.
I recommend going to comic festivals in the cooler months, Summer months in Tokyo can be very hot, and the festivals are always quite crowded.

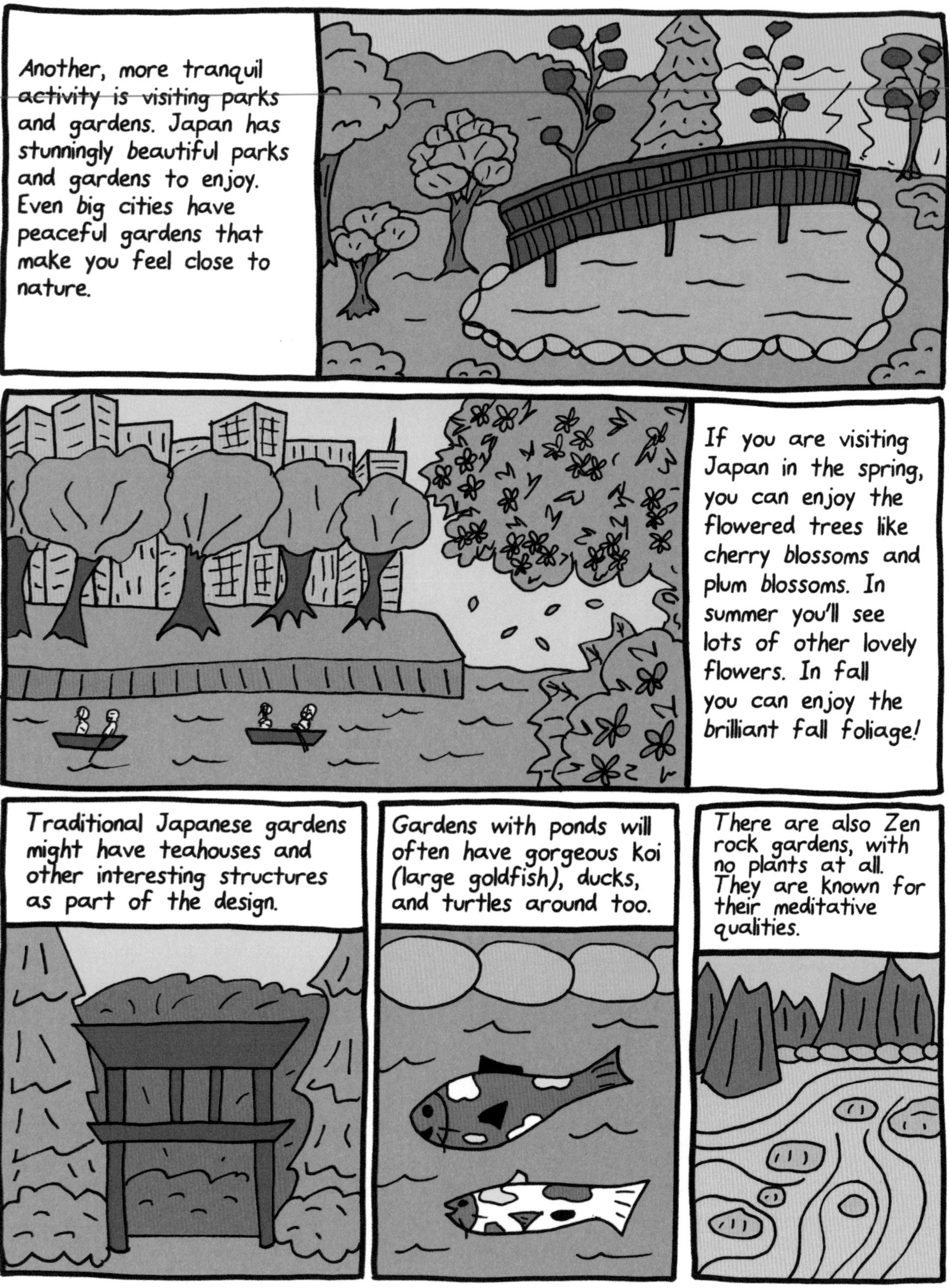
Another, more tranquil activity is visiting parks and gardens. Japan has stunningly beautiful parks and gardens to enjoy. Even big cities have peaceful gardens that make you feel close to nature.
If you are visiting Japan in the spring, you can enjoy the flowered trees like cherry blossoms and plum blossoms. In summer you'll see lots of other lovely flowers. In fall you can enjoy the brilliant fall foliage!
Traditional Japanese gardens might have teahouses and other interesting structures as part of the design.
Gardens with ponds will often have gorgeous koi (large goldfish), ducks, and turtles around too.
There are also Zen rock gardens, with no plants at all. They are known for their meditative qualities.

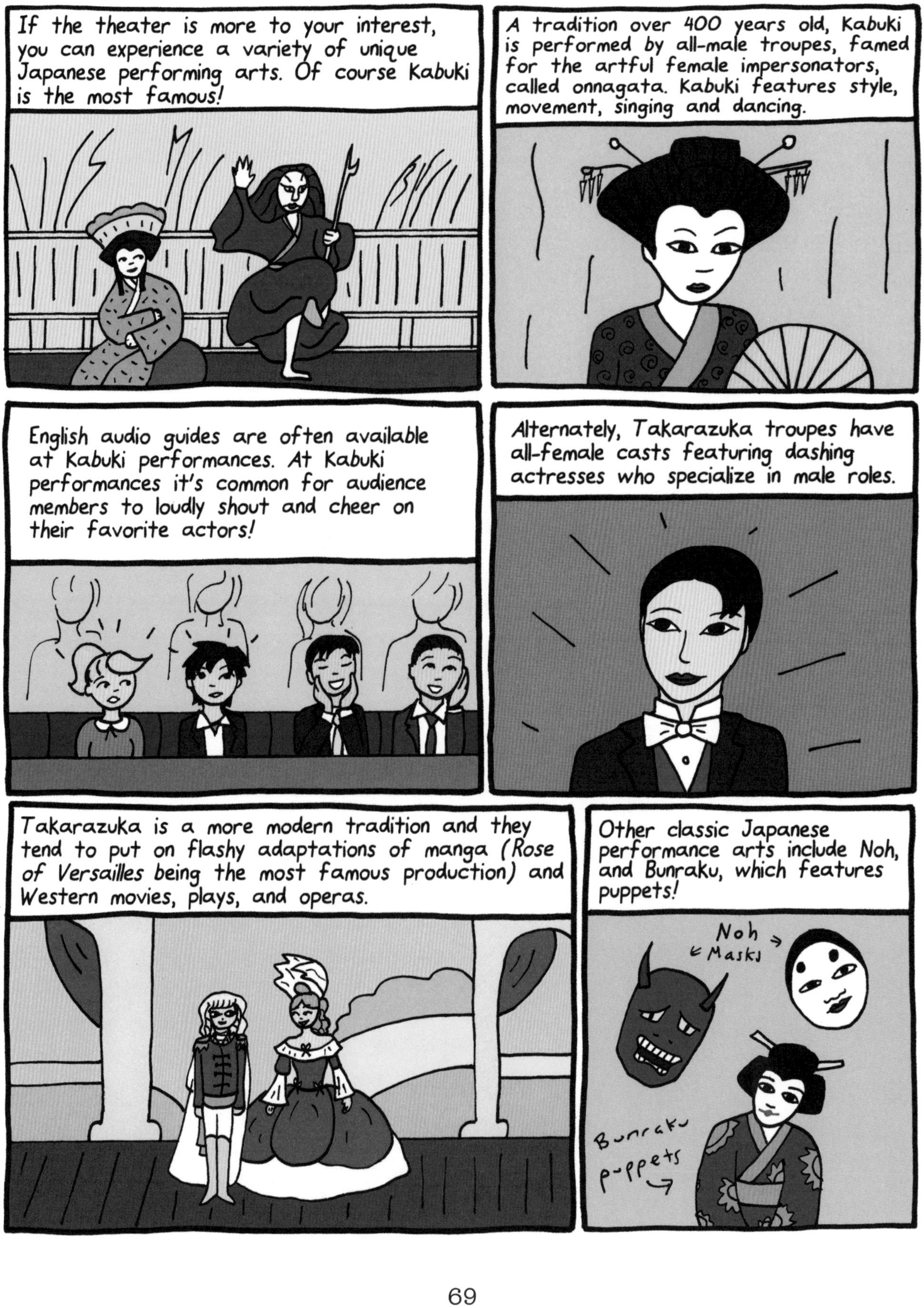
If the theater is more to your interest, you can experience a variety of unique Japanese performing arts. Of course Kabuki is the most famous!
A tradition over 400 years old, Kabuki is performed by all-male troupes, famed for the artful female impersonators, called onnagata. Kabuki features style, movement, singing and dancing.
English audio guides are often available at Kabuki performances. At Kabuki performances it's common for audience members to loudly shout and cheer on their favorite actors!
Alternately, Takarazuka troupes have all-female casts featuring dashing actresses who specialize in male roles.
Takarazuka is a more modern tradition and they tend to put on flashy adaptations of manga (*Rose of Versailles* being the most famous production) and Western movies, plays, and operas.
Other classic Japanese performance arts include Noh, and Bunraku, which features puppets!
Noh Masks
Bunraku puppets

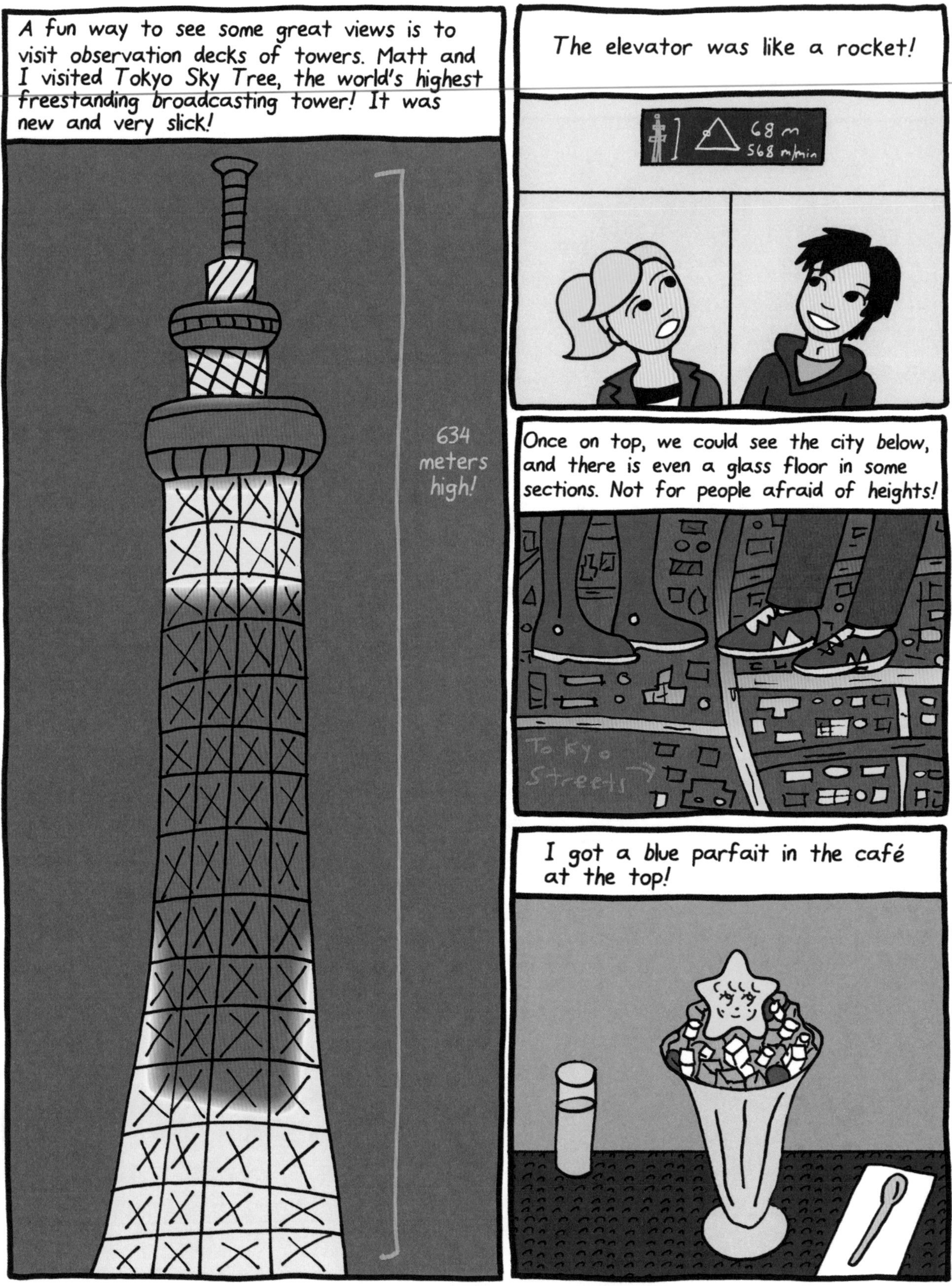
A fun way to see some great views is to visit observation decks of towers. Matt and I visited Tokyo Sky Tree, the world's highest freestanding broadcasting tower! It was new and very slick!
634 meters high!
The elevator was like a rocket!
68 m
568 m/min
Once on top, we could see the city below, and there is even a glass floor in some sections. Not for people afraid of heights!
Tokyo Streets
I got a blue parfait in the café at the top!

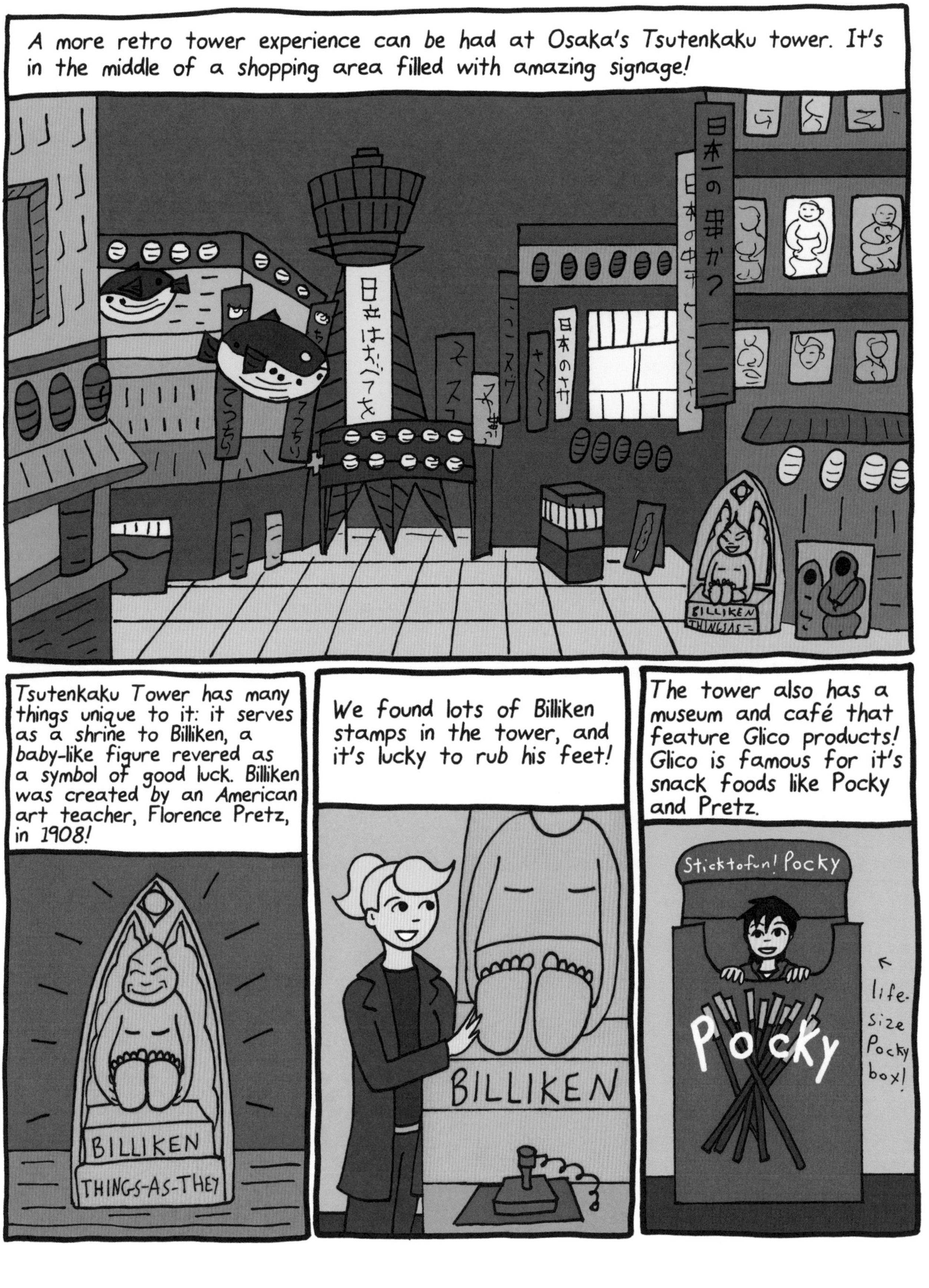
A more retro tower experience can be had at Osaka's Tsutenkaku tower. It's in the middle of a shopping area filled with amazing signage!
BILLIKEN
Tsutenkaku Tower has many things unique to it: it serves as a shrine to Billiken, a baby-like figure revered as a symbol of good luck. Billiken was created by an American art teacher, Florence Pretz, in 1908!
BILLIKEN
THINGS-AS-THEY
We found lots of Billiken stamps in the tower, and it's lucky to rub his feet!
BILLIKEN
The tower also has a museum and café that feature Glico products! Glico is famous for it's snack foods like Pocky and Pretz.
Sticktofun! Pocky
Pocky
life-size Pocky box!

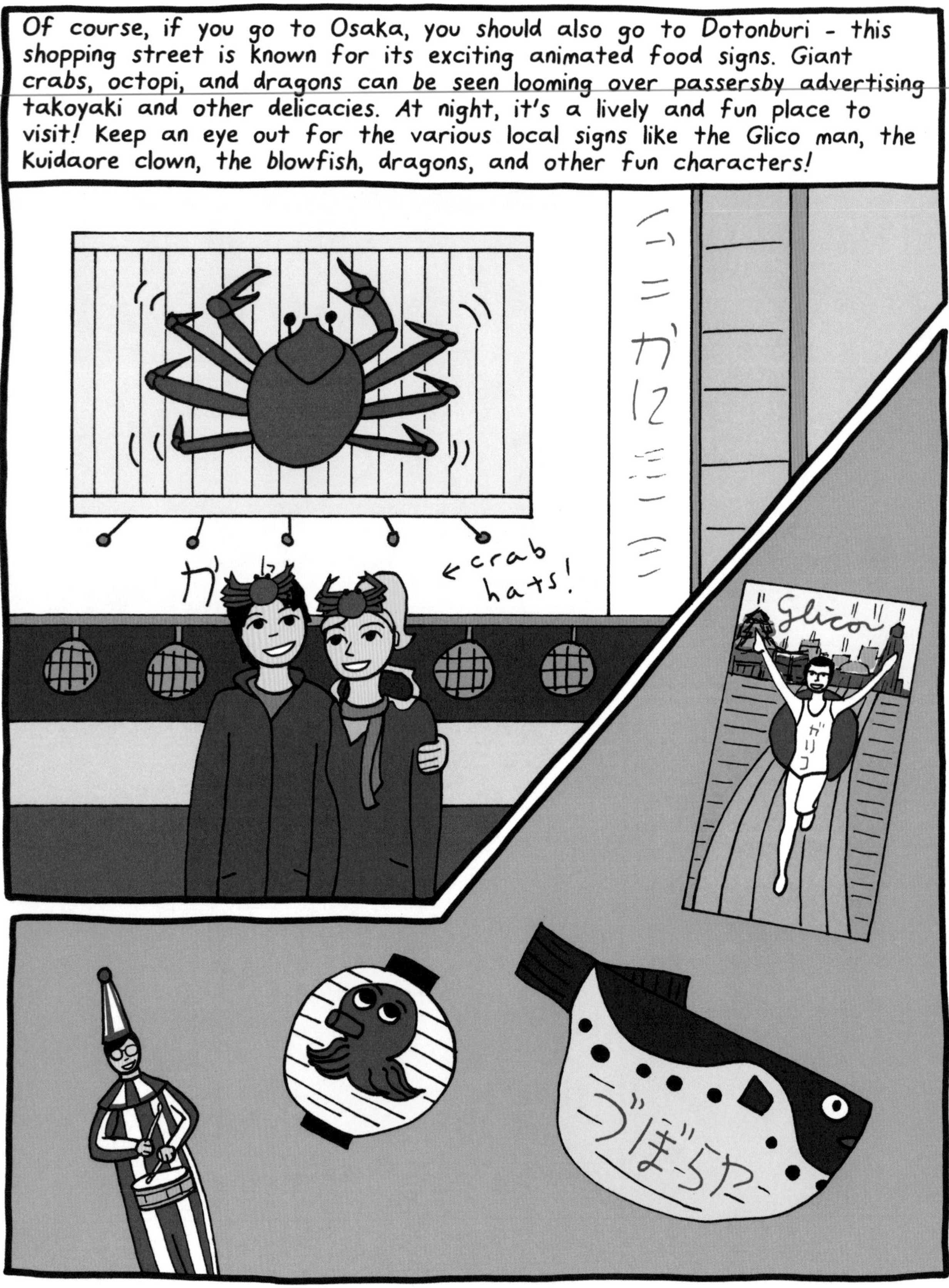
Of course, if you go to Osaka, you should also go to Dotonburi - this shopping street is known for its exciting animated food signs. Giant crabs, octopi, and dragons can be seen looming over passersby advertising takoyaki and other delicacies. At night, it's a lively and fun place to visit! Keep an eye out for the various local signs like the Glico man, the Kuidaore clown, the blowfish, dragons, and other fun characters!
← crab hats!
Glico
ガリコ
づぼらや

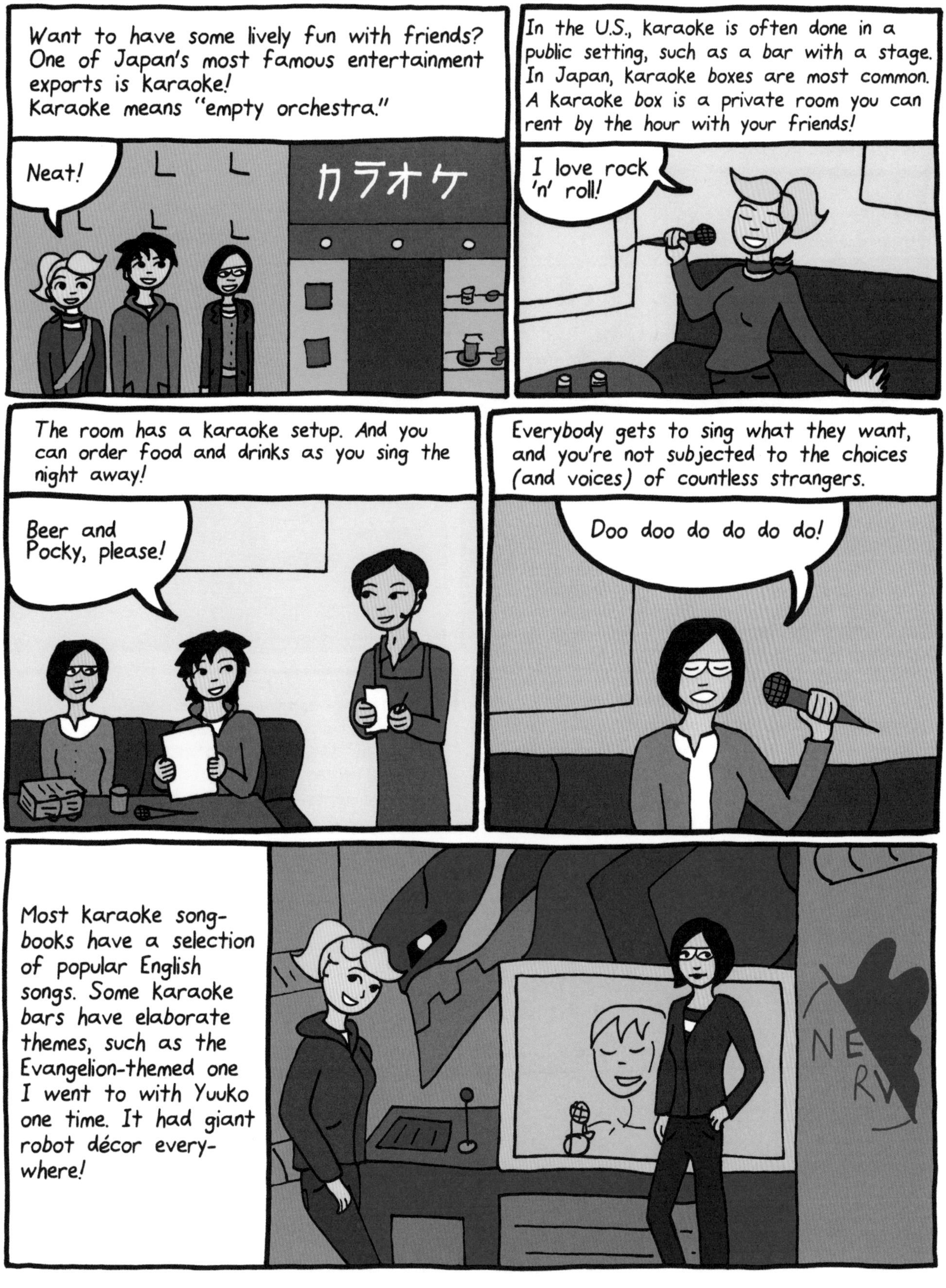
Want to have some lively fun with friends? One of Japan's most famous entertainment exports is karaoke! Karaoke means "empty orchestra."
Neat!
カラオケ
In the U.S., karaoke is often done in a public setting, such as a bar with a stage. In Japan, karaoke boxes are most common. A karaoke box is a private room you can rent by the hour with your friends!
I love rock 'n' roll!
The room has a karaoke setup. And you can order food and drinks as you sing the night away!
Beer and Pocky, please!
Everybody gets to sing what they want, and you're not subjected to the choices (and voices) of countless strangers.
Doo doo do do do do!
Most karaoke songbooks have a selection of popular English songs. Some karaoke bars have elaborate themes, such as the Evangelion-themed one I went to with Yuuko one time. It had giant robot décor everywhere!
NE
RV

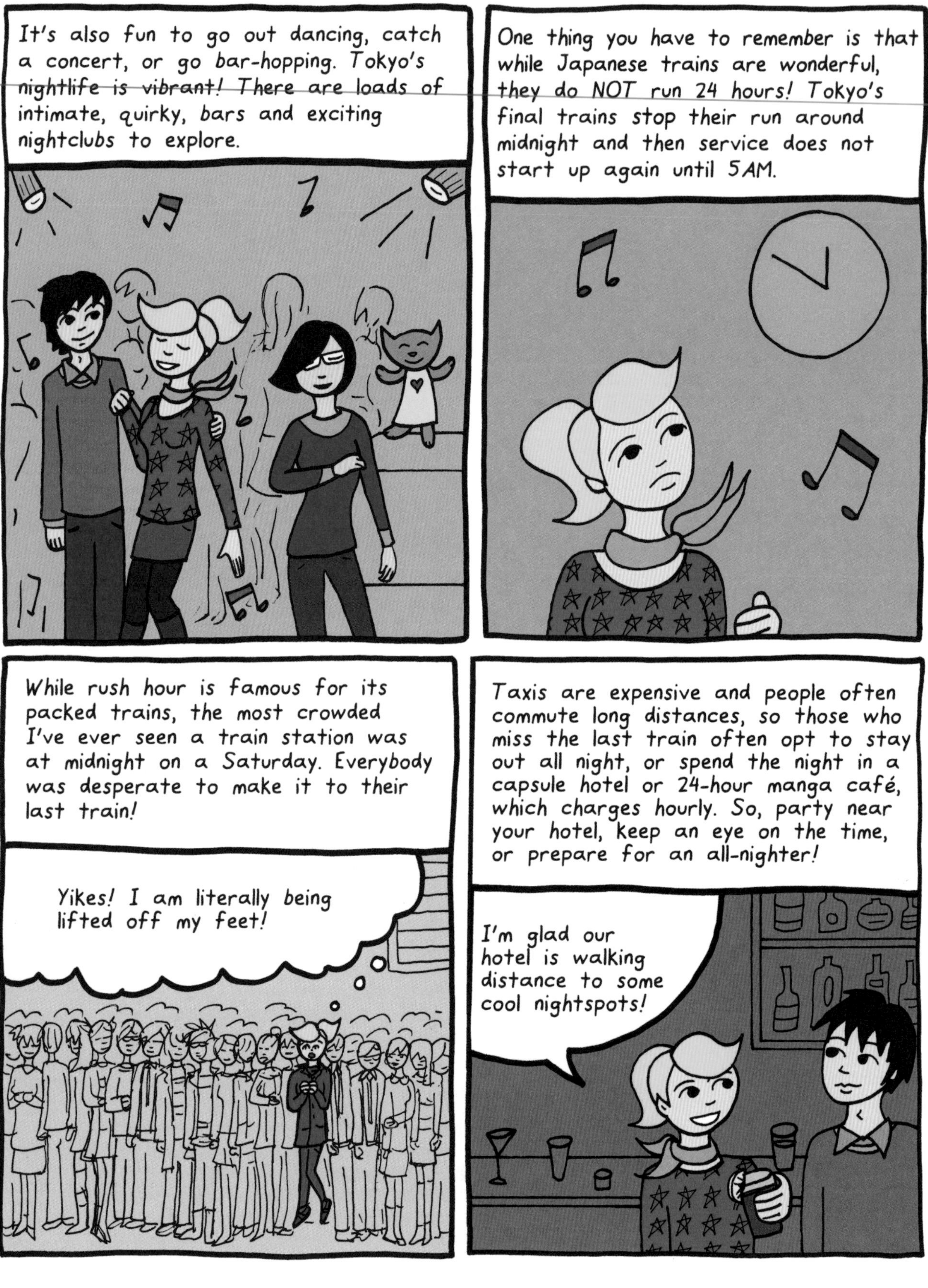
It's also fun to go out dancing, catch a concert, or go bar-hopping. Tokyo's nightlife is vibrant! There are loads of intimate, quirky, bars and exciting nightclubs to explore.
One thing you have to remember is that while Japanese trains are wonderful, they do NOT run 24 hours! Tokyo's final trains stop their run around midnight and then service does not start up again until 5AM.
While rush hour is famous for its packed trains, the most crowded I've ever seen a train station was at midnight on a Saturday. Everybody was desperate to make it to their last train!
Yikes! I am literally being lifted off my feet!
Taxis are expensive and people often commute long distances, so those who miss the last train often opt to stay out all night, or spend the night in a capsule hotel or 24-hour manga café, which charges hourly. So, party near your hotel, keep an eye on the time, or prepare for an all-nighter!
I'm glad our hotel is walking distance to some cool nightspots!

Ooedo-Onsen- Monogatari (2-6-3 Aomi, Koto, Tokyo 135-0064)
This is recommended for first time onsen visitors in the Tokyo area and
has free shuttle buses from various Tokyo locations.

http://www.ooedoonsen.jp/daiba/english/info.html

Comiket happens twice a year (once in August and once in December)
at Tokyo Big Sight (3-11-1 Ariake, Koto-ku, Tokyo, Japan 135-0063).

http://www.comiket.co.jp

Kaigai Festa happens once a year in the fall at Tokyo Big Sight.

http://kaigaimangafesta.com/en/

Kabuki performance information and locations can be found here:

http://www.kabuki-bito.jp/eng/contents/theatre/kabukiza.html

Takarazuka performance information and locations can be found here:

http://kageki.hankyu.co.jp/english/

Tokyo SkyTree (〒131-0045 Tokyo, Sumida, Oshiage, 1-1-2)
http://www.tokyo-skytree.jp/en/

Tsutenkaku Tower is in Osaka's Shinsekai district.
It is a short walk from Shin-Imamiya Station on
the JR Loop Line, Dobutsuen-mae Station on the
Midosuji and Tanimachi Subway Lines, and
Ebisucho Station on the Tanimachi Subway
Line.

Dotonbori is in the Minami (Namba) area
of Osaka, located around Namba Station.

Karaoke spots are usually pretty easy to
find. One of the biggest chains is called
Pasela. They often have luxurious and
themed accommodations. The Evangelion-themed
room we sang in is at Pasela Akiba.

http://www.pasela.co.jp/shop/akihabara/info/index.html

Tokyo nightlife and dancing is plentiful in
Roppongi and Shibuya. Golden Gai in Shinjuku has
over one hundred tiny unique bars lining its narrow alleys.
Gay nightlife can be found in the Shinjuku-ni-chome district.

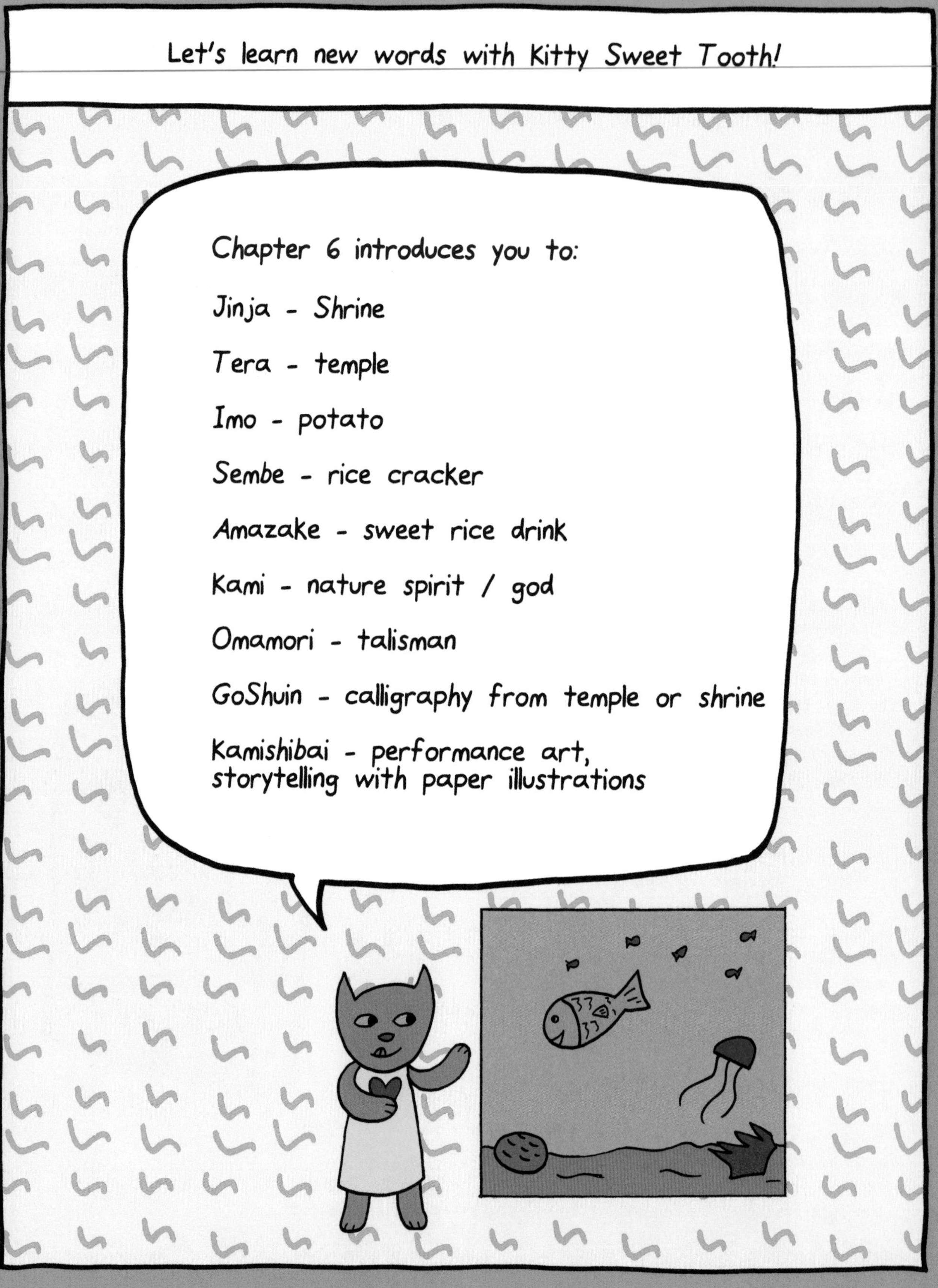
Let's learn new words with Kitty Sweet Tooth!
Chapter 6 introduces you to:
Jinja - Shrine
Tera - temple
Imo - potato
Sembe - rice cracker
Amazake - sweet rice drink
Kami - nature spirit / god
Omamori - talisman
GoShuin - calligraphy from temple or shrine
Kamishibai - performance art, storytelling with paper illustrations

Chapter 6

So Much to See!

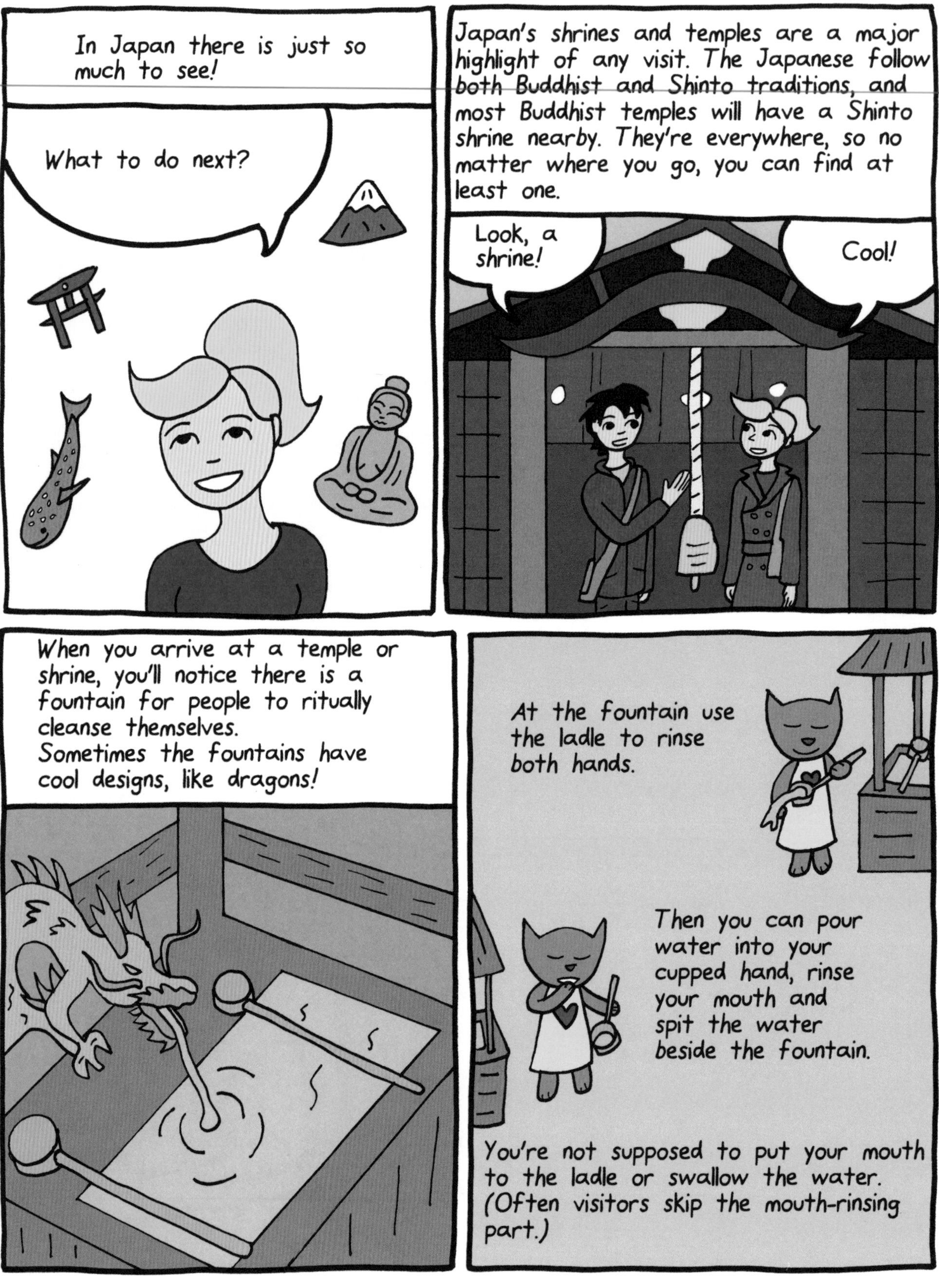
In Japan there is just so much to see!
What to do next?
Japan's shrines and temples are a major highlight of any visit. The Japanese follow both Buddhist and Shinto traditions, and most Buddhist temples will have a Shinto shrine nearby. They're everywhere, so no matter where you go, you can find at least one.
Look, a shrine!
Cool!
When you arrive at a temple or shrine, you'll notice there is a fountain for people to ritually cleanse themselves.
Sometimes the fountains have cool designs, like dragons!
At the fountain use the ladle to rinse both hands.
Then you can pour water into your cupped hand, rinse your mouth and spit the water beside the fountain.
You're not supposed to put your mouth to the ladle or swallow the water. (Often visitors skip the mouth-rinsing part.)

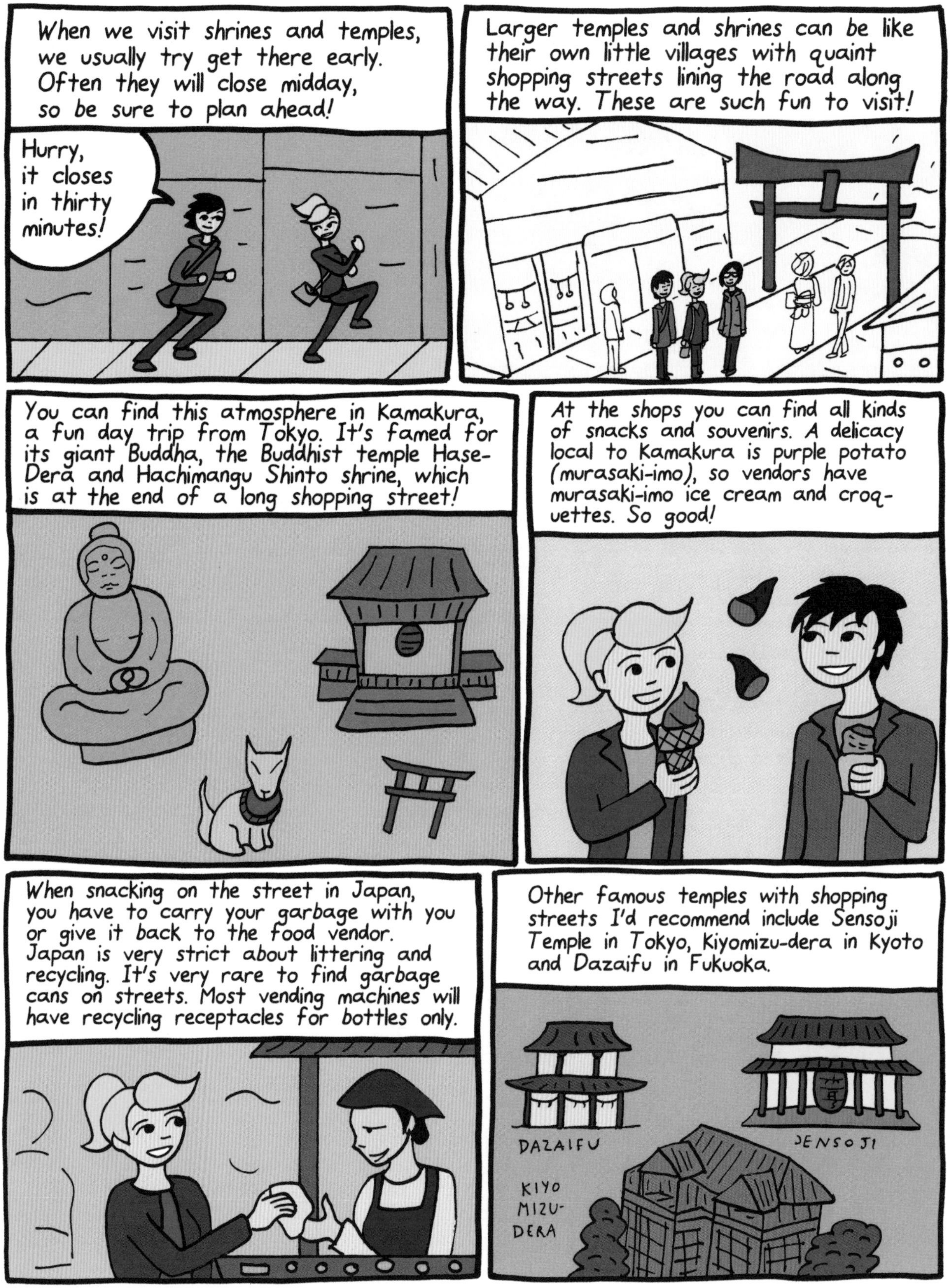
When we visit shrines and temples, we usually try get there early. Often they will close midday, so be sure to plan ahead!
Hurry, it closes in thirty minutes!
Larger temples and shrines can be like their own little villages with quaint shopping streets lining the road along the way. These are such fun to visit!
You can find this atmosphere in Kamakura, a fun day trip from Tokyo. It's famed for its giant Buddha, the Buddhist temple Hase-Dera and Hachimangu Shinto shrine, which is at the end of a long shopping street!
At the shops you can find all kinds of snacks and souvenirs. A delicacy local to Kamakura is purple potato (murasaki-imo), so vendors have murasaki-imo ice cream and croq-uettes. So good!
When snacking on the street in Japan, you have to carry your garbage with you or give it back to the food vendor. Japan is very strict about littering and recycling. It's very rare to find garbage cans on streets. Most vending machines will have recycling receptacles for bottles only.
Other famous temples with shopping streets I'd recommend include Sensoji Temple in Tokyo, Kiyomizu-dera in Kyoto and Dazaifu in Fukuoka.
DAZAIFU
SENSOJI
KIYO MIZU-DERA

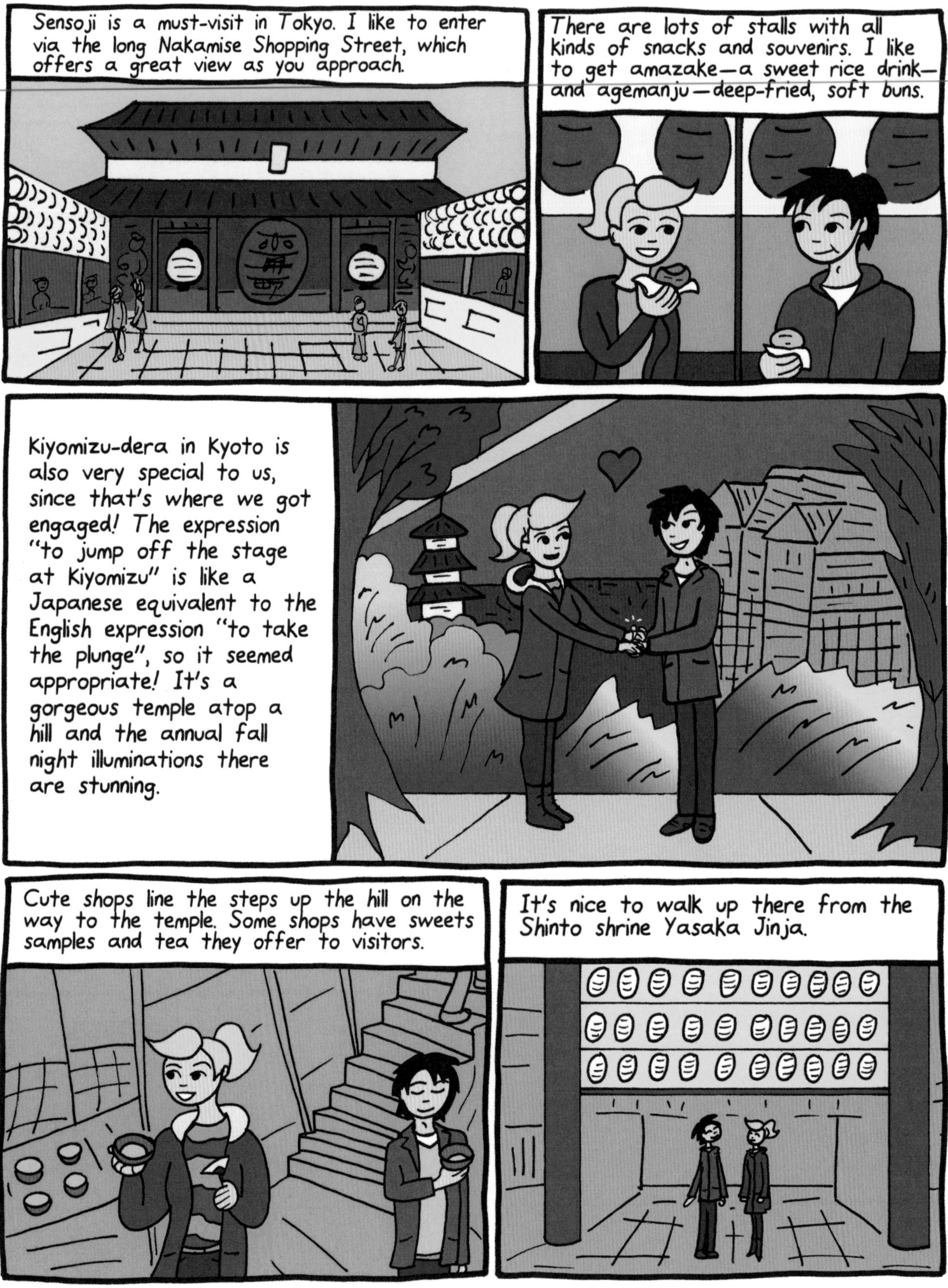
Sensoji is a must-visit in Tokyo. I like to enter via the long Nakamise Shopping Street, which offers a great view as you approach.
There are lots of stalls with all kinds of snacks and souvenirs. I like to get amazake—a sweet rice drink—and agemanju—deep-fried, soft buns.
Kiyomizu-dera in Kyoto is also very special to us, since that's where we got engaged! The expression "to jump off the stage at Kiyomizu" is like a Japanese equivalent to the English expression "to take the plunge", so it seemed appropriate! It's a gorgeous temple atop a hill and the annual fall night illuminations there are stunning.
Cute shops line the steps up the hill on the way to the temple. Some shops have sweets samples and tea they offer to visitors.
It's nice to walk up there from the Shinto shrine Yasaka Jinja.

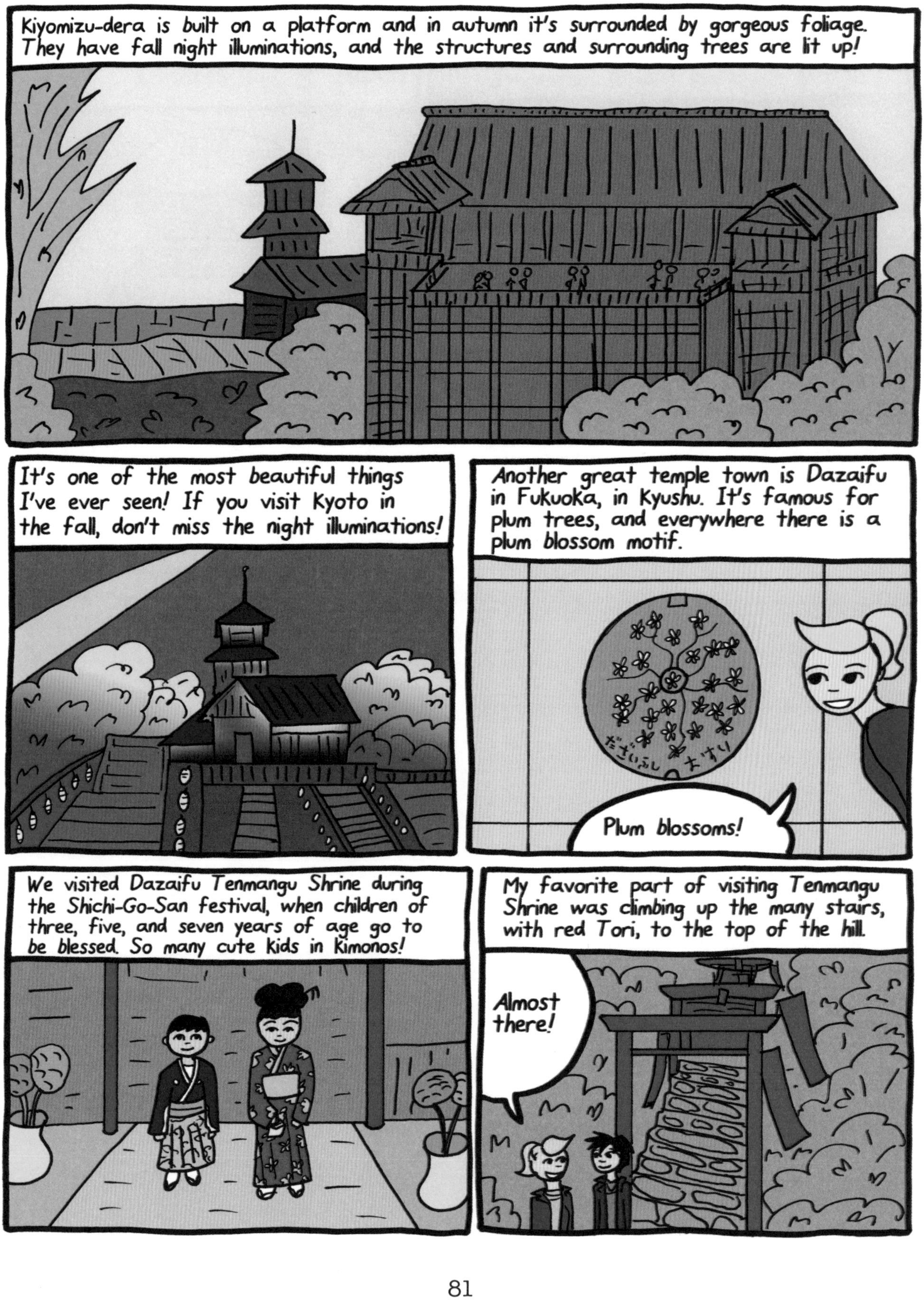
Kiyomizu-dera is built on a platform and in autumn it's surrounded by gorgeous foliage. They have fall night illuminations, and the structures and surrounding trees are lit up!
It's one of the most beautiful things I've ever seen! If you visit Kyoto in the fall, don't miss the night illuminations!
Another great temple town is Dazaifu in Fukuoka, in Kyushu. It's famous for plum trees, and everywhere there is a plum blossom motif.
だざいふし
Plum blossoms!
We visited Dazaifu Tenmangu Shrine during the Shichi-Go-San festival, when children of three, five, and seven years of age go to be blessed. So many cute kids in kimonos!
My favorite part of visiting Tenmangu Shrine was climbing up the many stairs, with red Tori, to the top of the hill.
Almost there!

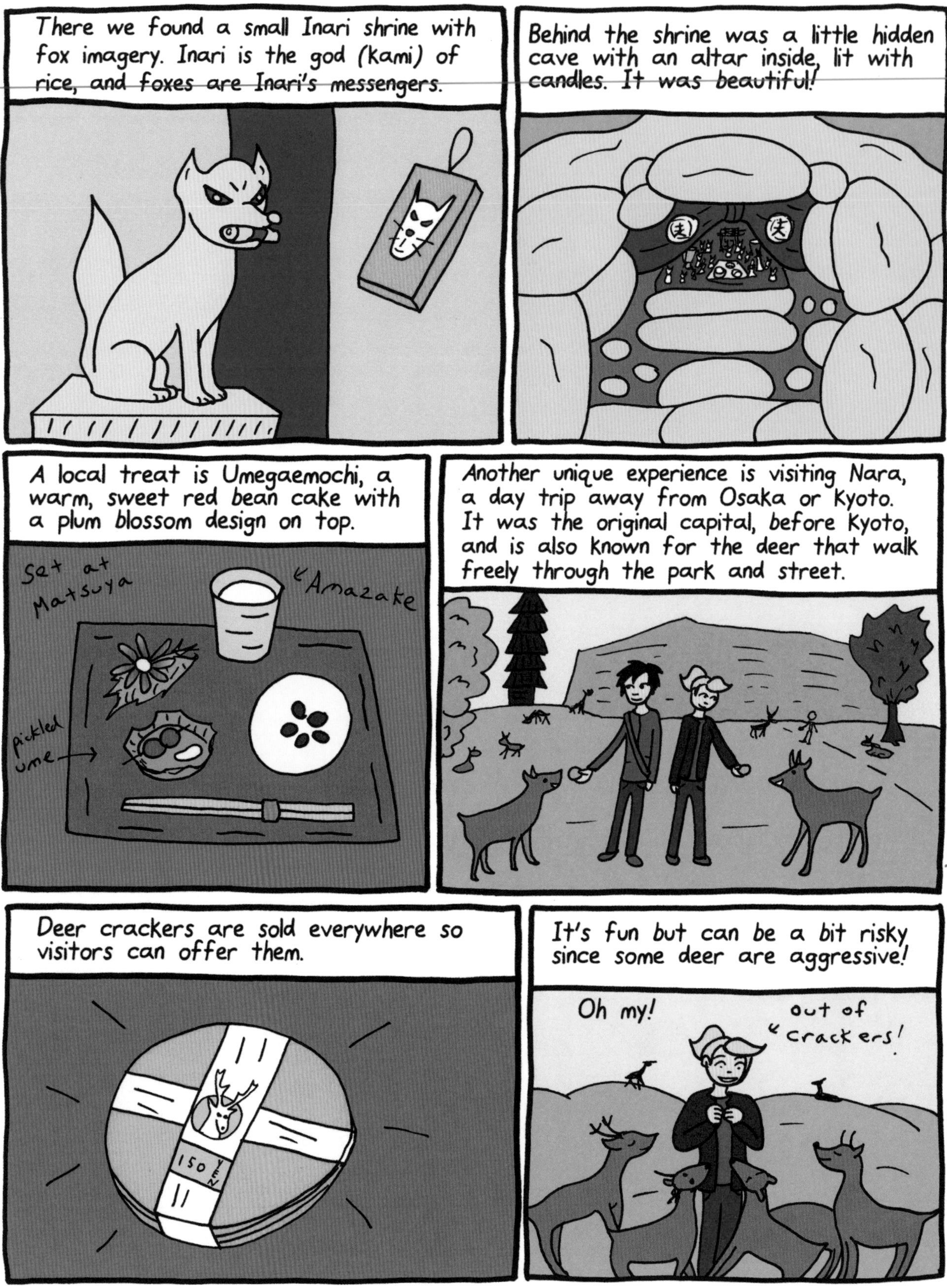
There we found a small Inari shrine with fox imagery. Inari is the god (kami) of rice, and foxes are Inari's messengers.
Behind the shrine was a little hidden cave with an altar inside, lit with candles. It was beautiful!
A local treat is Umegaemochi, a warm, sweet red bean cake with a plum blossom design on top.
Set at Matsuya
Amazake
pickled ume
Another unique experience is visiting Nara, a day trip away from Osaka or Kyoto. It was the original capital, before Kyoto, and is also known for the deer that walk freely through the park and street.
Deer crackers are sold everywhere so visitors can offer them.
150 YEN
It's fun but can be a bit risky since some deer are aggressive!
Oh my!
out of crackers!

A highlight of shrine and temple visits for me is shopping for omamori. These are amulets sold at temples and shrines.

I want them all!

They come in various styles, often little fabric pouches. They serve different purposes, such as bringing luck for safe travel, health and passing exams.

cat bell ←

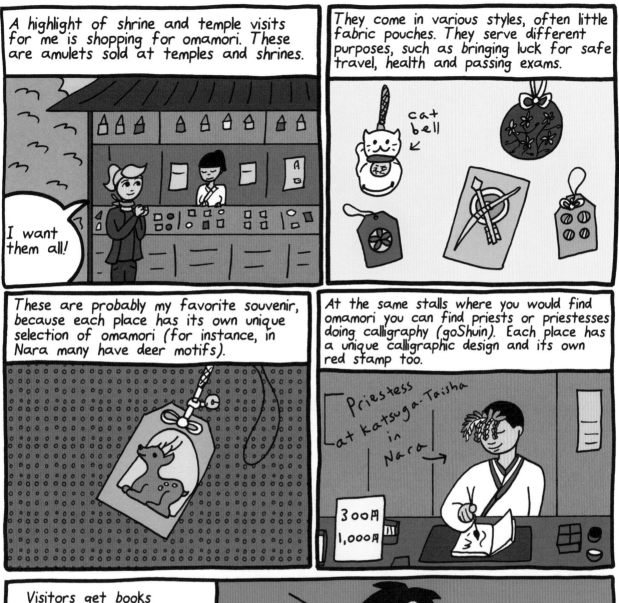

These are probably my favorite souvenir, because each place has its own unique selection of omamori (for instance, in Nara many have deer motifs).

At the same stalls where you would find omamori you can find priests or priestesses doing calligraphy (goShuin). Each place has a unique calligraphic design and its own red stamp too.

Priestess at Katsuga-Taisha in Nara →

300円
1,000円

Visitors get books (goShuinCho, usually available at the calligraphy stall) to collect calligraphy from different shrines and temples. These are wonderful mementos to collect during your travels. Typically the calligraphy is done in exchange for a donation of about 300 yen.

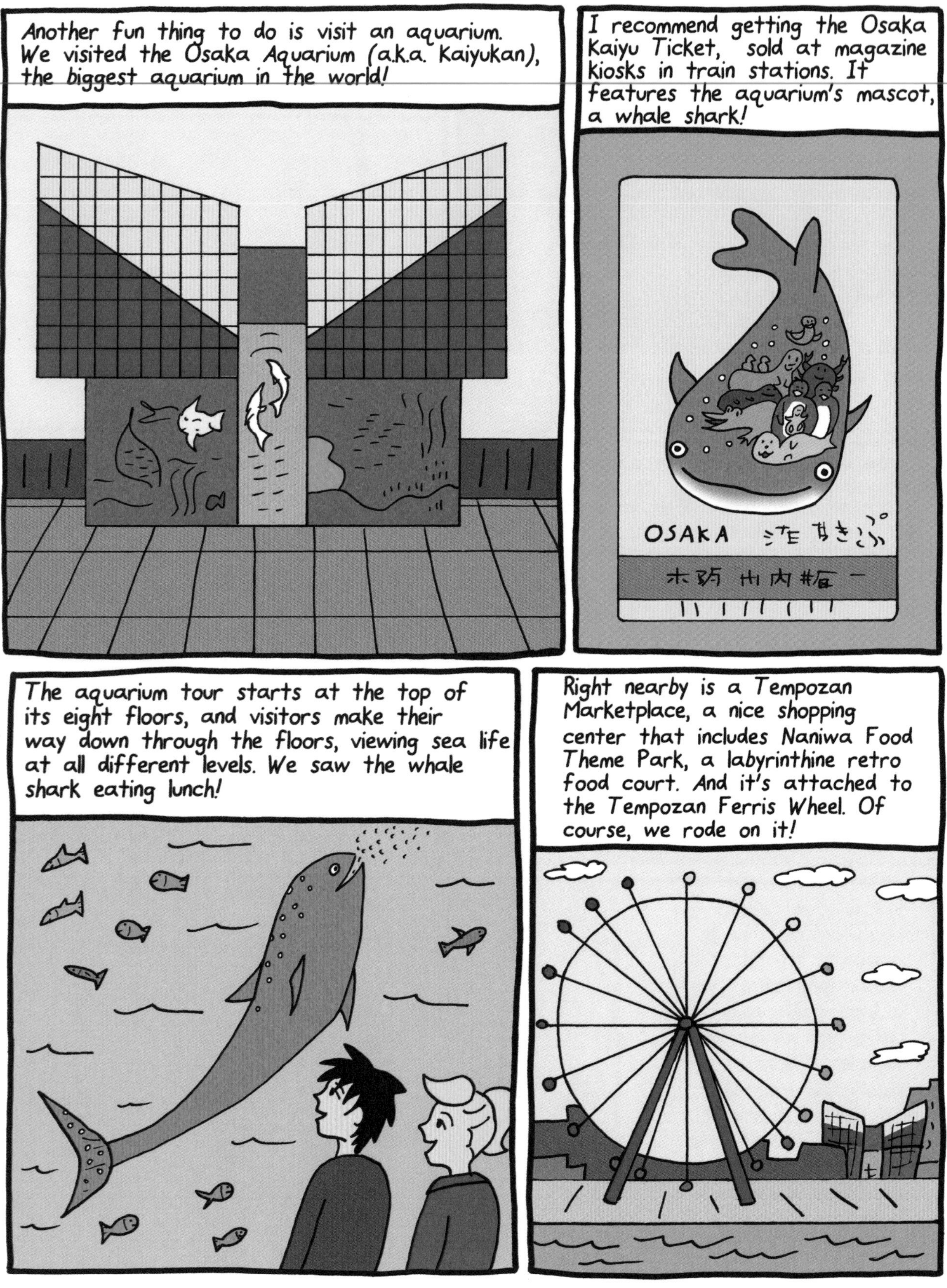
Another fun thing to do is visit an aquarium. We visited the Osaka Aquarium (a.k.a. Kaiyukan), the biggest aquarium in the world!
I recommend getting the Osaka Kaiyu Ticket, sold at magazine kiosks in train stations. It features the aquarium's mascot, a whale shark!
OSAKA
The aquarium tour starts at the top of its eight floors, and visitors make their way down through the floors, viewing sea life at all different levels. We saw the whale shark eating lunch!
Right nearby is a Tempozan Marketplace, a nice shopping center that includes Naniwa Food Theme Park, a labyrinthine retro food court. And it's attached to the Tempozan Ferris Wheel. Of course, we rode on it!

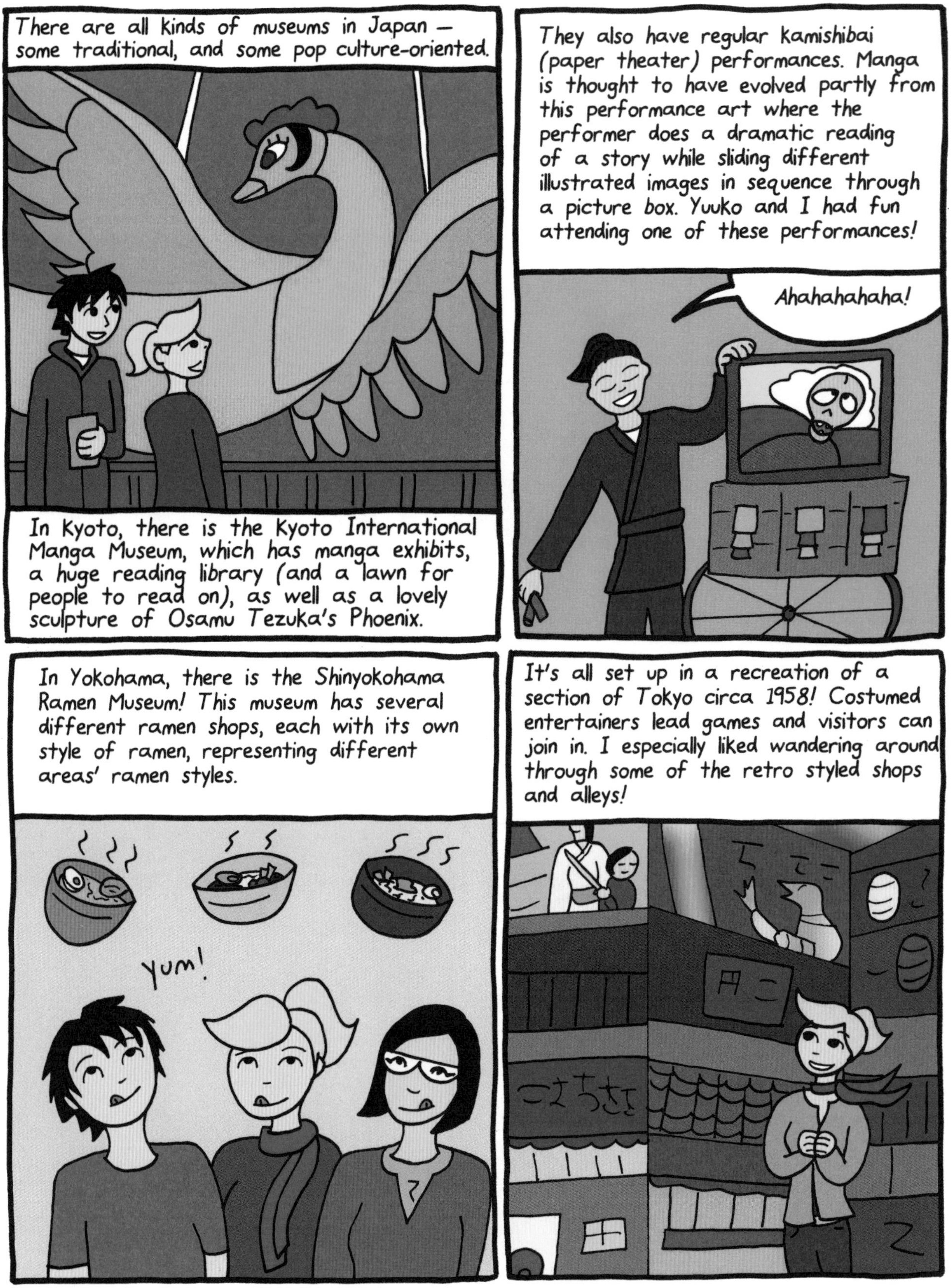
There are all kinds of museums in Japan — some traditional, and some pop culture-oriented.
In Kyoto, there is the Kyoto International Manga Museum, which has manga exhibits, a huge reading library (and a lawn for people to read on), as well as a lovely sculpture of Osamu Tezuka's Phoenix.
They also have regular kamishibai (paper theater) performances. Manga is thought to have evolved partly from this performance art where the performer does a dramatic reading of a story while sliding different illustrated images in sequence through a picture box. Yuuko and I had fun attending one of these performances!
Ahahahahaha!
In Yokohama, there is the Shinyokohama Ramen Museum! This museum has several different ramen shops, each with its own style of ramen, representing different areas' ramen styles.
yum!
It's all set up in a recreation of a section of Tokyo circa 1958! Costumed entertainers lead games and visitors can join in. I especially liked wandering around through some of the retro styled shops and alleys!

Fans of animation should certainly check out Tokyo's Ghibli Museum in nearby Mitaka, which imaginatively embodies the spirit of Studio Ghibli with a whimsical layout and features like the cat bus from *My Neighbor Totoro* and the giant robot from *Laputa*. This particular museum requires tourists to pre-reserve tickets via JTB travel agency. They can be purchased up to three months in advance of your visit.

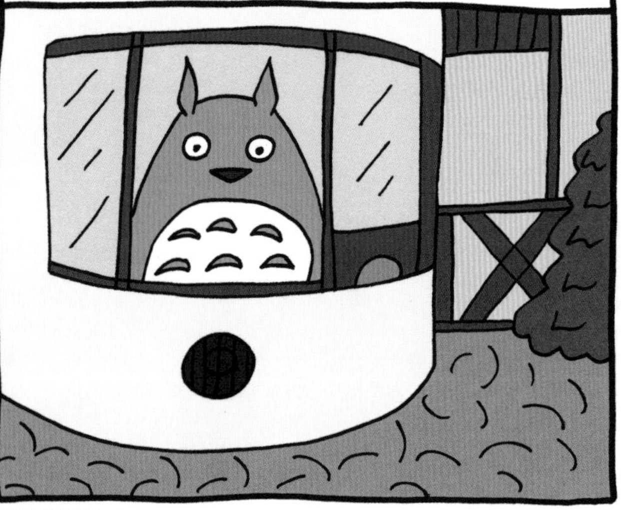

If you're a manga fan visiting the Osaka area, you'll want to check out the Osama Tezuka museum in the nearby town of Takarazuka (also famed for the Takarazuka performance revue). Tezuka, known as the god of manga, created Astro Boy, Black Jack, and countless other beloved characters. A trip to the museum and catching a performance by the revue could be a fun day trip from Osaka or Kyoto!

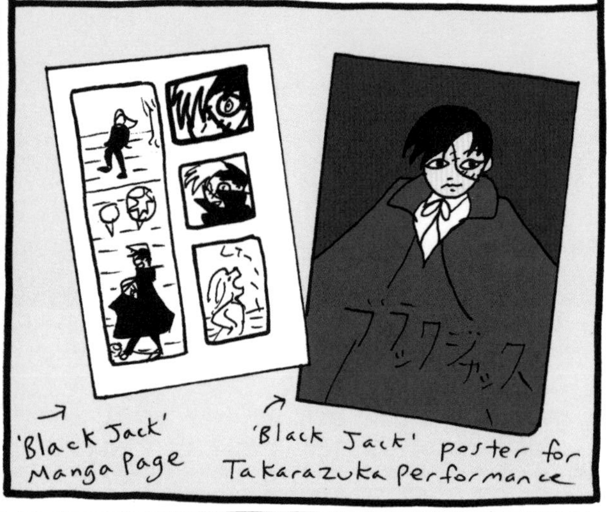
'Black Jack' Manga Page
'Black Jack' poster for Takarazuka performance

For more traditional types of museums in the Tokyo area, you can check out the Edo-Tokyo Museum and the Tokyo National Museum.

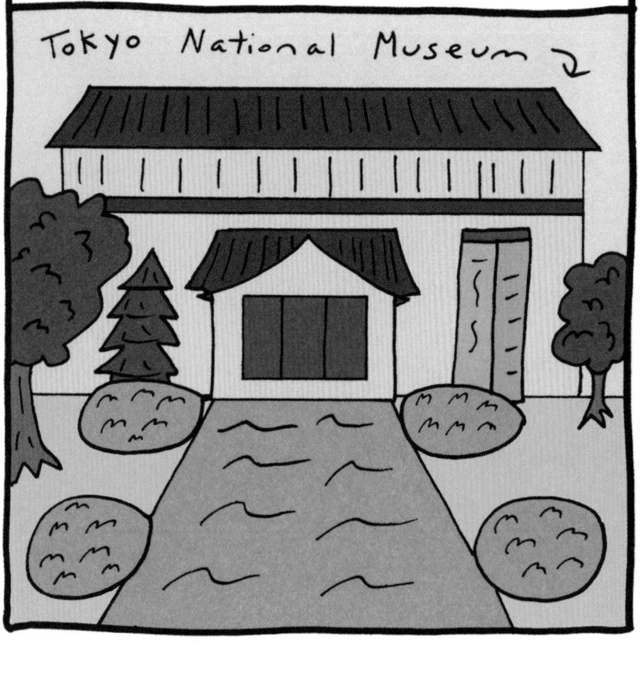
Tokyo National Museum

To see several museums (including Tokyo National Museum) in one spot, as well as some lovely shrines and temples, visit Tokyo's Ueno Park. A great idea if you're short on time!

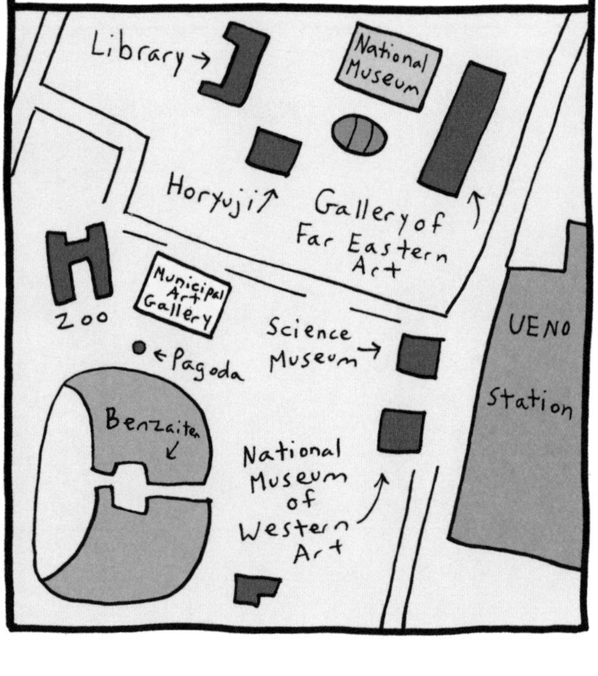
Library
National Museum
Horyuji
Gallery of Far Eastern Art
Zoo
Municipal Art Gallery
Science Museum
Pagoda
UENO Station
Benzaiten
National Museum of Western Art

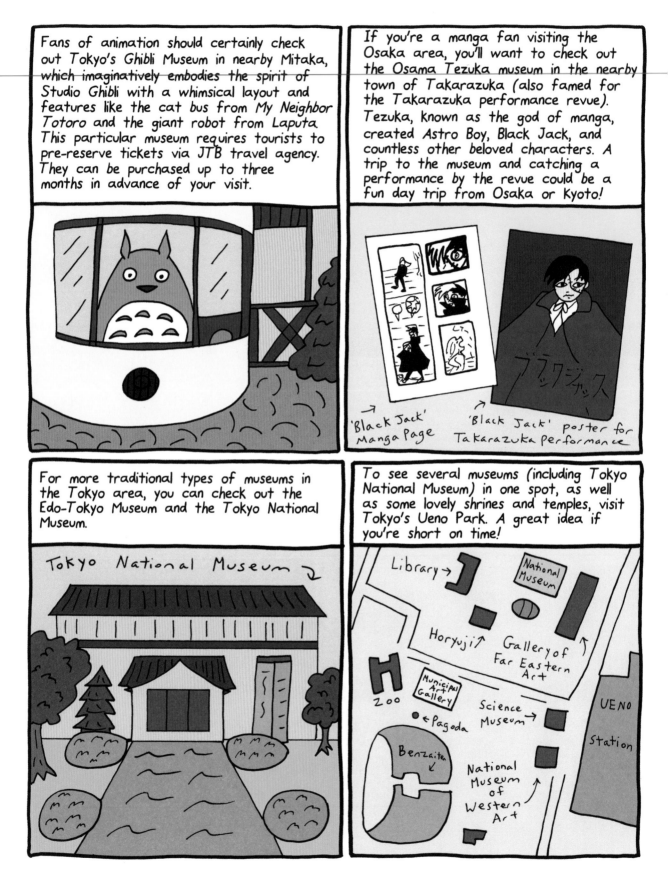

In Japan, you'll notice these cute lucky beckoning cat statues in shops and restaurants. This is the Maneki Neko. It is believed that the cat with its right paw raised invites money and the one with its left paw raised invites people. There are a few legends of the Maneki Neko. One is about a feudal lord during the Edo period who was beckoned by a cat to a temple gate. Once he was inside the temple, a severe thunderstorm suddenly struck. Out of gratitude, the lord made a large donation to the temple and designated it the temple of his family. When the cat died, Shobyodo temple was built on the grounds and the cat was deified and called Shobyo Kannon. Visitors started to offer Maneki Neko statues to show gratitude when their wishes came true. This charming temple ground, Gotoku-ji, is in Setagaya. It is an easy day trip within Tokyo, and highly recommended for cat lovers!

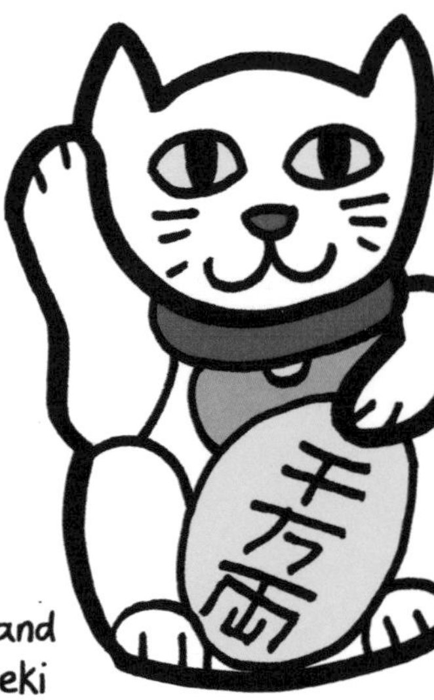
千万両

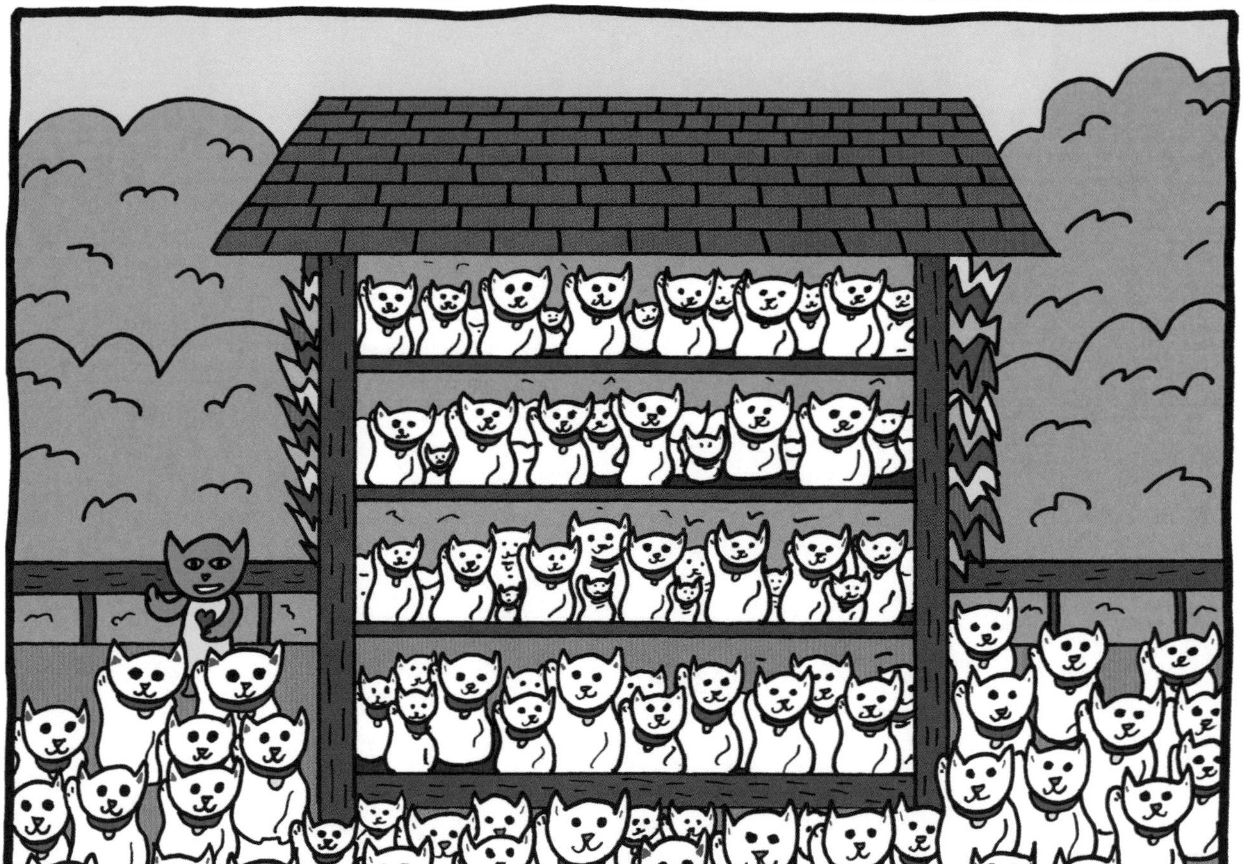

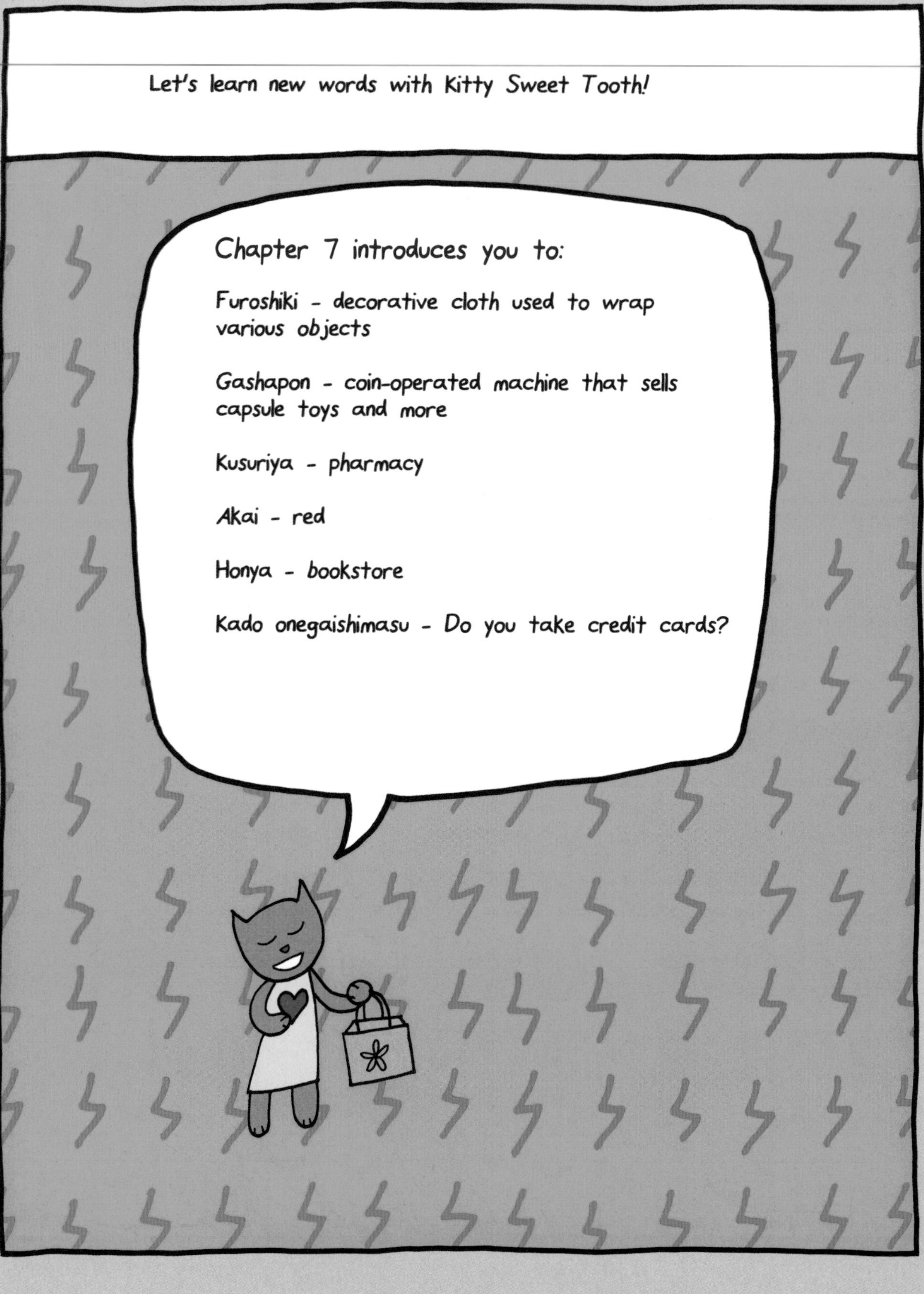
Let's learn new words with Kitty Sweet Tooth!
Chapter 7 introduces you to:
Furoshiki - decorative cloth used to wrap various objects
Gashapon - coin-operated machine that sells capsule toys and more
Kusuriya - pharmacy
Akai - red
Honya - bookstore
Kado onegaishimasu - Do you take credit cards?

Chapter 7

Did Somebody Say "Shopping"?

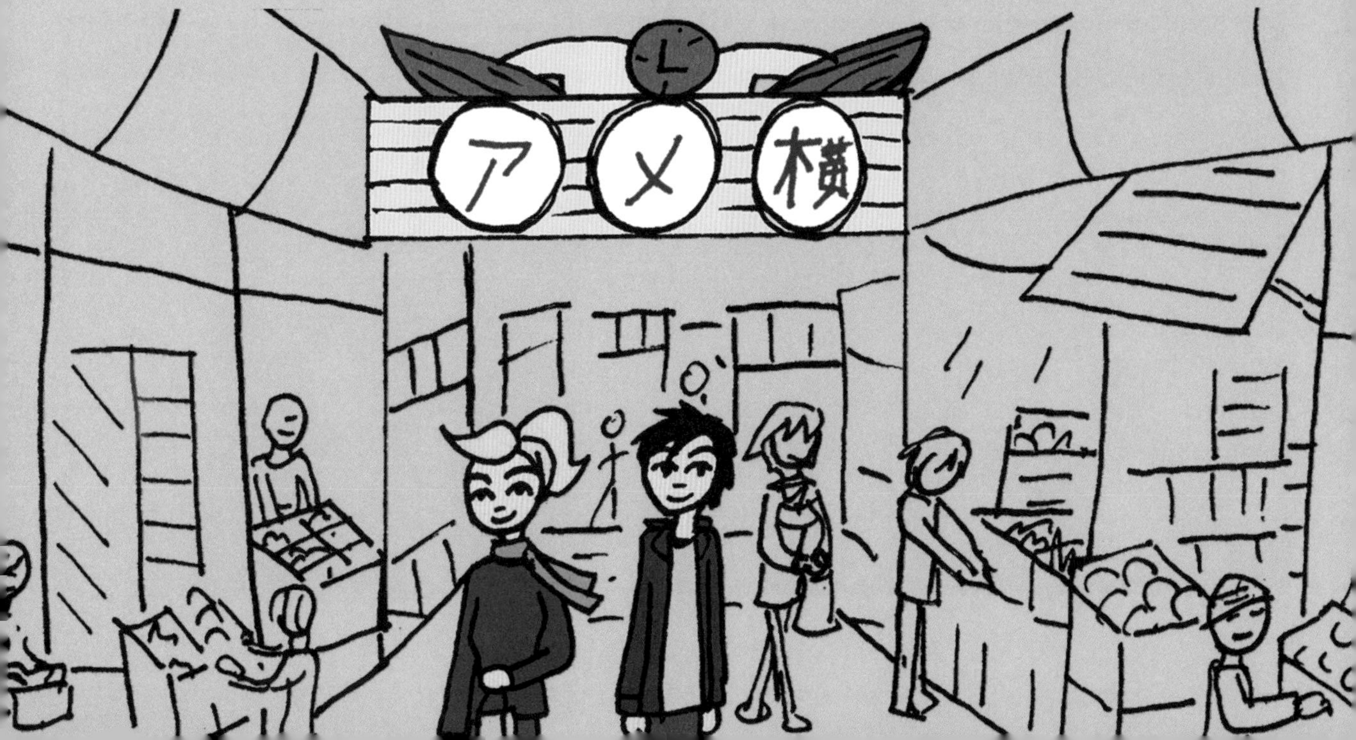
アメ横

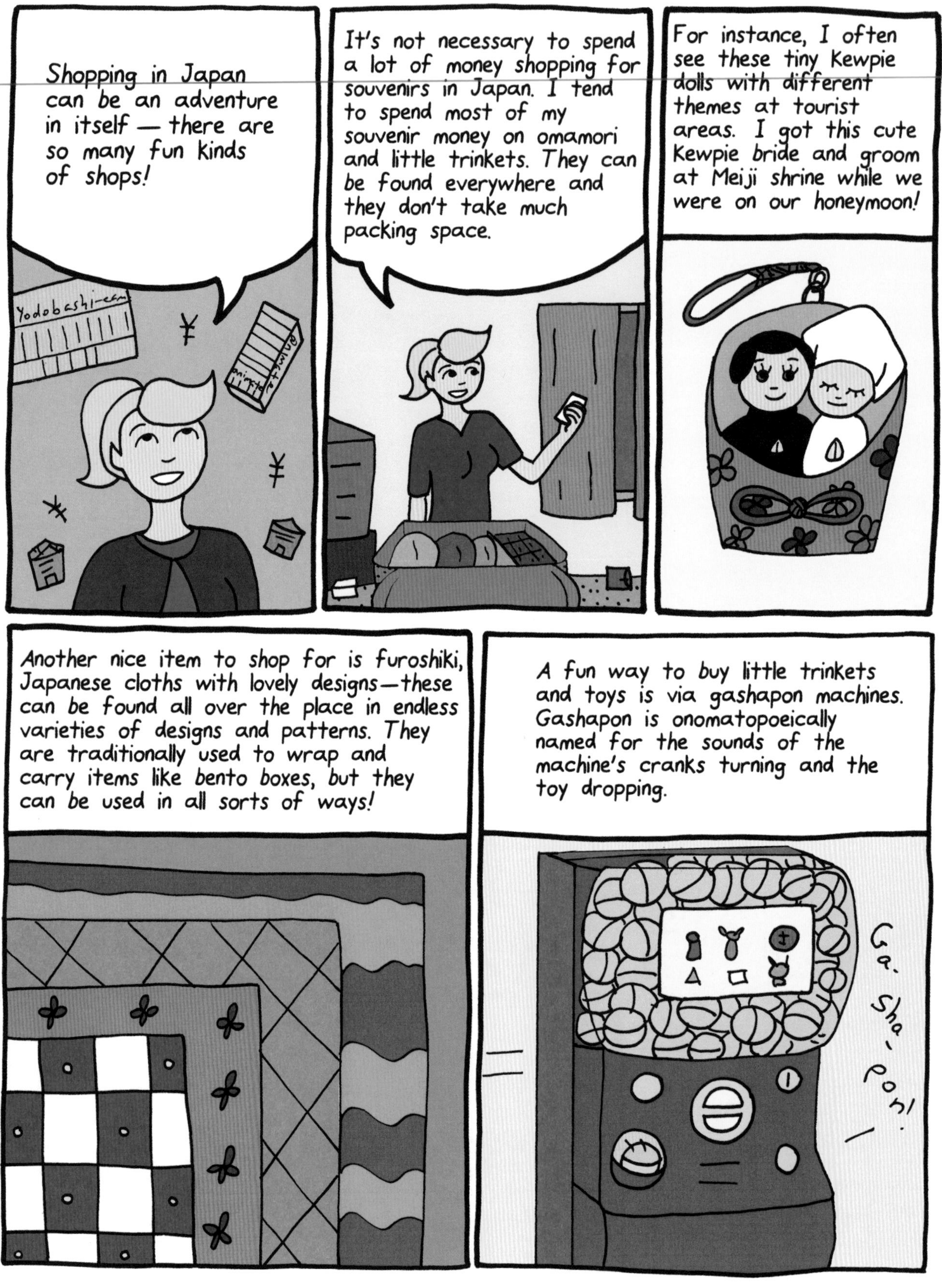

Shopping in Japan can be an adventure in itself — there are so many fun kinds of shops!
It's not necessary to spend a lot of money shopping for souvenirs in Japan. I tend to spend most of my souvenir money on omamori and little trinkets. They can be found everywhere and they don't take much packing space.
For instance, I often see these tiny Kewpie dolls with different themes at tourist areas. I got this cute Kewpie bride and groom at Meiji shrine while we were on our honeymoon!
Another nice item to shop for is furoshiki, Japanese cloths with lovely designs—these can be found all over the place in endless varieties of designs and patterns. They are traditionally used to wrap and carry items like bento boxes, but they can be used in all sorts of ways!
A fun way to buy little trinkets and toys is via gashapon machines. Gashapon is onomatopoeically named for the sounds of the machine's cranks turning and the toy dropping.
Ga-Sha-Pon!

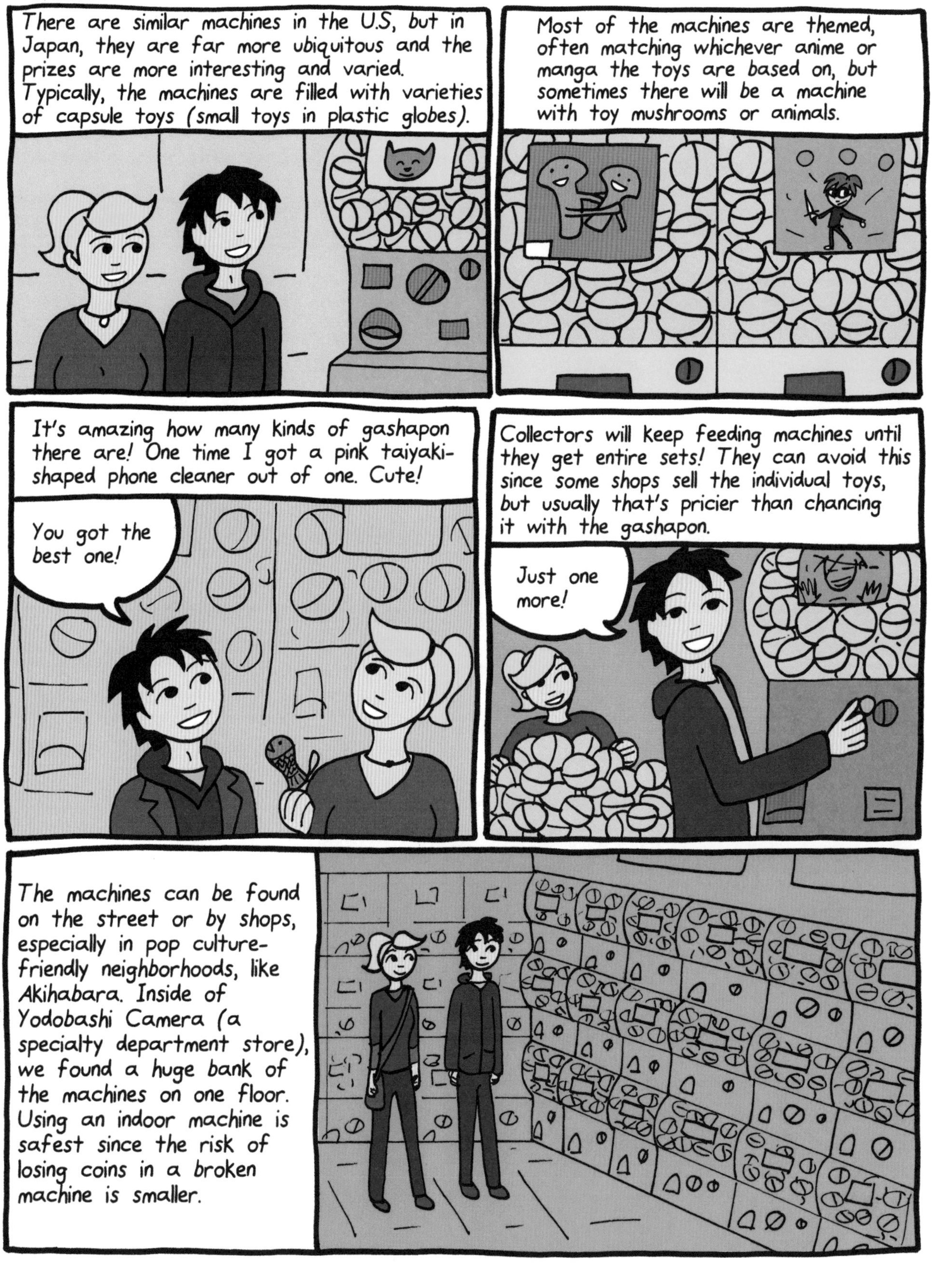
There are similar machines in the U.S, but in Japan, they are far more ubiquitous and the prizes are more interesting and varied. Typically, the machines are filled with varieties of capsule toys (small toys in plastic globes).
Most of the machines are themed, often matching whichever anime or manga the toys are based on, but sometimes there will be a machine with toy mushrooms or animals.
It's amazing how many kinds of gashapon there are! One time I got a pink taiyaki-shaped phone cleaner out of one. Cute!
You got the best one!
Collectors will keep feeding machines until they get entire sets! They can avoid this since some shops sell the individual toys, but usually that's pricier than chancing it with the gashapon.
Just one more!
The machines can be found on the street or by shops, especially in pop culture-friendly neighborhoods, like Akihabara. Inside of Yodobashi Camera (a specialty department store), we found a huge bank of the machines on one floor. Using an indoor machine is safest since the risk of losing coins in a broken machine is smaller.

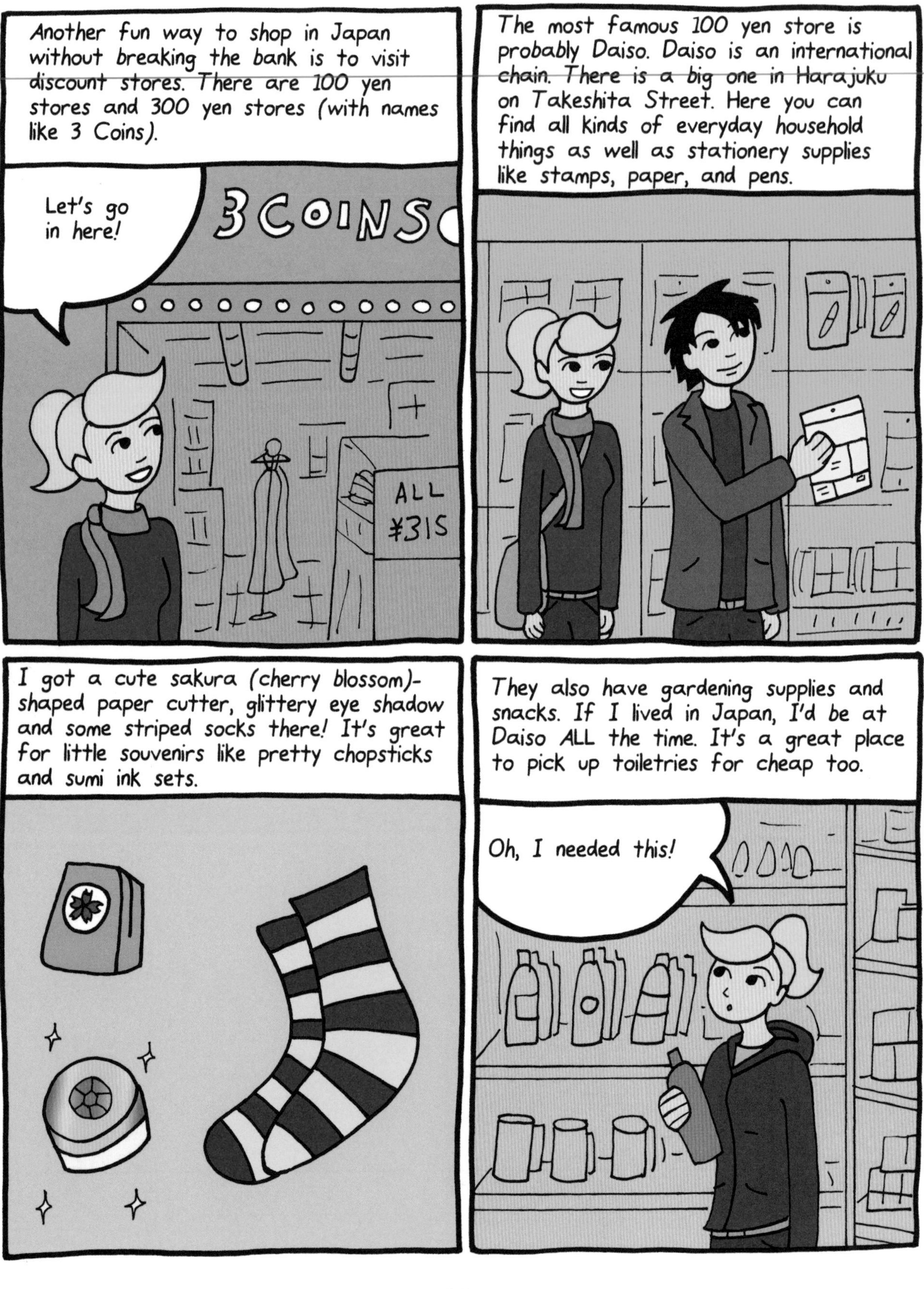
Another fun way to shop in Japan without breaking the bank is to visit discount stores. There are 100 yen stores and 300 yen stores (with names like 3 Coins).
Let's go in here!
3COINS
ALL ¥315
The most famous 100 yen store is probably Daiso. Daiso is an international chain. There is a big one in Harajuku on Takeshita Street. Here you can find all kinds of everyday household things as well as stationery supplies like stamps, paper, and pens.
I got a cute sakura (cherry blossom)-shaped paper cutter, glittery eye shadow and some striped socks there! It's great for little souvenirs like pretty chopsticks and sumi ink sets.
They also have gardening supplies and snacks. If I lived in Japan, I'd be at Daiso ALL the time. It's a great place to pick up toiletries for cheap too.
Oh, I needed this!

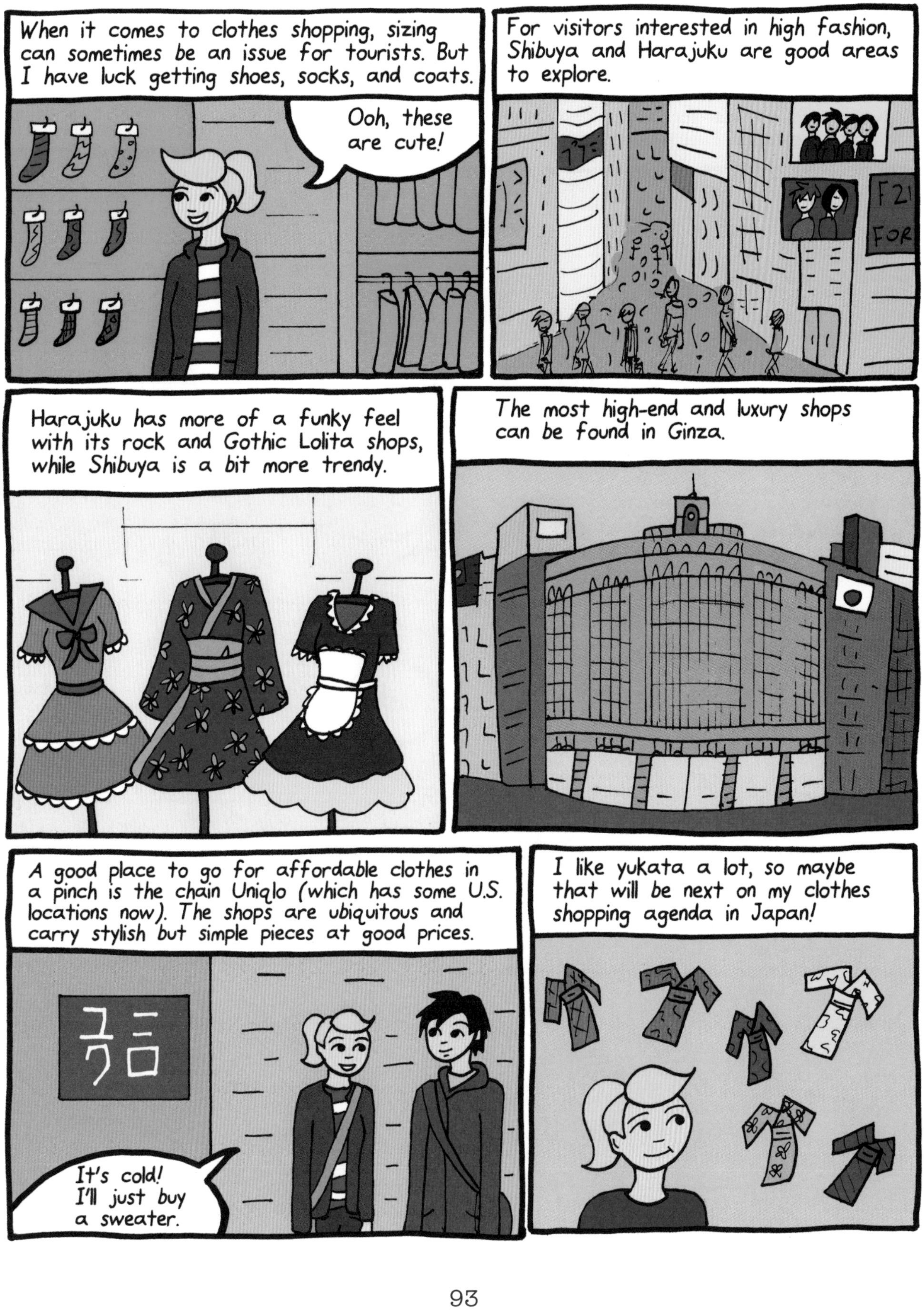
When it comes to clothes shopping, sizing can sometimes be an issue for tourists. But I have luck getting shoes, socks, and coats.
Ooh, these are cute!
For visitors interested in high fashion, Shibuya and Harajuku are good areas to explore.
F21
FOR
Harajuku has more of a funky feel with its rock and Gothic Lolita shops, while Shibuya is a bit more trendy.
The most high-end and luxury shops can be found in Ginza.
A good place to go for affordable clothes in a pinch is the chain Uniqlo (which has some U.S. locations now). The shops are ubiquitous and carry stylish but simple pieces at good prices.
It's cold! I'll just buy a sweater.
I like yukata a lot, so maybe that will be next on my clothes shopping agenda in Japan!

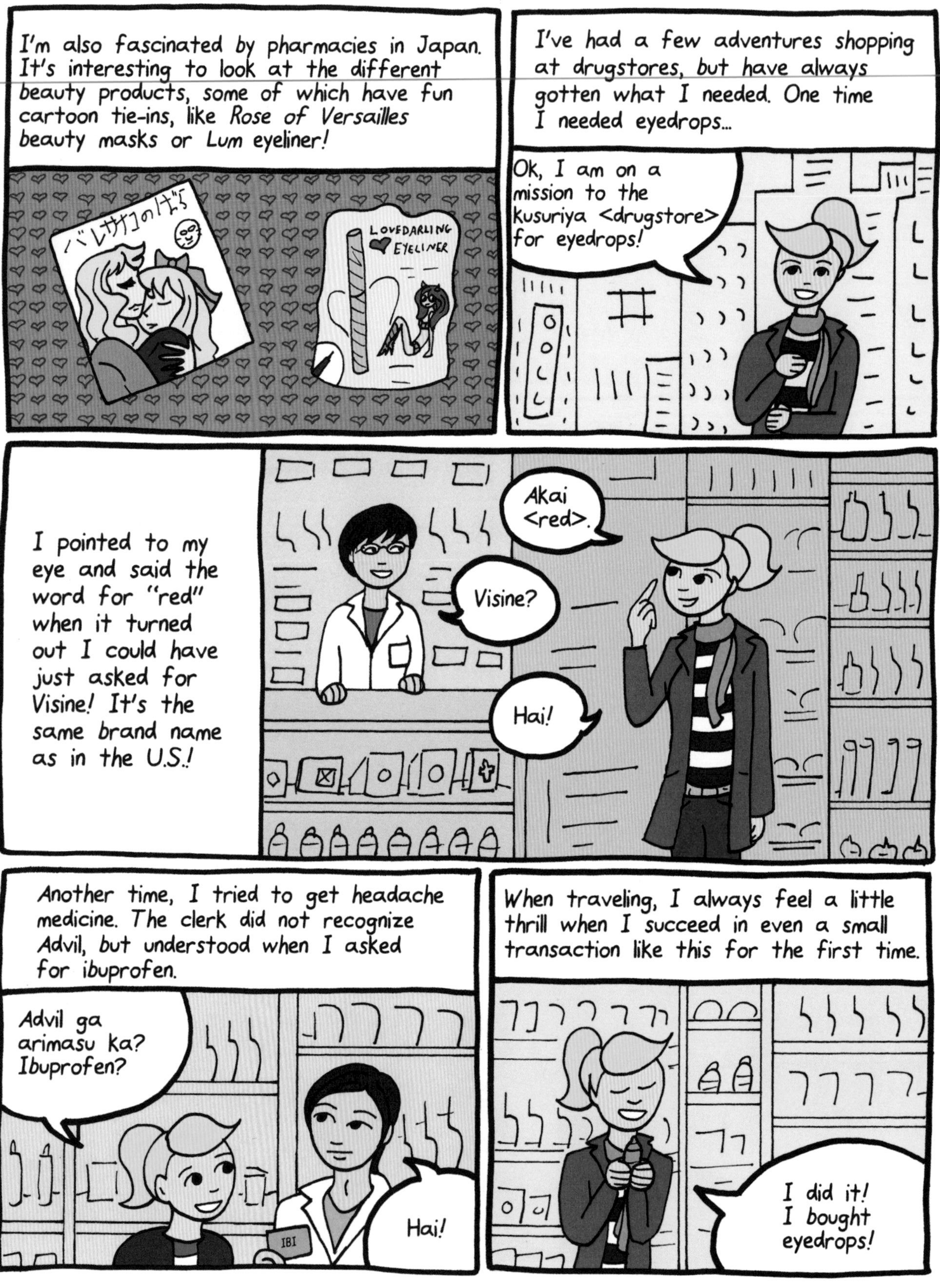
I'm also fascinated by pharmacies in Japan. It's interesting to look at the different beauty products, some of which have fun cartoon tie-ins, like *Rose of Versailles* beauty masks or *Lum* eyeliner!
LOVEDARLING EYELINER
I've had a few adventures shopping at drugstores, but have always gotten what I needed. One time I needed eyedrops...
Ok, I am on a mission to the kusuriya <drugstore> for eyedrops!
I pointed to my eye and said the word for "red" when it turned out I could have just asked for Visine! It's the same brand name as in the U.S.!
Akai <red>.
Visine?
Hai!
Another time, I tried to get headache medicine. The clerk did not recognize Advil, but understood when I asked for ibuprofen.
Advil ga arimasu ka? Ibuprofen?
Hai!
IBI
When traveling, I always feel a little thrill when I succeed in even a small transaction like this for the first time.
I did it! I bought eyedrops!

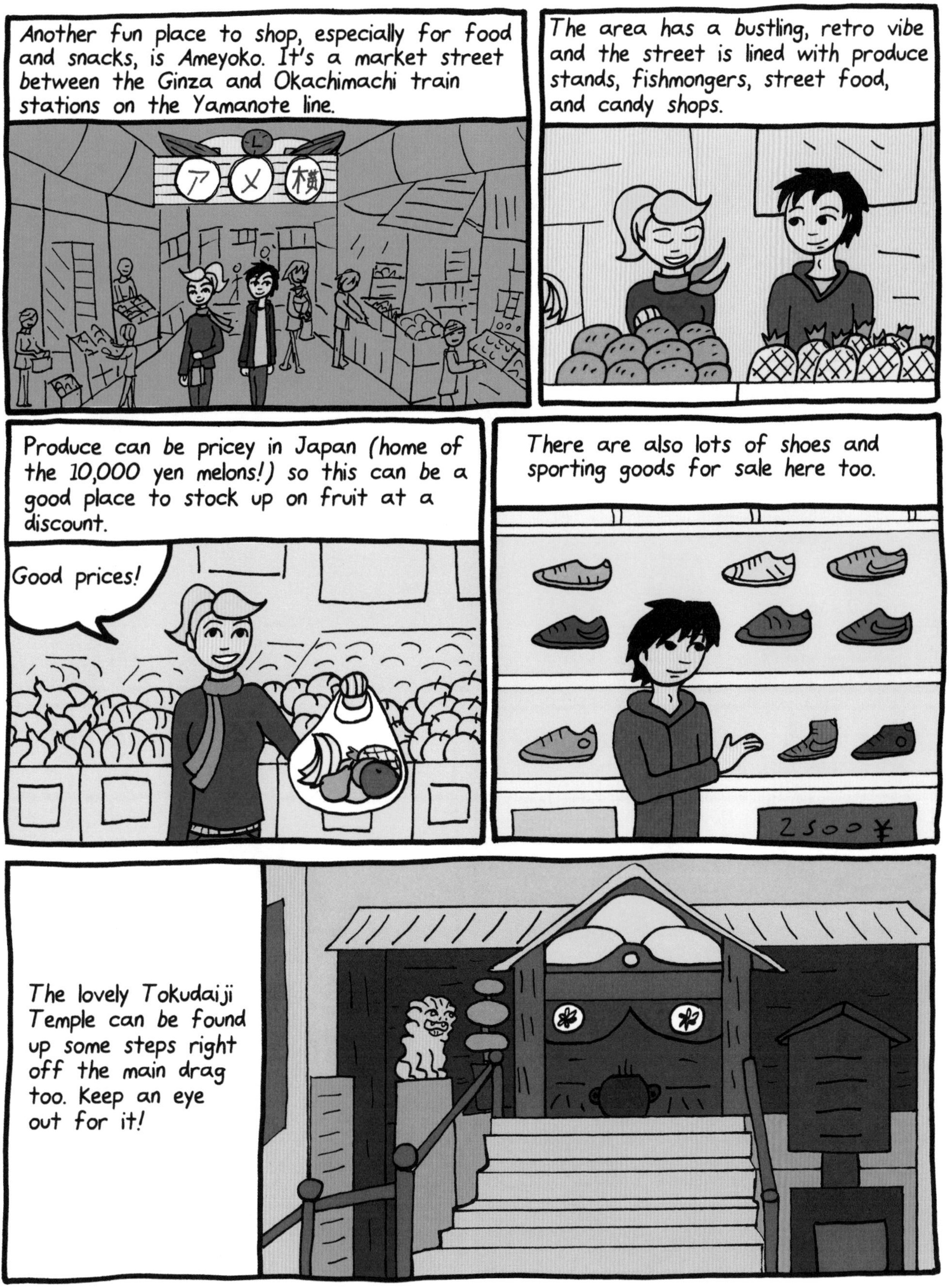
Another fun place to shop, especially for food and snacks, is Ameyoko. It's a market street between the Ginza and Okachimachi train stations on the Yamanote line.
アメ横
The area has a bustling, retro vibe and the street is lined with produce stands, fishmongers, street food, and candy shops.
Produce can be pricey in Japan (home of the 10,000 yen melons!) so this can be a good place to stock up on fruit at a discount.
Good prices!
There are also lots of shoes and sporting goods for sale here too.
2500¥
The lovely Tokudaiji Temple can be found up some steps right off the main drag too. Keep an eye out for it!

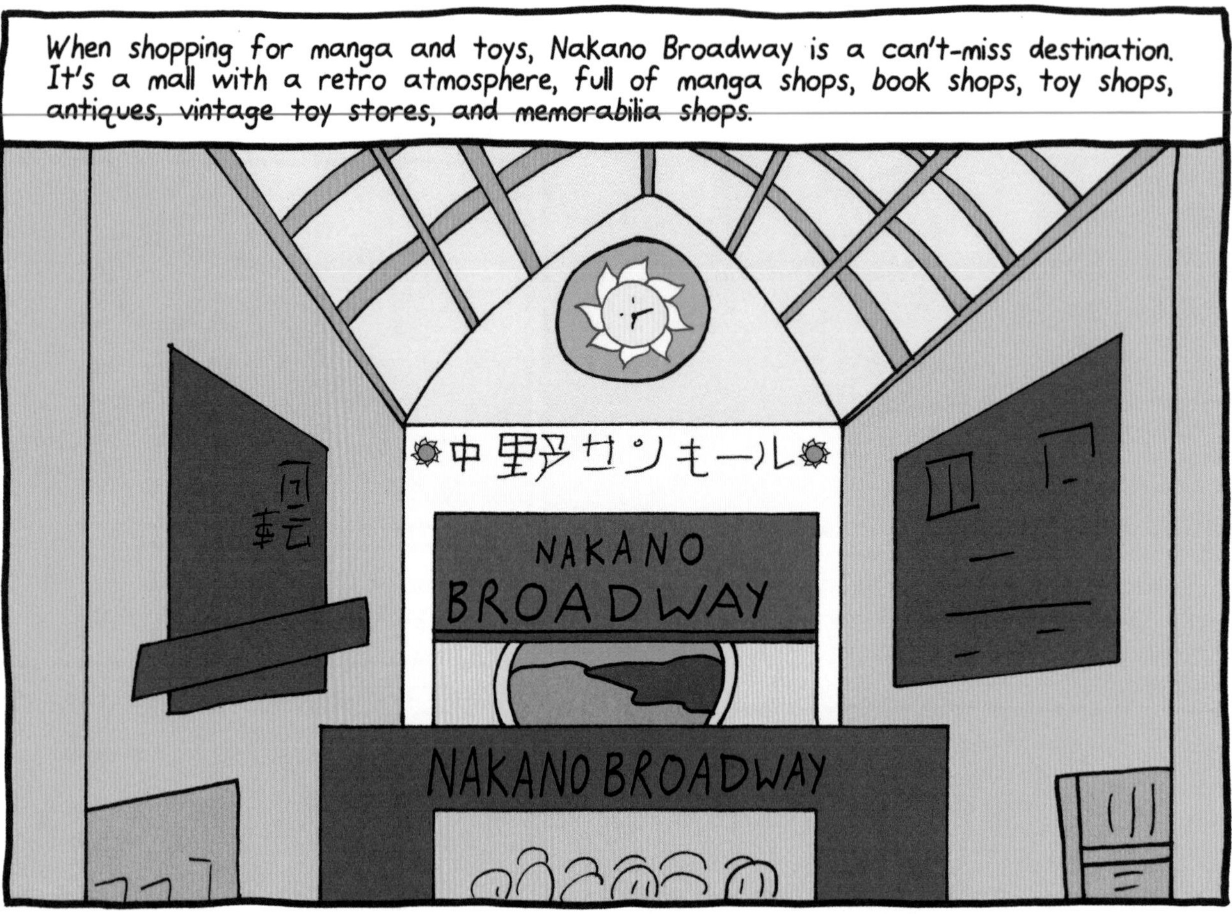
When shopping for manga and toys, Nakano Broadway is a can't-miss destination. It's a mall with a retro atmosphere, full of manga shops, book shops, toy shops, antiques, vintage toy stores, and memorabilia shops.
中野サンモール
NAKANO BROADWAY
NAKANO BROADWAY

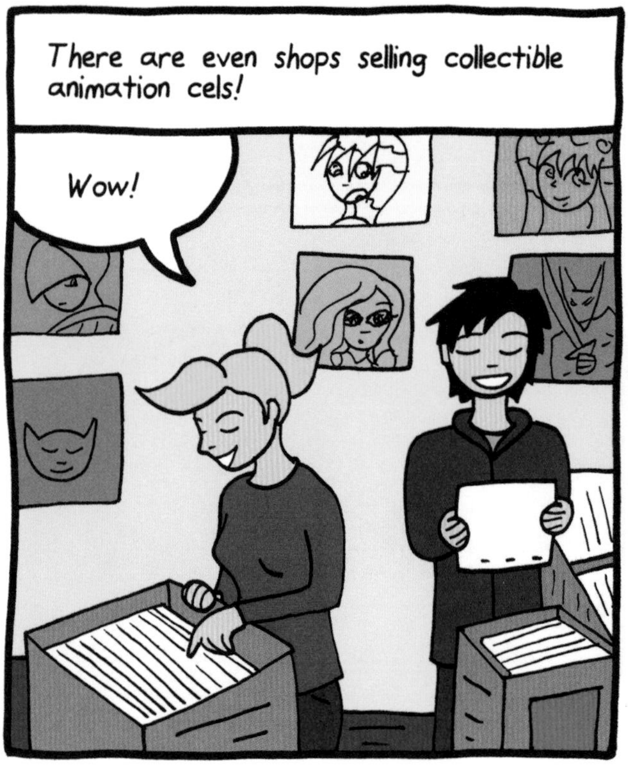
There are even shops selling collectible animation cels!
Wow!

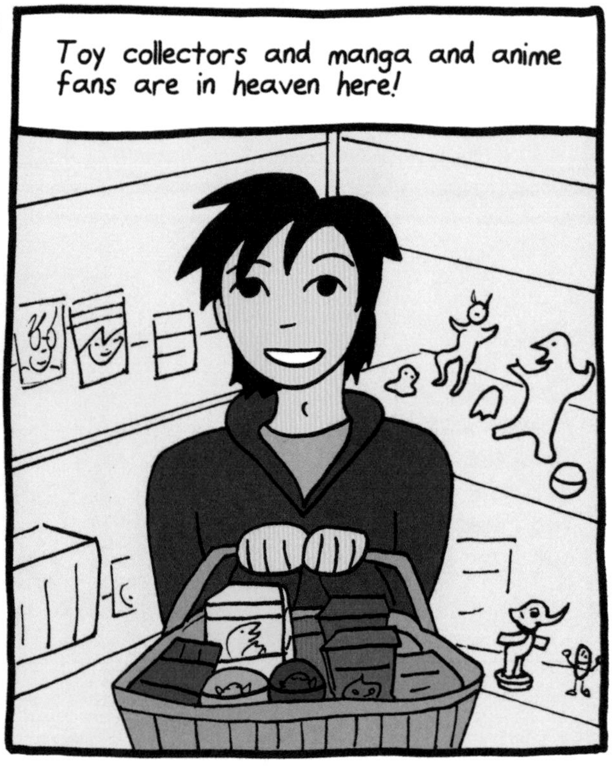
Toy collectors and manga and anime fans are in heaven here!

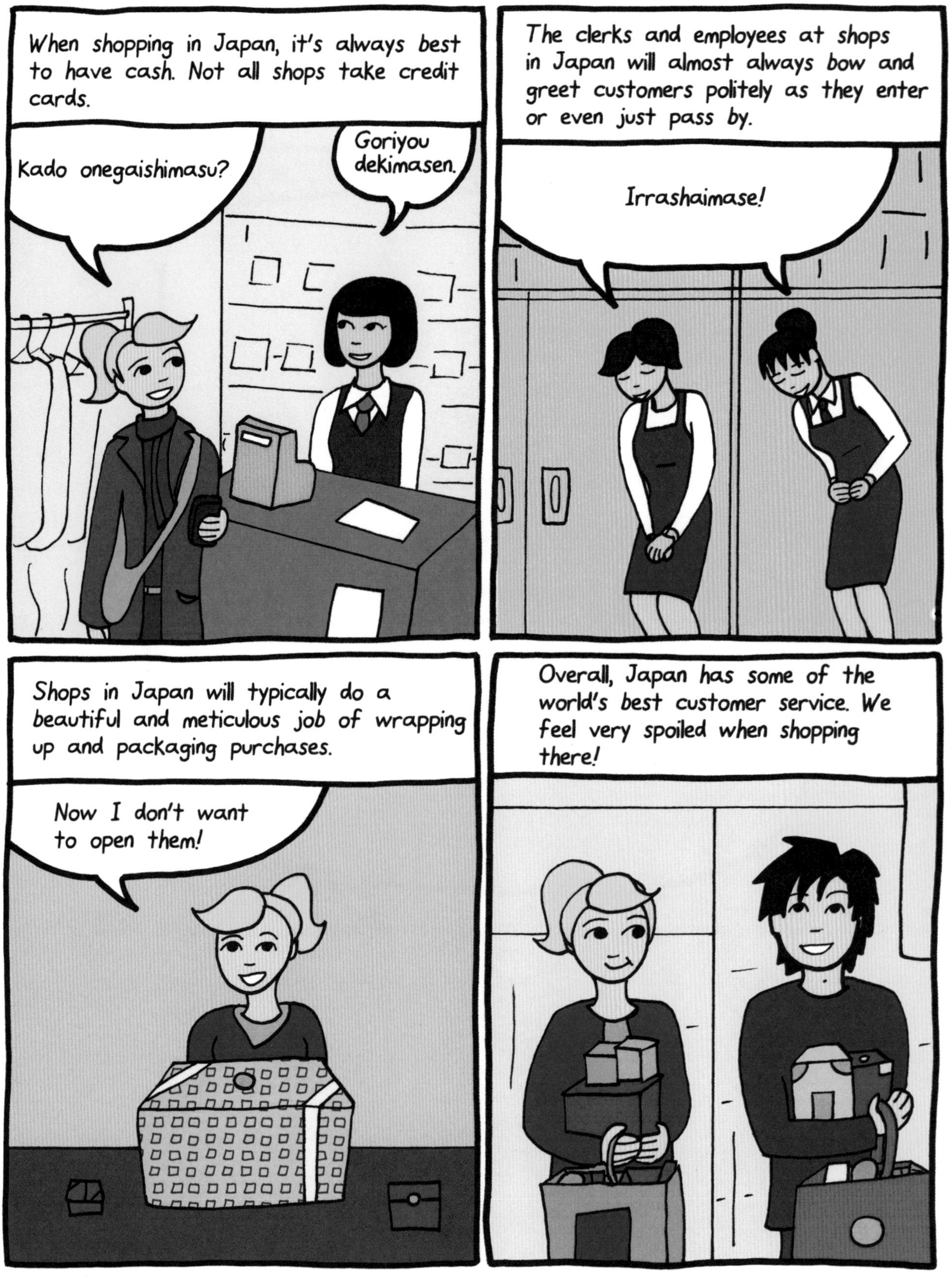
When shopping in Japan, it's always best to have cash. Not all shops take credit cards.
Kado onegaishimasu?
Goriyou dekimasen.
The clerks and employees at shops in Japan will almost always bow and greet customers politely as they enter or even just pass by.
Irrashaimase!
Shops in Japan will typically do a beautiful and meticulous job of wrapping up and packaging purchases.
Now I don't want to open them!
Overall, Japan has some of the world's best customer service. We feel very spoiled when shopping there!

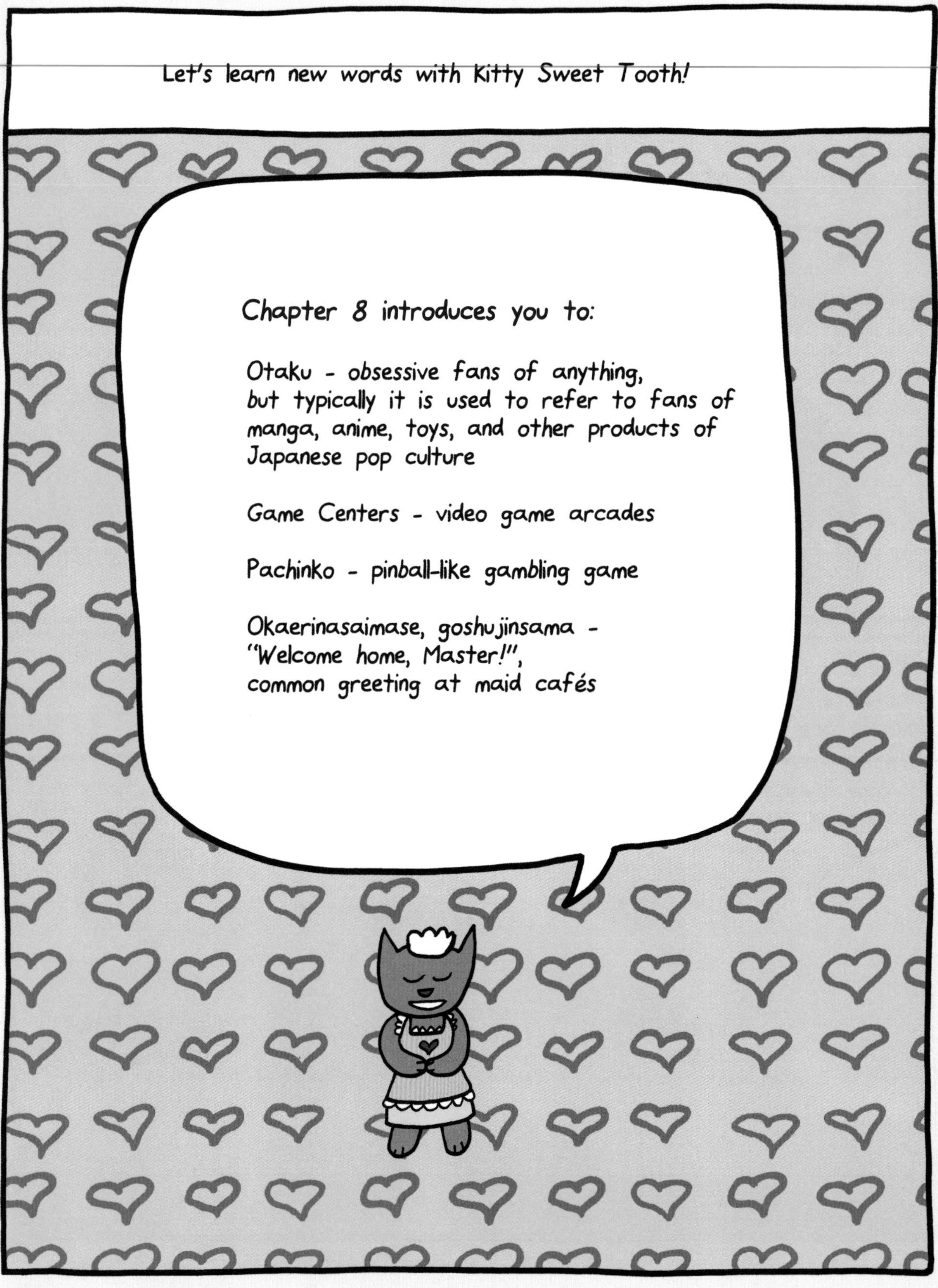
Let's learn new words with Kitty Sweet Tooth!
Chapter 8 introduces you to:
Otaku - obsessive fans of anything, but typically it is used to refer to fans of manga, anime, toys, and other products of Japanese pop culture
Game Centers - video game arcades
Pachinko - pinball-like gambling game
Okaerinasaimase, goshujinsama - "Welcome home, Master!", common greeting at maid cafés

Chapter 8

Manga and Anime and Video Games—Oh My!

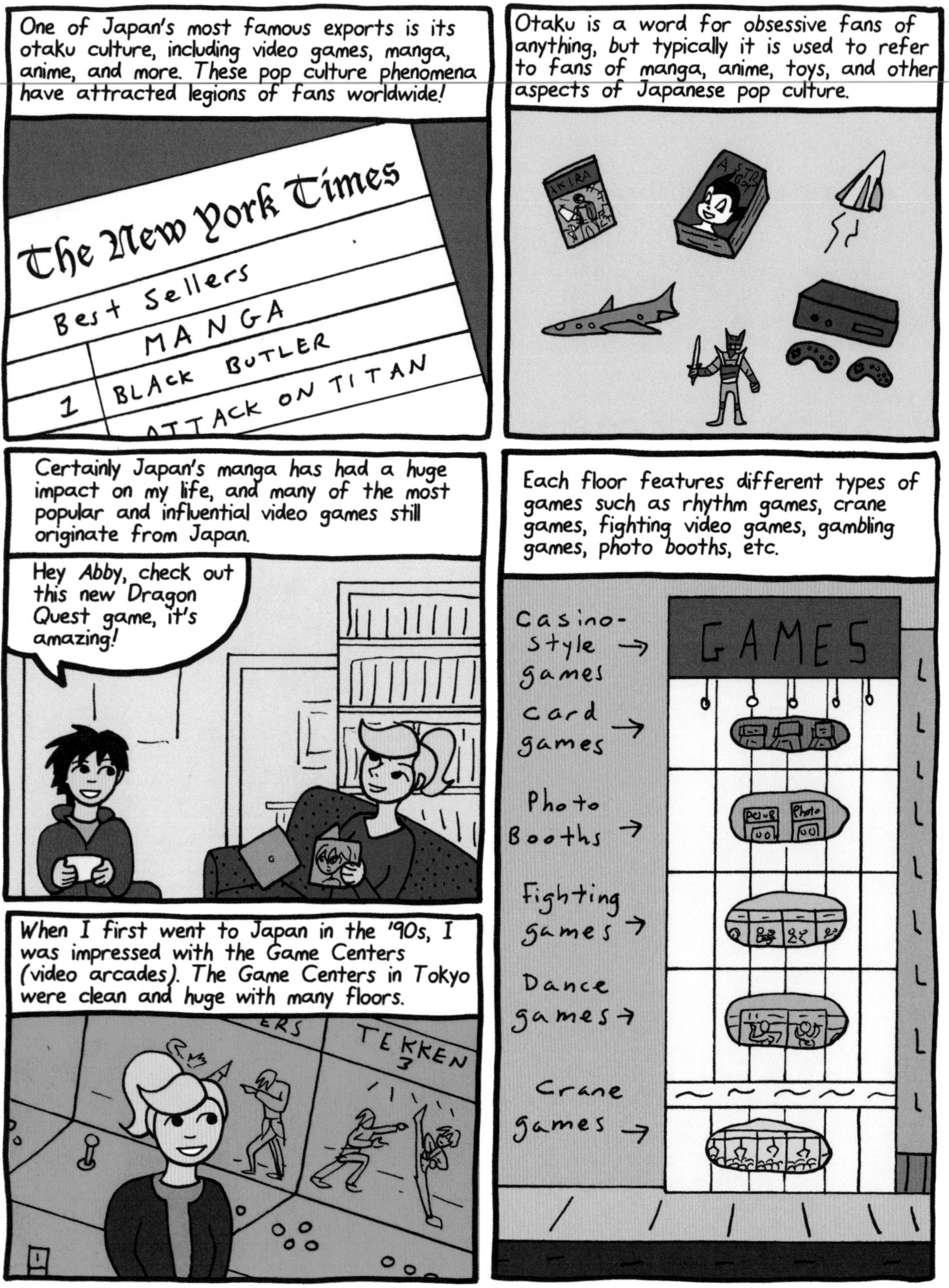
One of Japan's most famous exports is its otaku culture, including video games, manga, anime, and more. These pop culture phenomena have attracted legions of fans worldwide!
The New York Times
Best Sellers
MANGA
1
BLACK BUTLER
ATTACK ON TITAN
Otaku is a word for obsessive fans of anything, but typically it is used to refer to fans of manga, anime, toys, and other aspects of Japanese pop culture.
AKIRA
Certainly Japan's manga has had a huge impact on my life, and many of the most popular and influential video games still originate from Japan.
Hey Abby, check out this new Dragon Quest game, it's amazing!
When I first went to Japan in the '90s, I was impressed with the Game Centers (video arcades). The Game Centers in Tokyo were clean and huge with many floors.
ERS
TEKKEN 3
Each floor features different types of games such as rhythm games, crane games, fighting video games, gambling games, photo booths, etc.
GAMES
Casino-style games
card games
Photo Booths
Fighting games
Dance games
Crane games

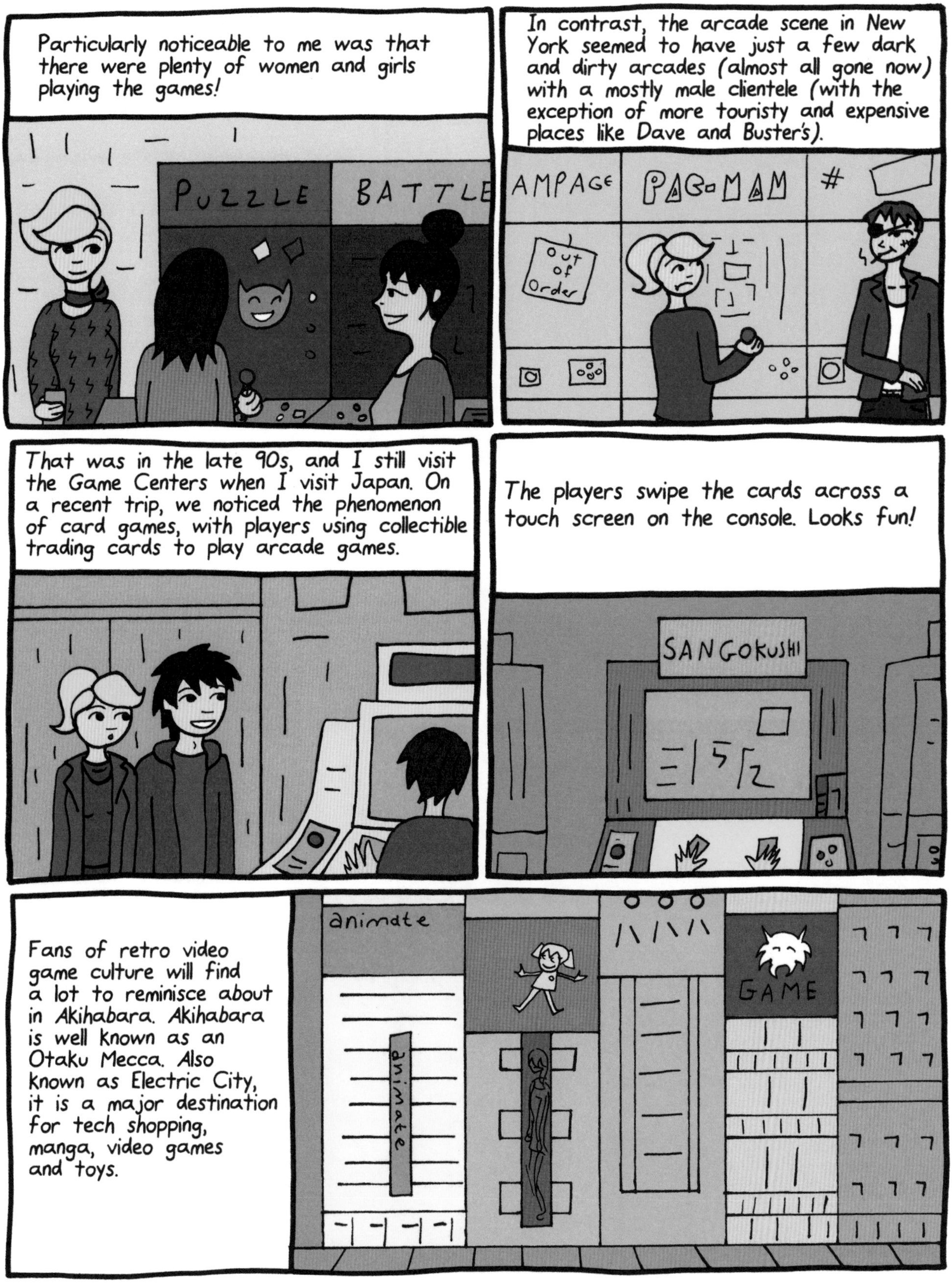

Particularly noticeable to me was that there were plenty of women and girls playing the games!
PUZZLE
BATTLE
In contrast, the arcade scene in New York seemed to have just a few dark and dirty arcades (almost all gone now) with a mostly male clientele (with the exception of more touristy and expensive places like Dave and Buster's).
AMPAGE
PAC-MAN
#
Out of Order
That was in the late 90s, and I still visit the Game Centers when I visit Japan. On a recent trip, we noticed the phenomenon of card games, with players using collectible trading cards to play arcade games.
The players swipe the cards across a touch screen on the console. Looks fun!
SANGOKUSHI
Fans of retro video game culture will find a lot to reminisce about in Akihabara. Akihabara is well known as an Otaku Mecca. Also known as Electric City, it is a major destination for tech shopping, manga, video games and toys.
animate
animate
GAME

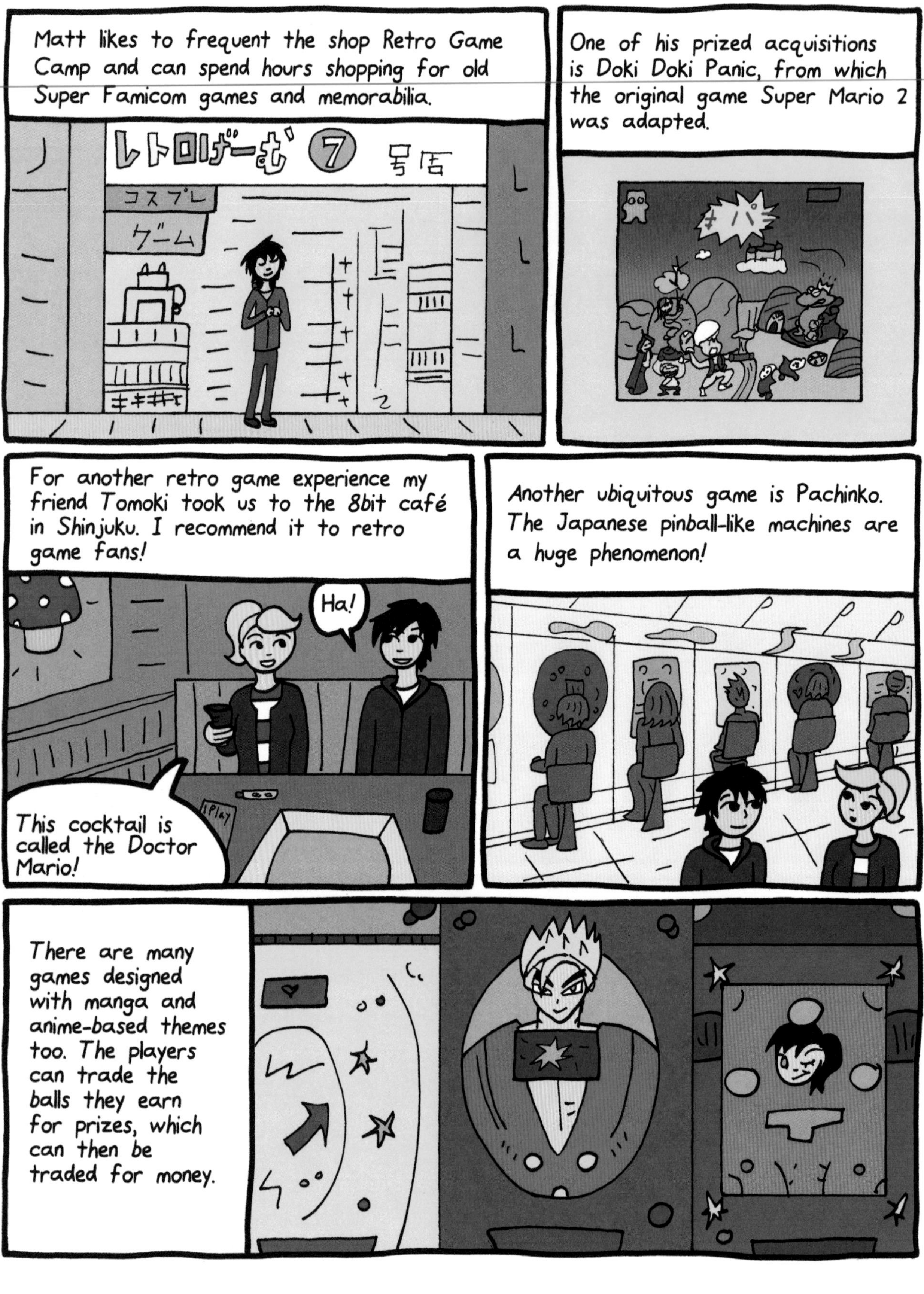
Matt likes to frequent the shop Retro Game Camp and can spend hours shopping for old Super Famicom games and memorabilia.
レトロげーむ 7 号店
コスプレ
ゲーム
One of his prized acquisitions is Doki Doki Panic, from which the original game Super Mario 2 was adapted.
For another retro game experience my friend Tomoki took us to the 8bit café in Shinjuku. I recommend it to retro game fans!
Ha!
This cocktail is called the Doctor Mario!
1 Play
Another ubiquitous game is Pachinko. The Japanese pinball-like machines are a huge phenomenon!
There are many games designed with manga and anime-based themes too. The players can trade the balls they earn for prizes, which can then be traded for money.

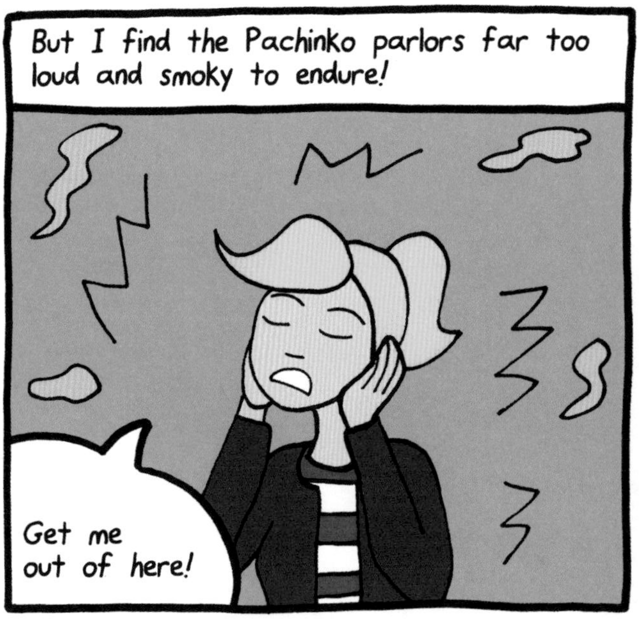
But I find the Pachinko parlors far too loud and smoky to endure!
Get me out of here!

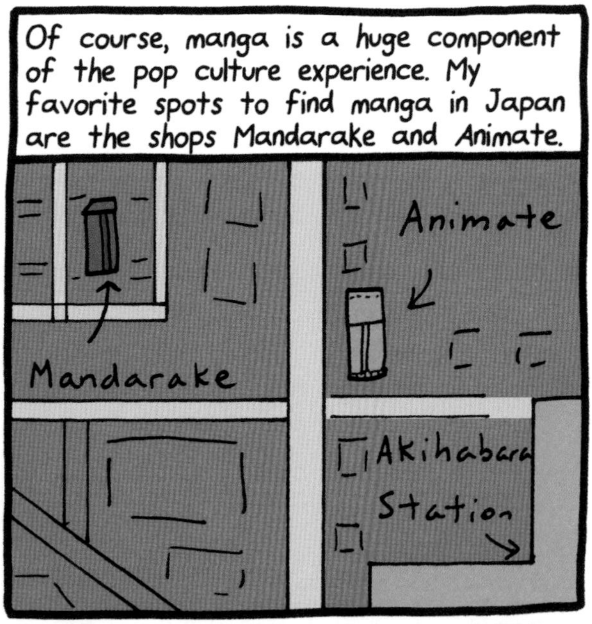
Of course, manga is a huge component of the pop culture experience. My favorite spots to find manga in Japan are the shops Mandarake and Animate.
Mandarake
Animate
Akihabara Station

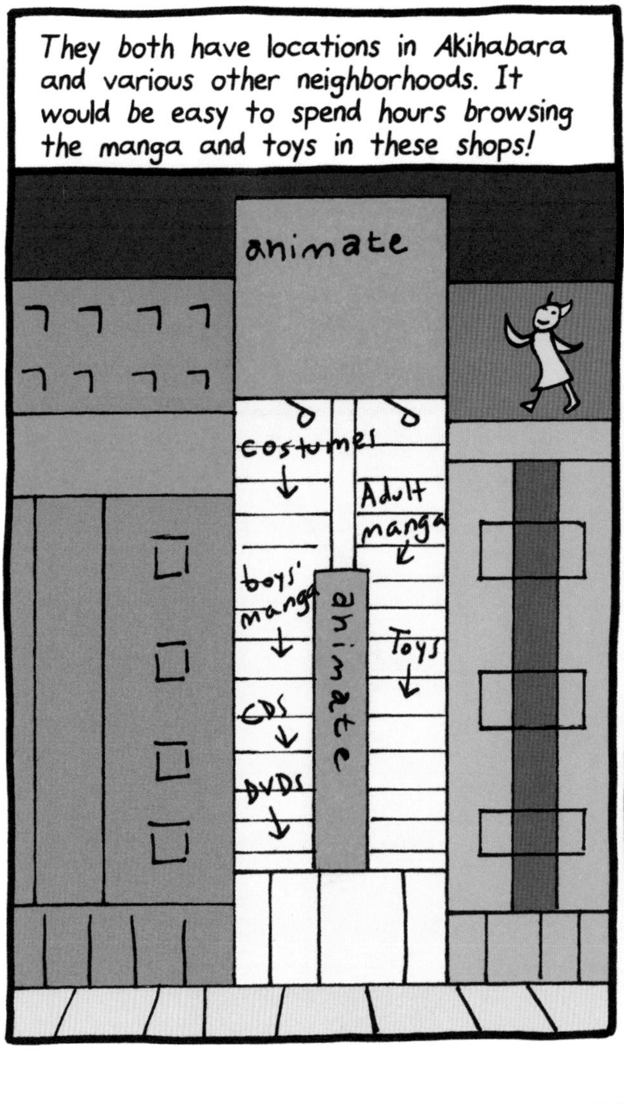
They both have locations in Akihabara and various other neighborhoods. It would be easy to spend hours browsing the manga and toys in these shops!
animate
costumes
Adult manga
boys' manga
animate
Toys
CDs
DVDs

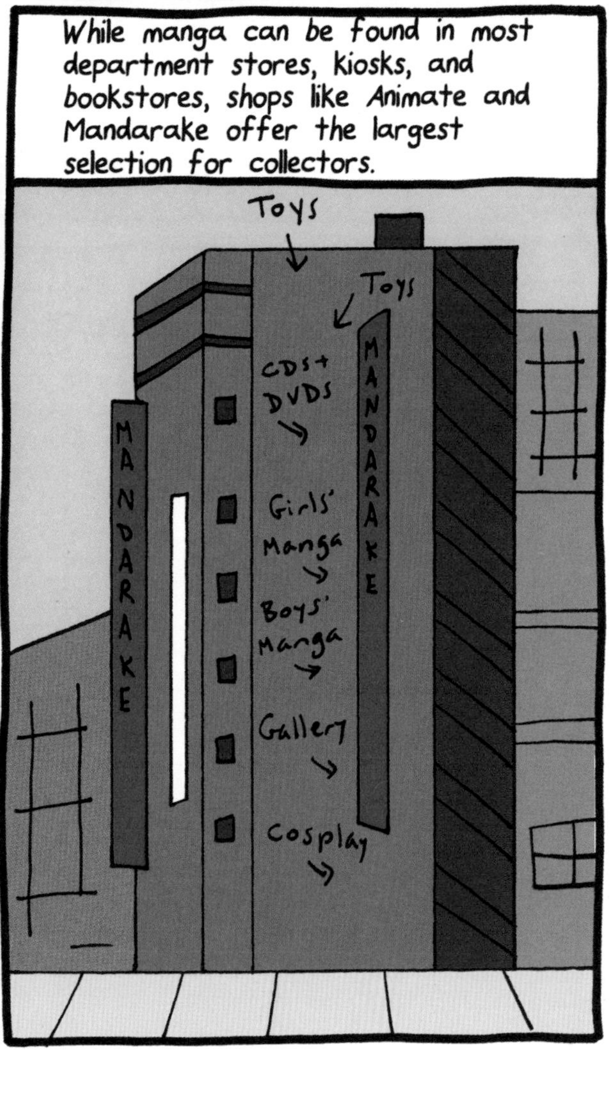
While manga can be found in most department stores, kiosks, and bookstores, shops like Animate and Mandarake offer the largest selection for collectors.
Toys
Toys
CDs + DVDs
MANDARAKE
MANDARAKE
Girls' Manga
Boys' Manga
Gallery
Cosplay

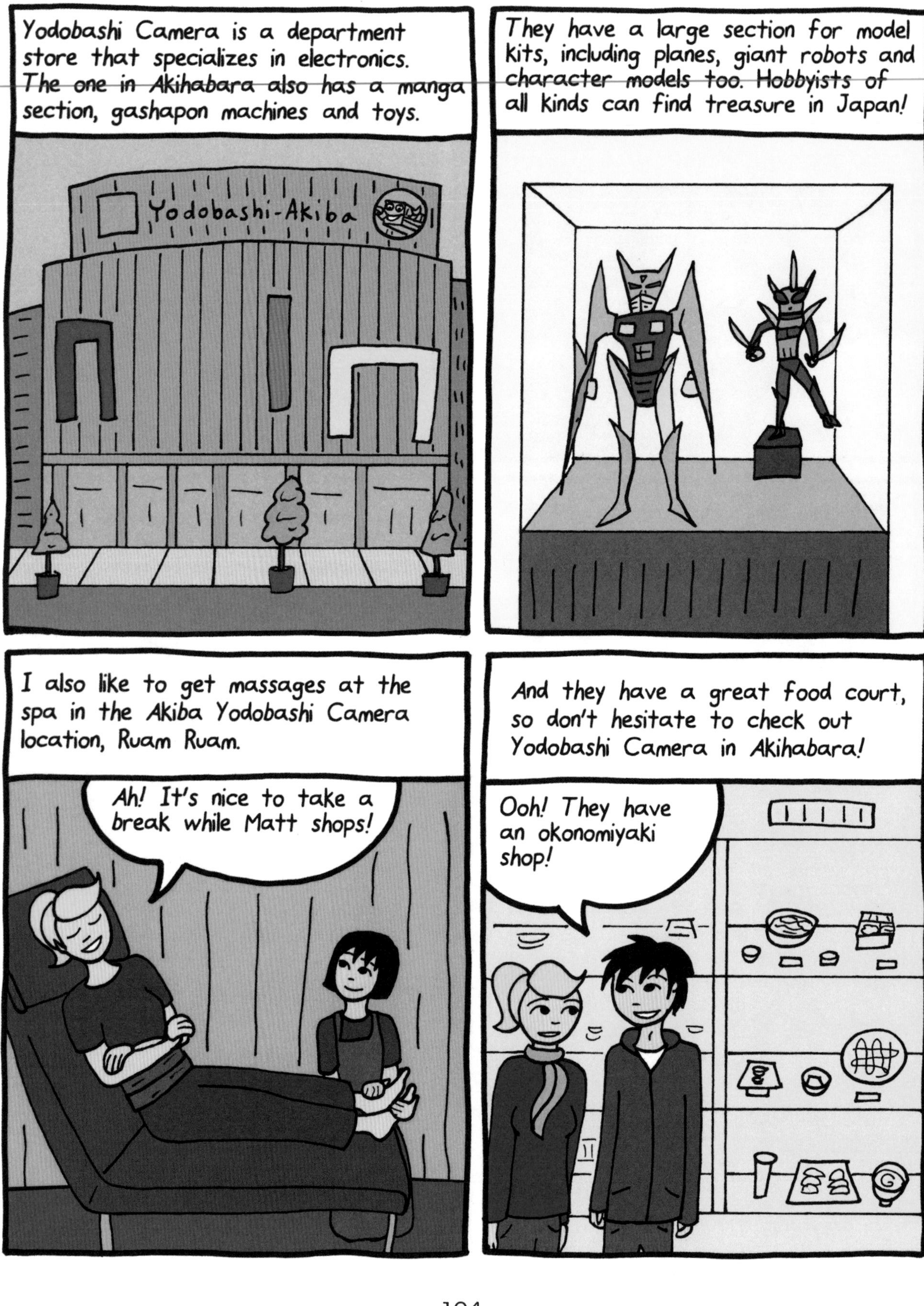
Yodobashi Camera is a department store that specializes in electronics. The one in Akihabara also has a manga section, gashapon machines and toys.
Yodobashi-Akiba
They have a large section for model kits, including planes, giant robots and character models too. Hobbyists of all kinds can find treasure in Japan!
I also like to get massages at the spa in the Akiba Yodobashi Camera location, Ruam Ruam.
Ah! It's nice to take a break while Matt shops!
And they have a great food court, so don't hesitate to check out Yodobashi Camera in Akihabara!
Ooh! They have an okonomiyaki shop!

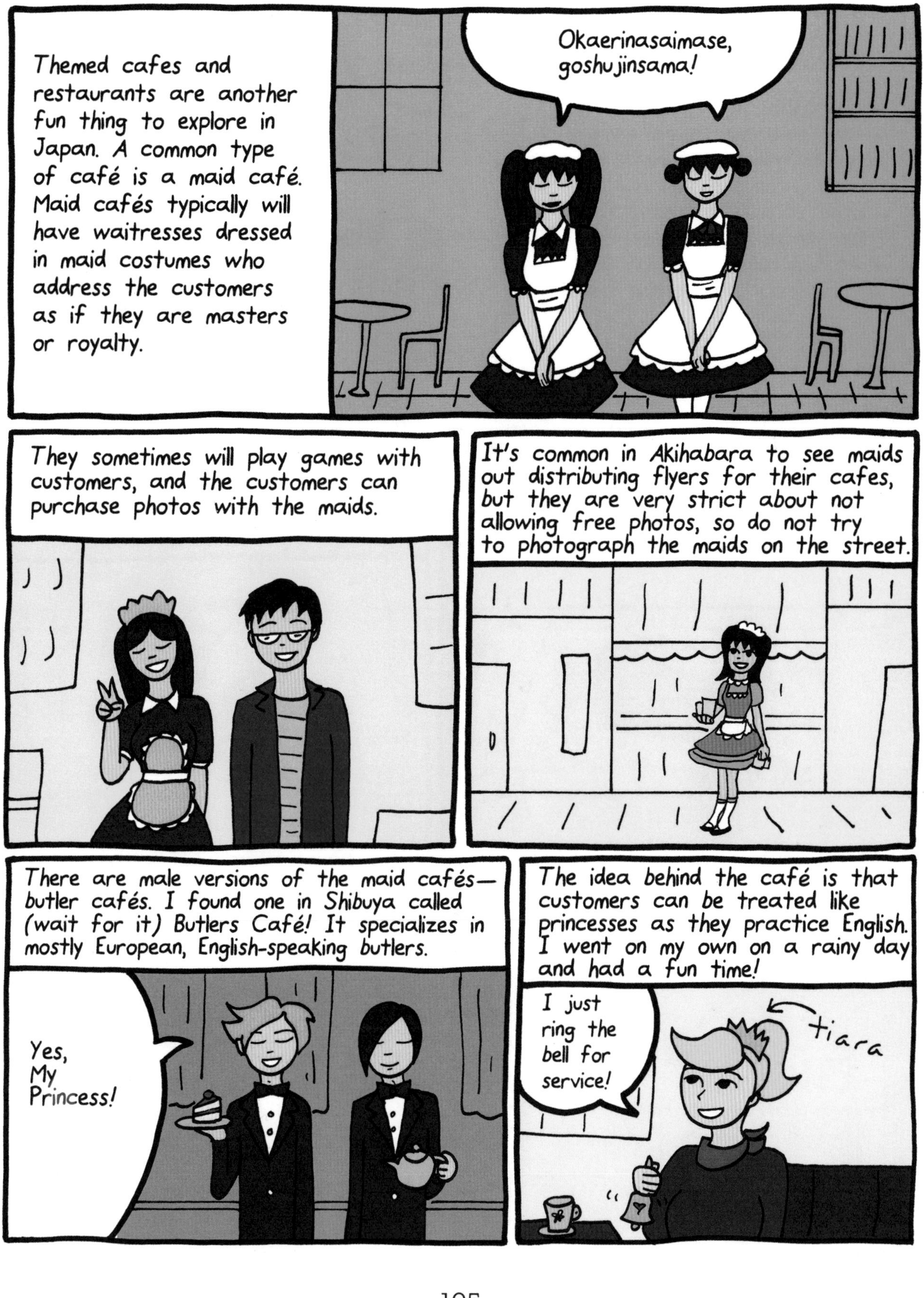
Themed cafes and restaurants are another fun thing to explore in Japan. A common type of café is a maid café. Maid cafés typically will have waitresses dressed in maid costumes who address the customers as if they are masters or royalty.
Okaerinasaimase, goshujinsama!
They sometimes will play games with customers, and the customers can purchase photos with the maids.
It's common in Akihabara to see maids out distributing flyers for their cafes, but they are very strict about not allowing free photos, so do not try to photograph the maids on the street.
There are male versions of the maid cafés—butler cafés. I found one in Shibuya called (wait for it) Butlers Café! It specializes in mostly European, English-speaking butlers.
Yes, My Princess!
The idea behind the café is that customers can be treated like princesses as they practice English. I went on my own on a rainy day and had a fun time!
I just ring the bell for service!
tiara

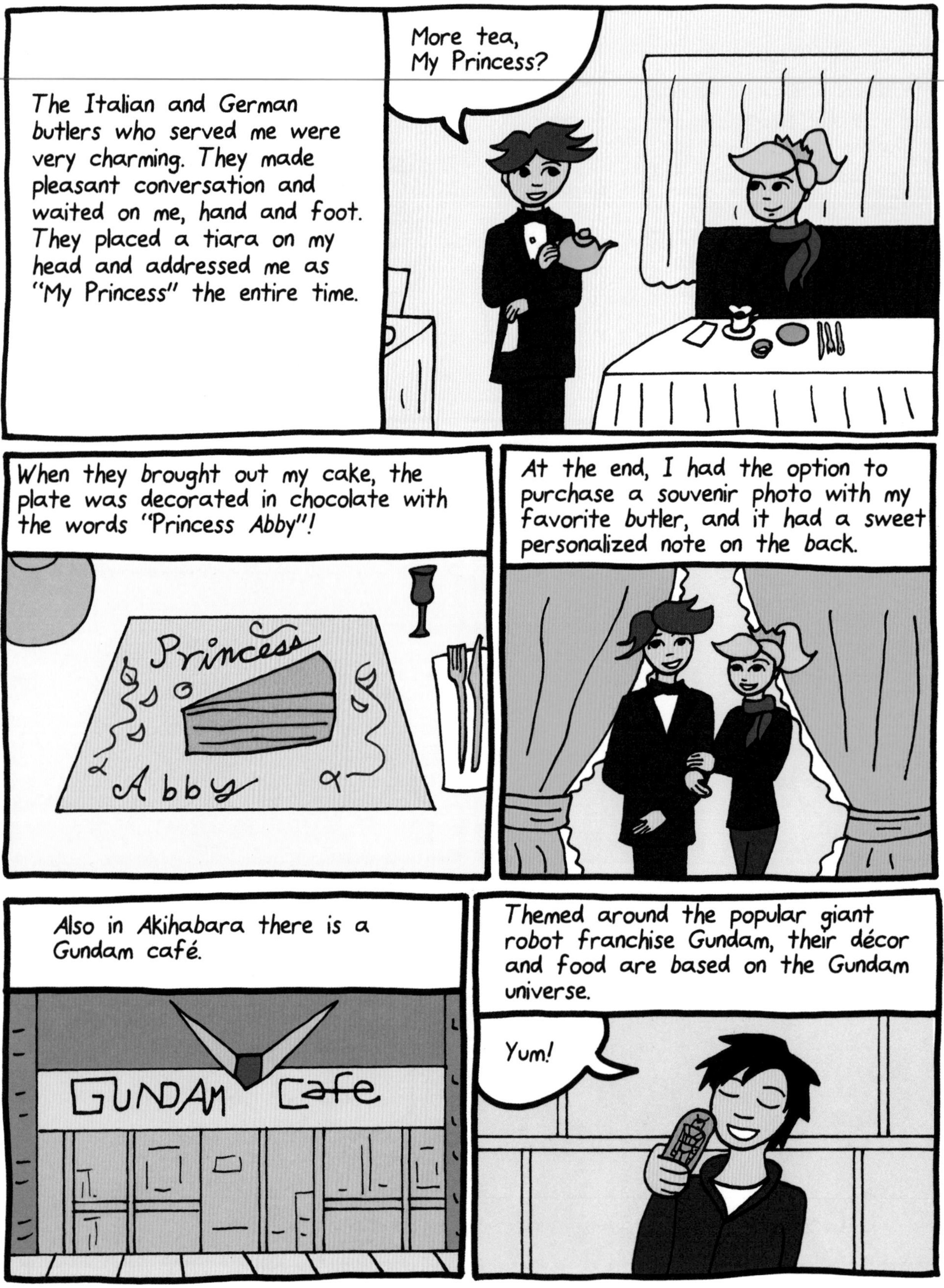
The Italian and German butlers who served me were very charming. They made pleasant conversation and waited on me, hand and foot. They placed a tiara on my head and addressed me as "My Princess" the entire time.
More tea, My Princess?
When they brought out my cake, the plate was decorated in chocolate with the words "Princess Abby"!
Princess
Abby
At the end, I had the option to purchase a souvenir photo with my favorite butler, and it had a sweet personalized note on the back.
Also in Akihabara there is a Gundam café.
GUNDAM Cafe
Themed around the popular giant robot franchise Gundam, their décor and food are based on the Gundam universe.
Yum!

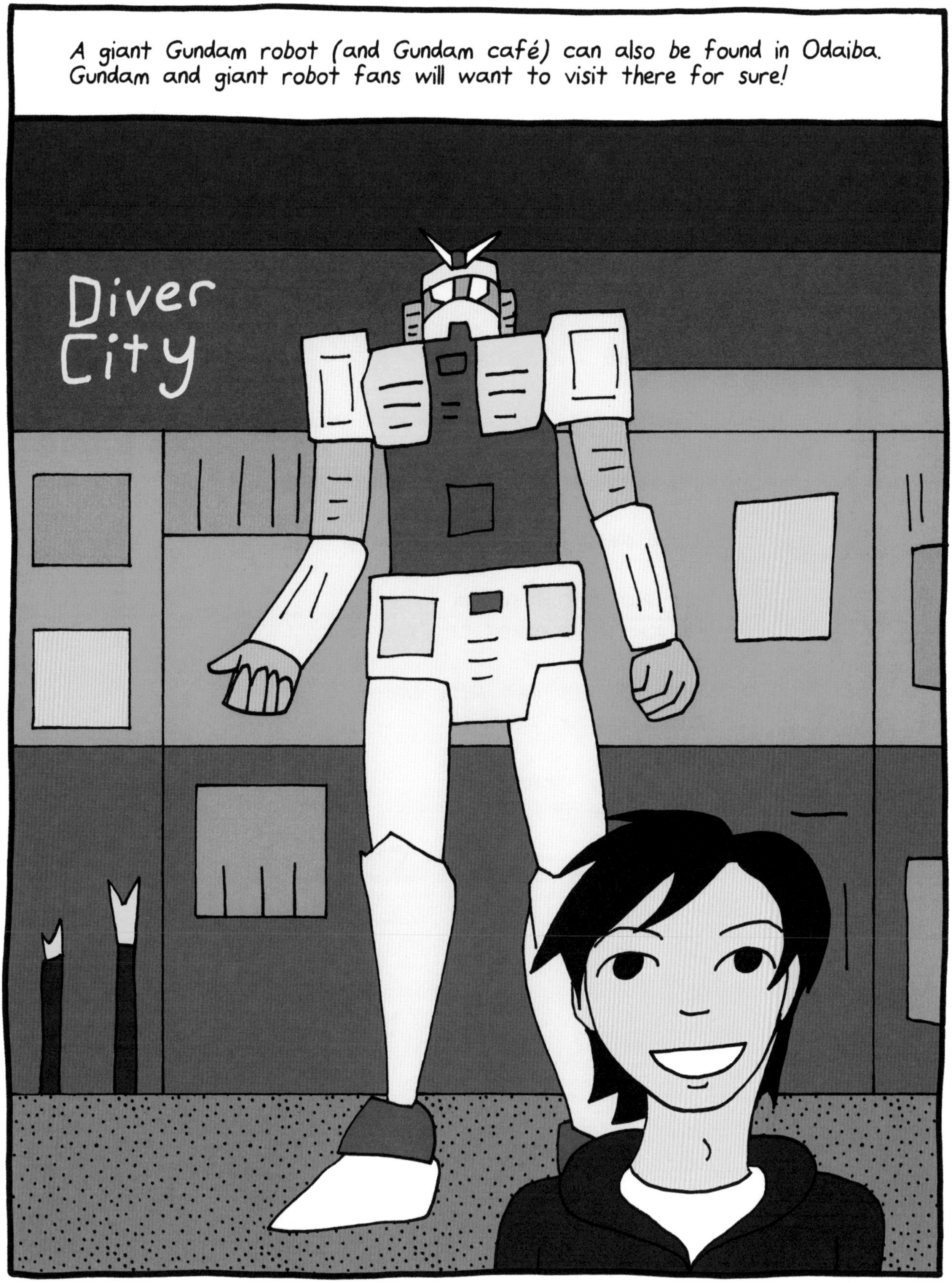
A giant Gundam robot (and Gundam café) can also be found in Odaiba. Gundam and giant robot fans will want to visit there for sure!
Diver City

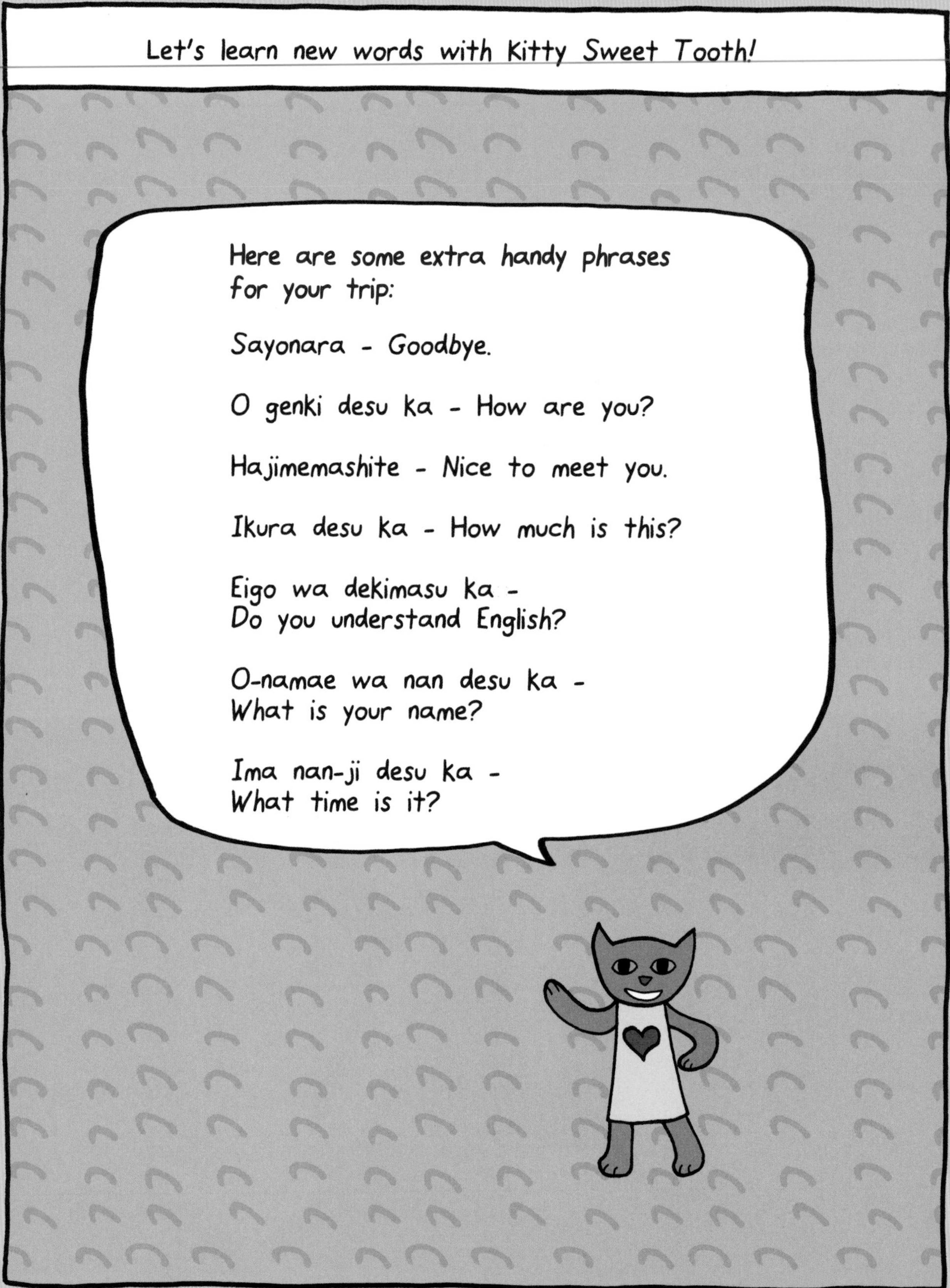
Let's learn new words with Kitty Sweet Tooth!
Here are some extra handy phrases for your trip:
Sayonara - Goodbye.
O genki desu ka - How are you?
Hajimemashite - Nice to meet you.
Ikura desu ka - How much is this?
Eigo wa dekimasu ka - Do you understand English?
O-namae wa nan desu ka - What is your name?
Ima nan-ji desu ka - What time is it?

Chapter 9

Do We Have to Leave?

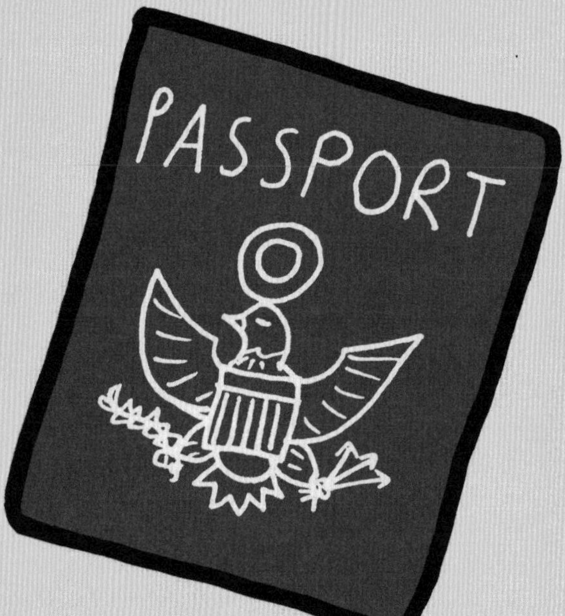
PASSPORT

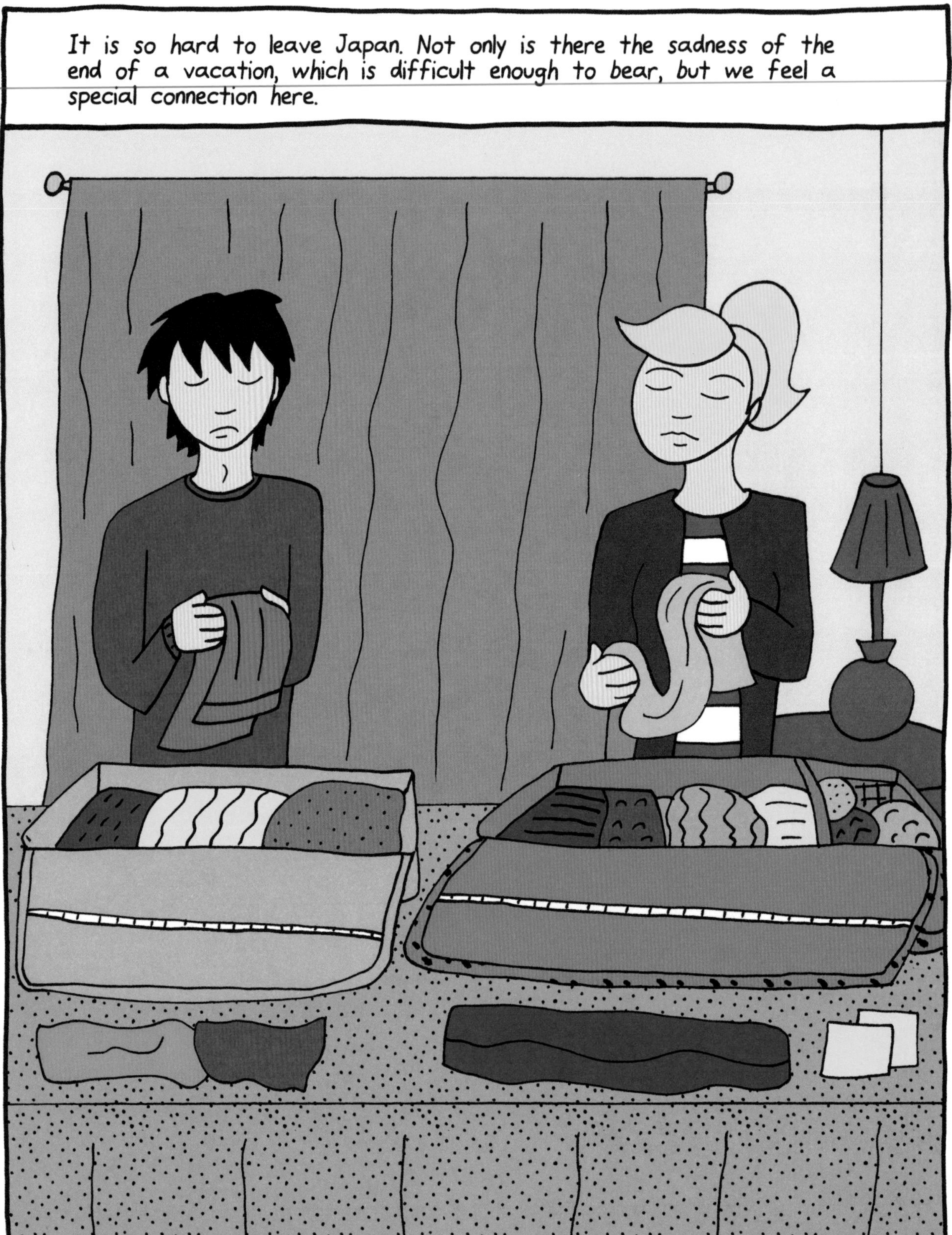
It is so hard to leave Japan. Not only is there the sadness of the end of a vacation, which is difficult enough to bear, but we feel a special connection here.

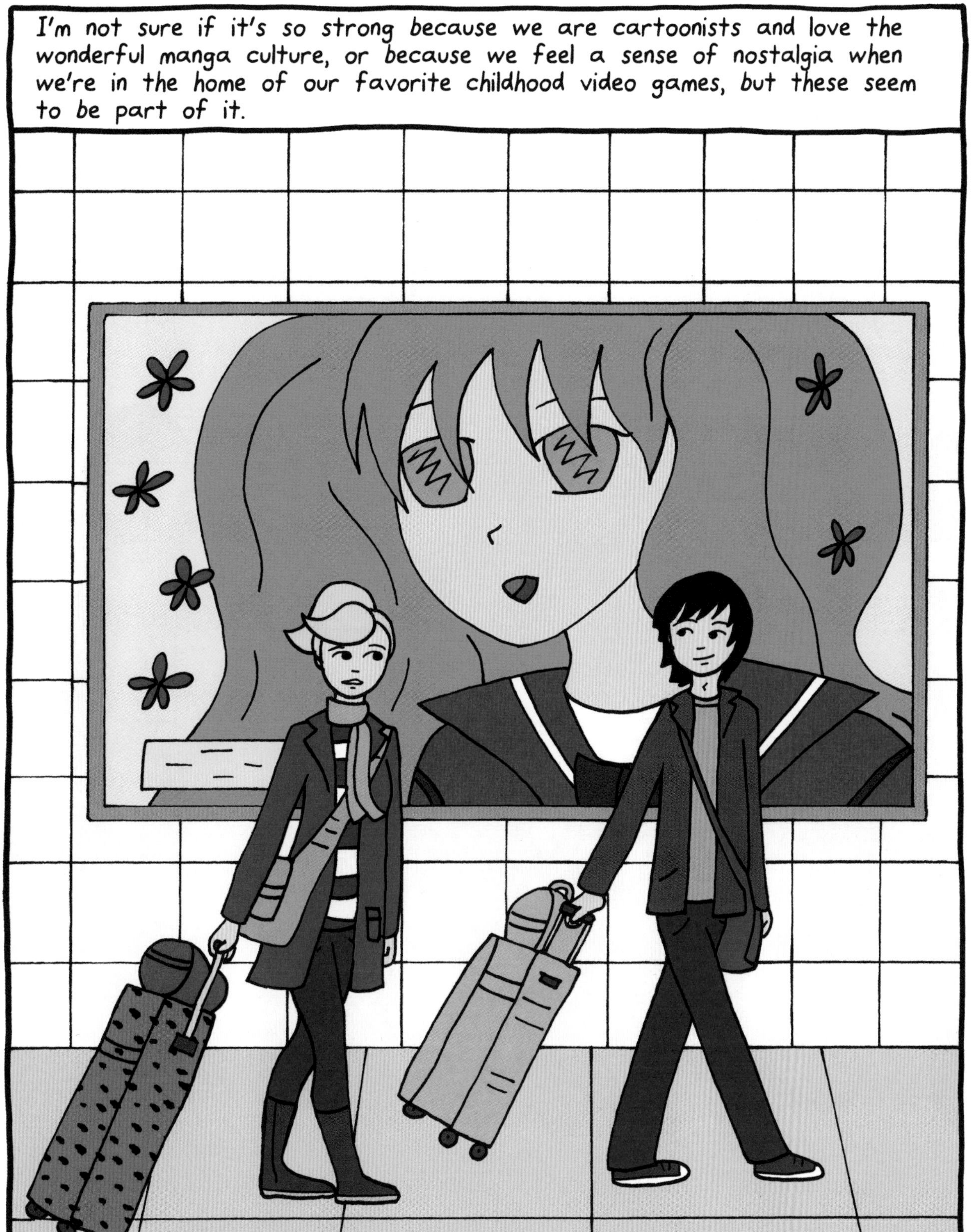
I'm not sure if it's so strong because we are cartoonists and love the wonderful manga culture, or because we feel a sense of nostalgia when we're in the home of our favorite childhood video games, but these seem to be part of it.

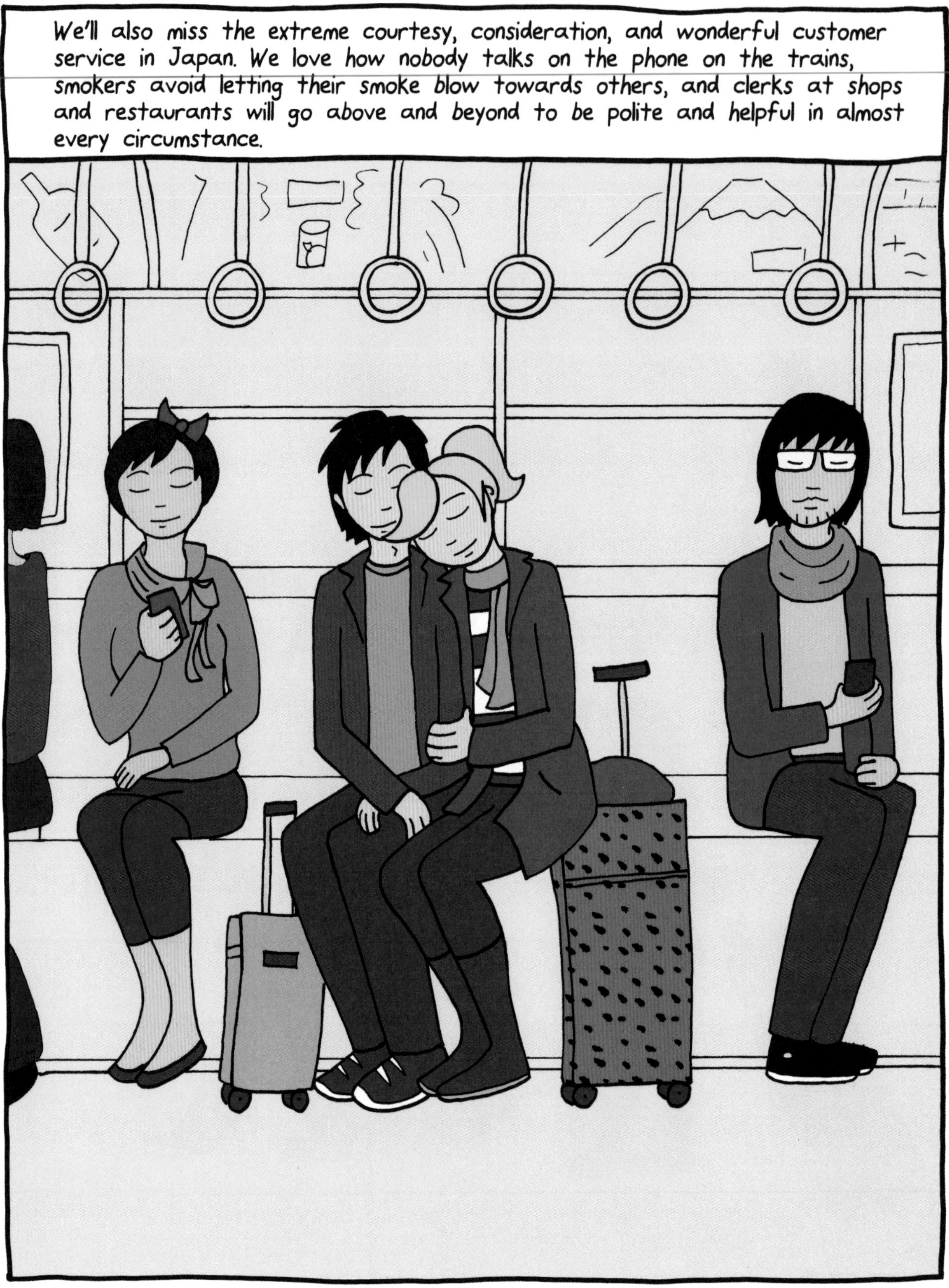
We'll also miss the extreme courtesy, consideration, and wonderful customer service in Japan. We love how nobody talks on the phone on the trains, smokers avoid letting their smoke blow towards others, and clerks at shops and restaurants will go above and beyond to be polite and helpful in almost every circumstance.

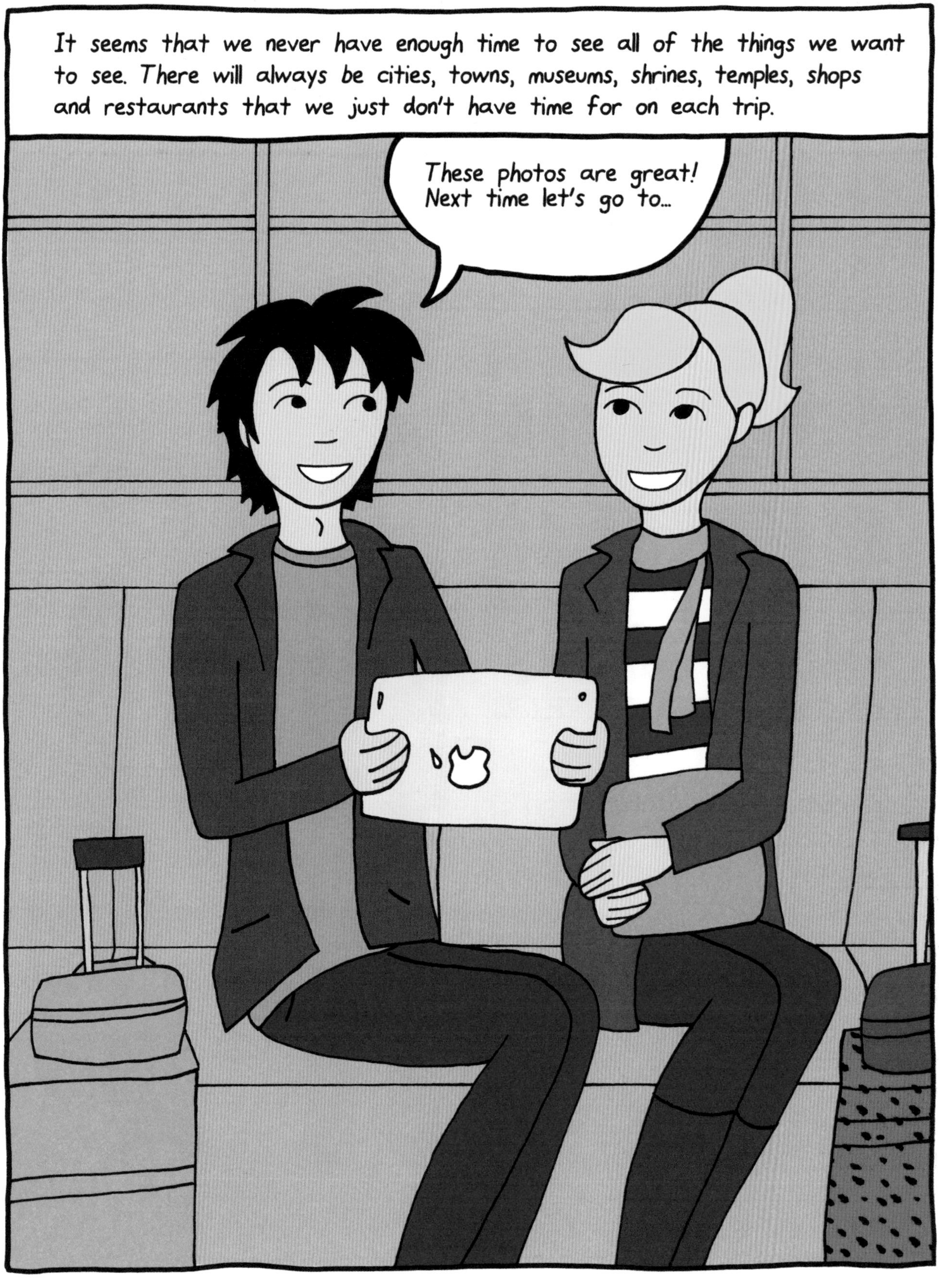
It seems that we never have enough time to see all of the things we want to see. There will always be cities, towns, museums, shrines, temples, shops and restaurants that we just don't have time for on each trip.
These photos are great! Next time let's go to...

And we certainly will miss the conveniences of Japan, the high-tech devices, delivery services, convenience stores, snacks and vending machines.

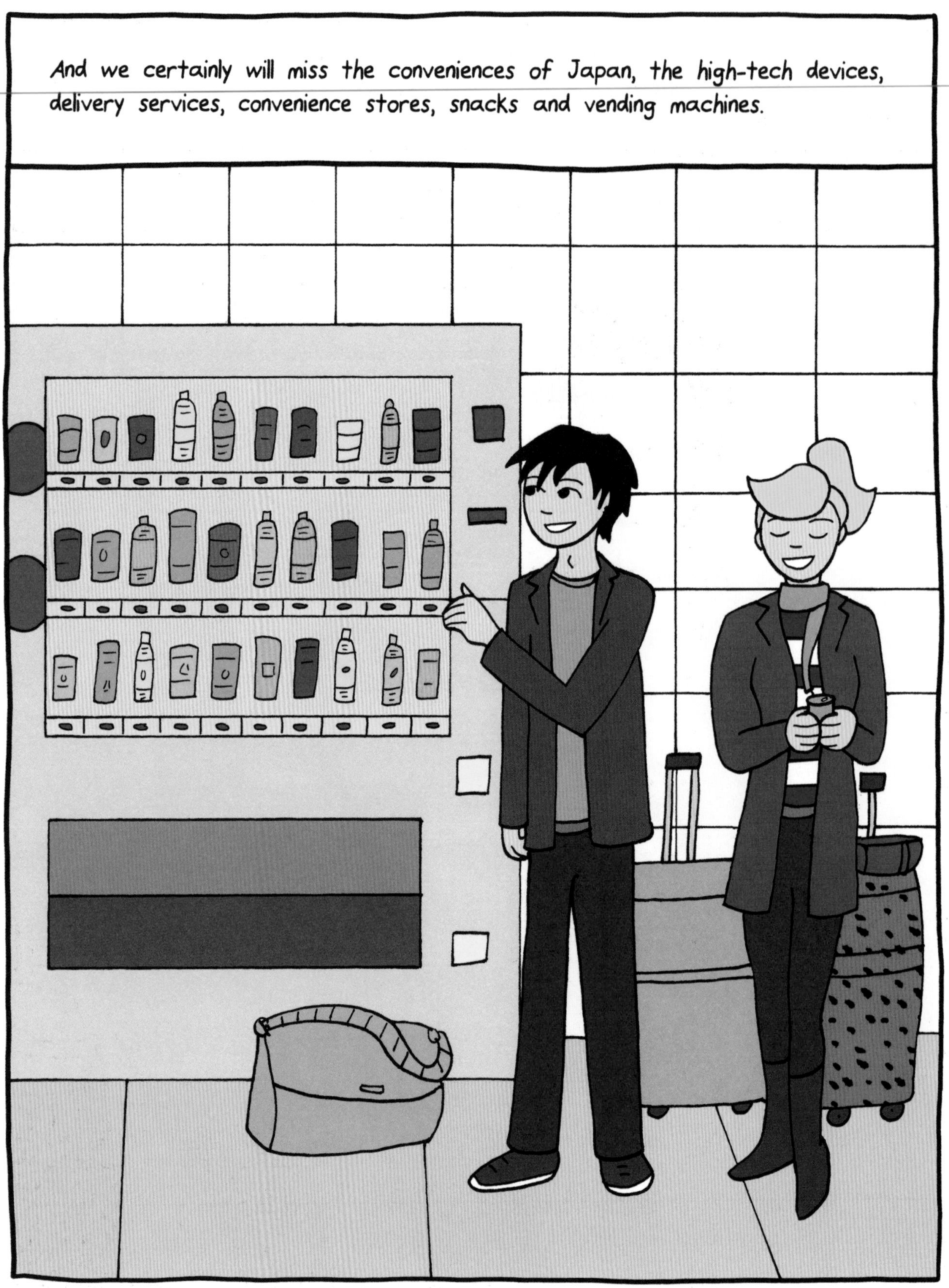

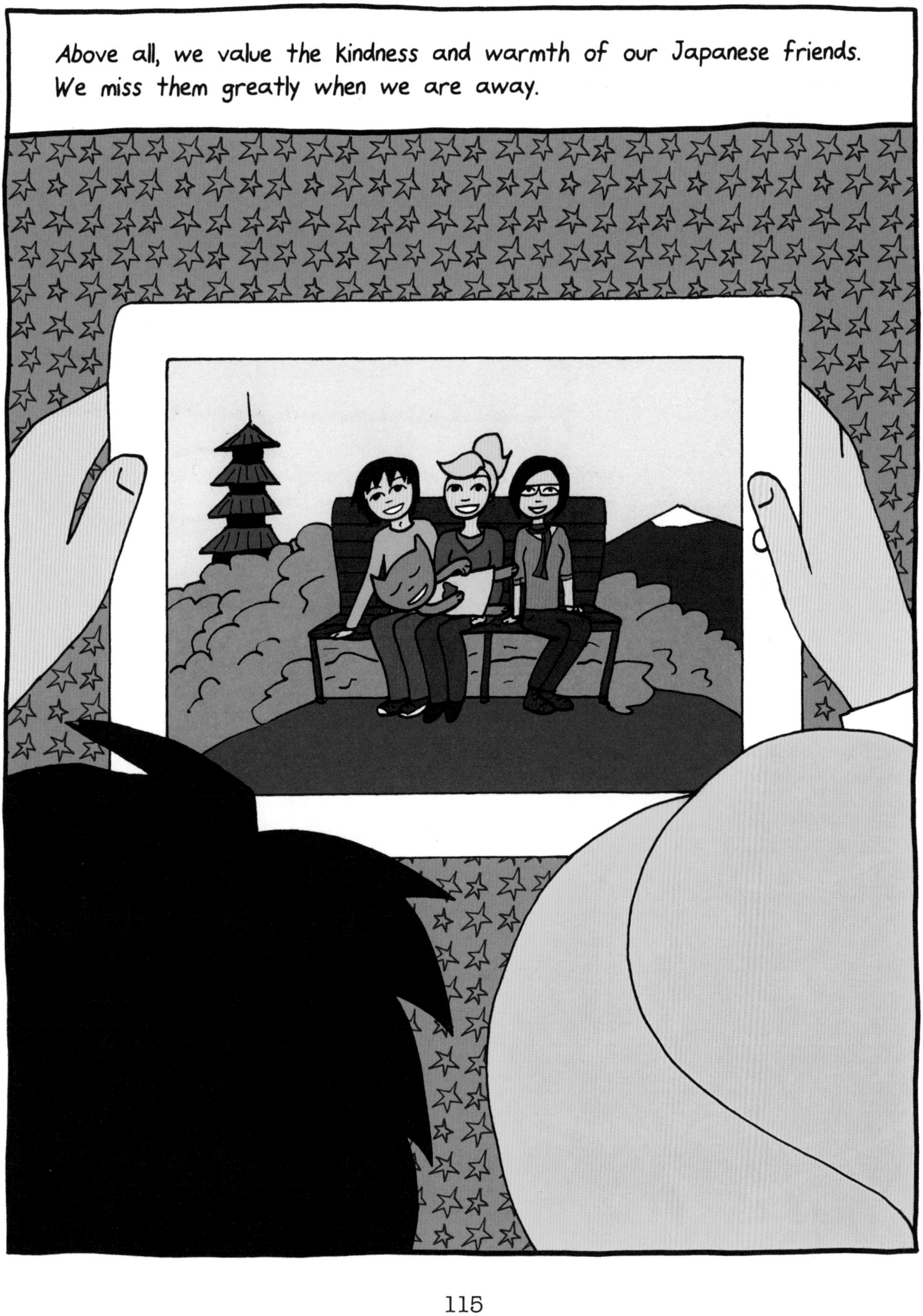
Above all, we value the kindness and warmth of our Japanese friends.
We miss them greatly when we are away.

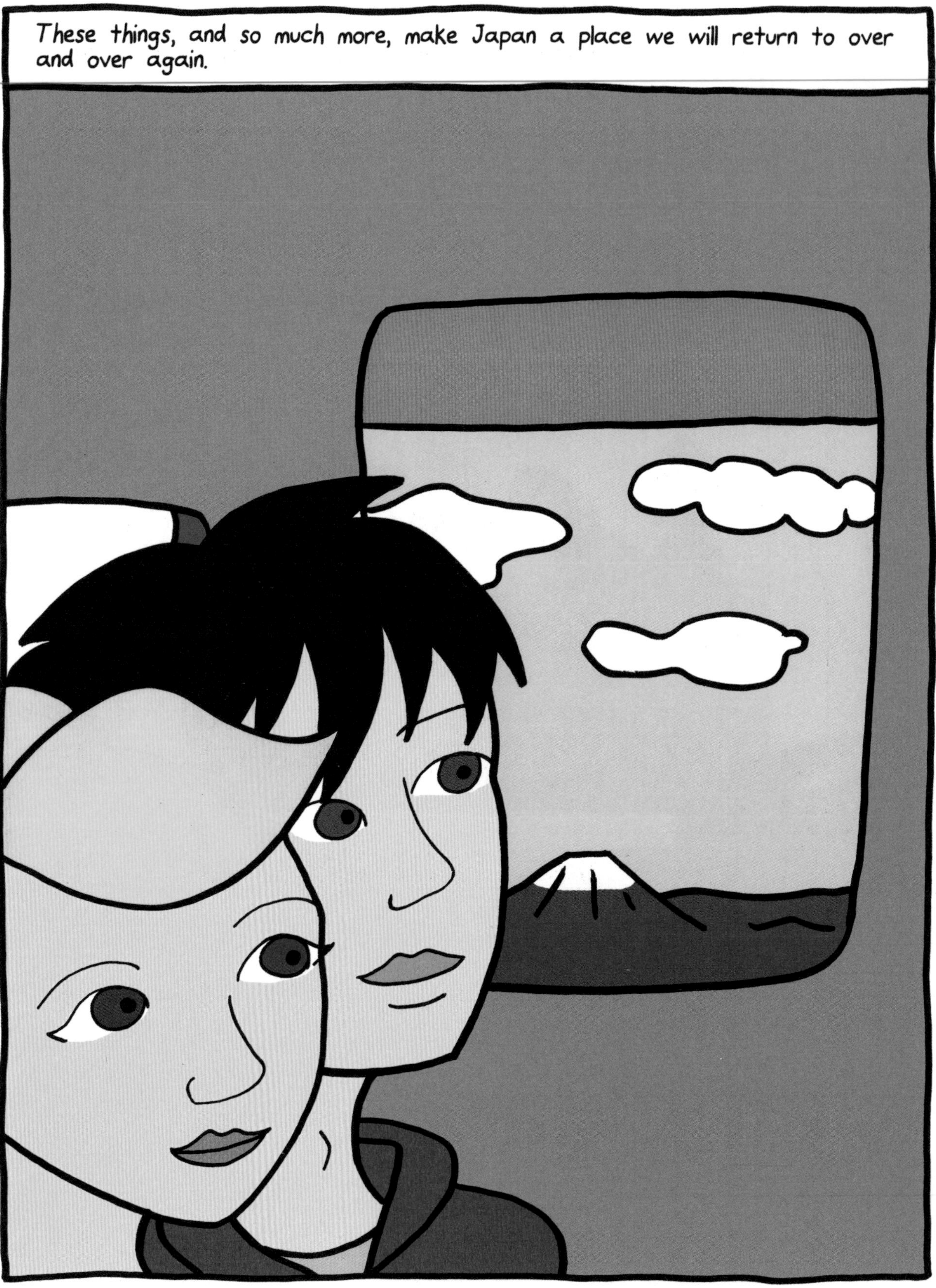
These things, and so much more, make Japan a place we will return to over and over again.

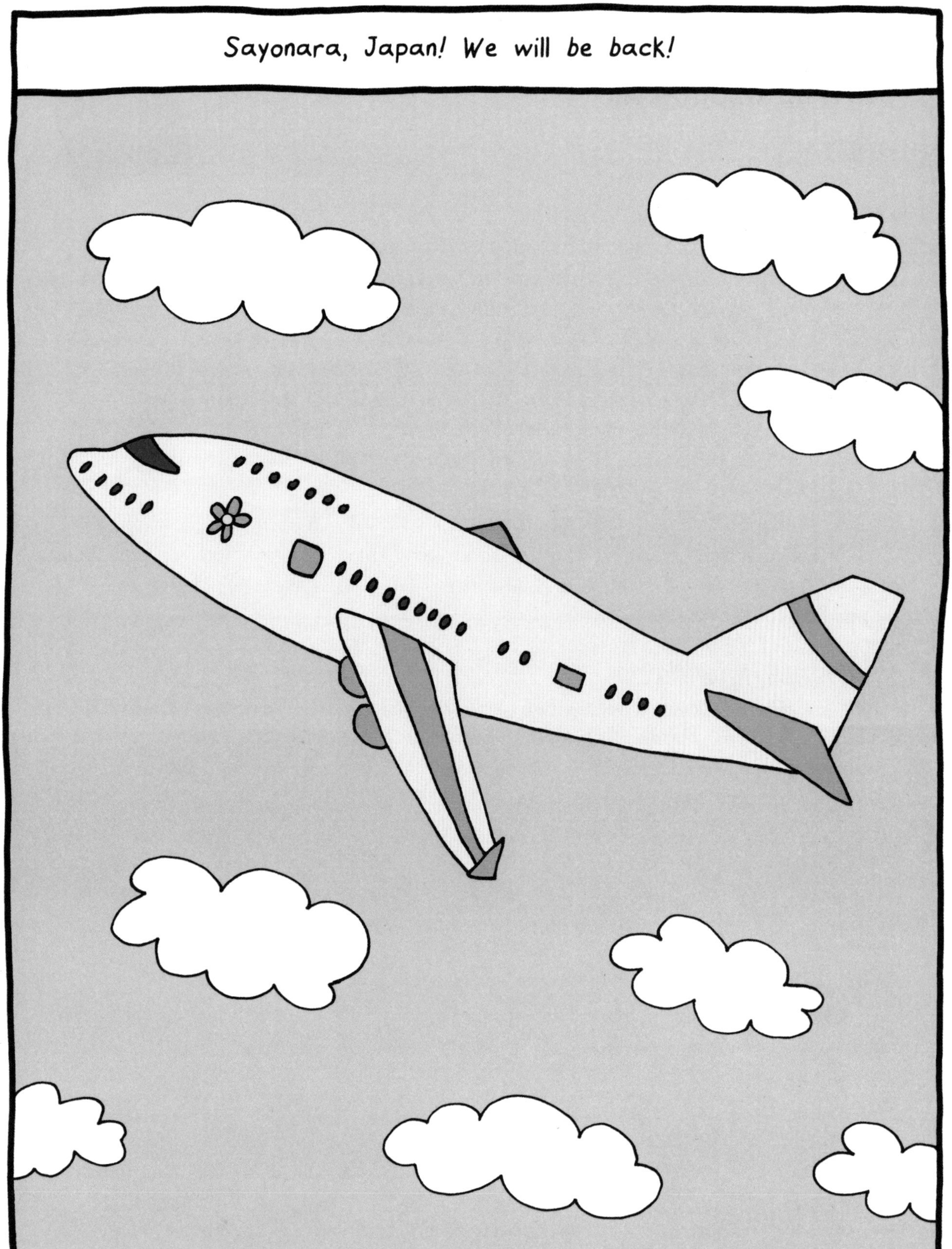
Sayonara, Japan! We will be back!

TRAVEL RESOURCES

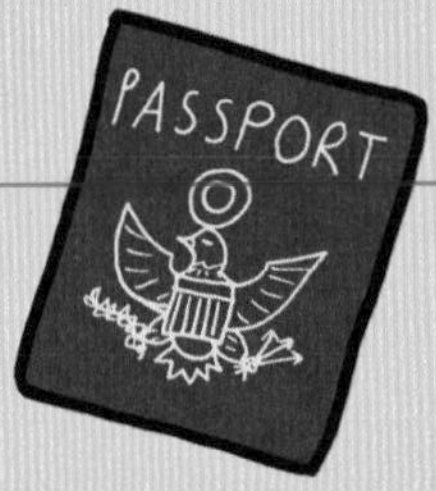
PASSPORT

WEBSITES:

http://www.japan-guide.com
This is my favorite Japan travel site for planning, especially from a logistical standpoint! It has a lot of great information about destinations with details about rates, routes and train fares. The site is regularly updated with information and dates for specific seasons and festivals, including cherry blossom season and fall color tracking. There's even information alerting visitors when a given area will be undergoing maintenance or new construction.

http://www.jnto.go.jp/eng
This is the official site of the Japan National Tourism Organization. This comprehensive site is a great resource for information on whatever might interest you in and about Japan. The site sometimes features promotions and contests as well.

http://www.hyperdia.com
Hyperdia's site shows the routes and the timetables of the railway and aviation of Japan. I highly recommend using this site to check out the timetables for Shinkansen in advance of your trip, especially if you are using a Japan Rail pass.

Hotels.com
I find it easy to book and search for hotels on this site. Also, you can get a free night for every 10 nights you book with them!

Tripadvisor.com
This is a great place to do some more in-depth research on hotels and restaurants before you book. They post tons of reviews.

Kayak.com
This site lets you compare the prices offered by different online travel sites, so it's a good way to shop using a single search. The site also has a page (Click MORE on the main menu) for more general information, so you can compare airline baggage costs and get a sense of flight costs your area to other parts of the country/world.

HANDY JAPAN APPS

For Getting Around:

trains.jp
This is a lifesaver for riding trains in the Tokyo area. Just type in your origin and destination stations, then you get a choice of routes, with ride duration, fares, and transfers easily outlined—all in English.

Hyperdia
This site and app includes Shinkansen and train routes all over Japan. The app has a 30-day free trial, after which you can buy a subscription. Handy if you are doing more countrywide travel.

Google Maps
Map apps are great, and a phone with GPS is indispensible especially in Japan, where directions can be very confusing.

For speaking the language:

Kotaba
A basic Japanese language study app, helpful for beginners.

Human Japanese
This is a popular, friendly app for learning the written and spoken language.

Learn Japanese
If you're traveling with an iPhone, the Learn Japanese app (this series is available for other languages as well) is great for finding the phrases you need and learning how to say them. There's even an option for hearing the phrase spoken slowly, to make them easier to repeat.

SOME OTHER RECOMMENDED DESTINATIONS

This book focuses on destinations in Japan that I've traveled to personally, so it is by no means a complete guide. Every time I return I go somewhere new! Here are a few of the places I visited after the art for this book was completed.

Hiroshima
Rebuilt after the aftermath of World War II, this city has monuments, museums and parks dedicated to the pursuit of peace. If you have a JR Pass, you can use it on the Maple Loop tour bus. Handy!

Miyajima
Home of the iconic red torii gate of Itsukushima Shrine that stands up out of the water at high tide, Miyajima is a must-see, and it is an easy day trip from Hiroshima. Miyajima also has deer (similar to Nara, but visitors are forbidden to feed them) and Mount Misen for fans of hiking as well as gorgeous mountain views.

Onomichi
Onomichi is a charming town in Hiroshima Prefecture. The main attraction is the 25-temple walk, a scenic route that goes up and down winding hills on a path connecting 25 temples.

Yokohama Chinatown
Japan's largest Chinatown is bordered by ornate and lovely gates. The colorful Kanteibyo temple is a must-see and there are plenty of interesting food stands with dumplings and other delicacies! Pandas are a major theme here, so remember to pick up a cute panda souvenir.

IMPORTANT INFO IN CASE OF EMERGENCIES

Police Boxes are stationed in major metropolitan areas and they can often assist with directions. In Japanese a police box is called "Koban".

In emergencies, the numbers to call are 110 (police) or 119 (ambulance/fire).

The U.S. Embassy in Tokyo's Telephone #* is 81-3-3224-5000.

Earthquakes are a fairly common occurrence in Japan. Typically they are not severe. When checking into your hotel make sure to take note of the emergency exits and instructions in the hotel's room guide. Here are some more tips:

1) Don't panic.
2) When inside, stay inside and take cover. Get under a desk, table, or doorjamb to avoid falling objects.
3) When outside, take cover if you can. If you can't find anything to cover you, drop to the ground and cover your head and neck until it passes.
4) Keep away from windows and don't use elevators.
5) If in a public building, follow the lead of the employees.

FEATURED AND RECOMMENDED PLACES TO VISIT

SHRINES & TEMPLES

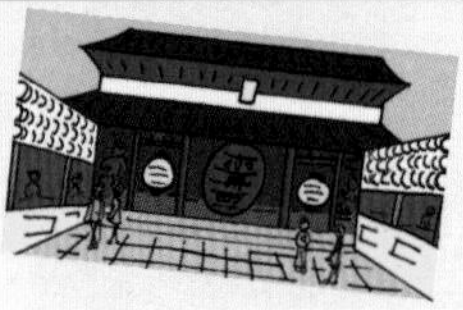

Sensoji Temple
2-3-4 Asakusa
Taito, Tokyo 111-0032
+81-3-3842-0181

Tokudaiji
4-6-2 Ueno, Taito-ku
Ueno and Yanaka, Tokyo, 110-0005
+81-3-3831-7926

Kiyomizudera Temple
94 Kiyomizu 1-chome, Higashiyama Ward,
Kyoto 605-0862
+81-7-5551-1234

Yasaka Shrine
625 Gion Kitagawa, Higashiyama-ku,
Kyoto 605-0073
+81-7-5561-6155

Dazaifu Tenmangu
4-7-1 Saifu
Dazaifu, Fukuoka Prefecture 818-0195
+81-9-2922-8225

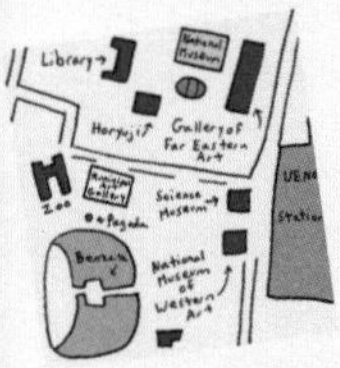
Library
National Museum
Horyuji
Gallery of Far Eastern Art
Zoo
Science Museum
National Museum of Western Art

MUSEUMS & ATTRACTIONS

Ghibli Museum
1-1-83 Shimorenjaku
Mitaka, Tokyo 181-0013
+81-5-7005-5777

Shinyokohama Ramen Museum
2-14-21 Shinyokohama, Kohoku Ward,
Yokohama, Kanagawa Prefecture 222-0033
+81-4-5471-0503

Ooedo Onsen Monogatari
2-6-3 Aomi, Koto-ku, Tokyo Prefecture
135-0064
+81-3-5500-1126

Tokyo Sky Tree
1-1-2 Oshiage
Sumida, Tokyo 131-0045
+81-3-5302-3470

Osaka Aquarium (Kaiyukan)
1-1-10 Kaigandori
Minato Ward, Osaka 552-0022
+81-6-6576-5501

Osamu Tezuka Manga Museum
7-65 Mukogawacho, Takarazuka, Hyogo
Prefecture 665-0844
+81 797-81-2970

Tsutenkaku Tower
1 18 6 Ebisuhigashi,
Naniwa ku, Osaka, 556 0002
+81-6-6641-9555

Kyoto International Manga Museum
Karasuma-dori Oike-agaru
Kyoto 604-0846
+81-7-5254-7414 or +81-797-81-2970

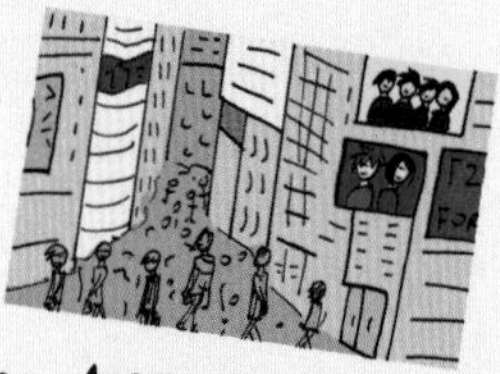

SHOPPING

Ameyoko Shopping Area
(Ueno, Taito-ku) and Nakano Broadway
(5-52-15 Nakano, Nakano-ku) are two
major Tokyo shopping areas

Animate* Ikebukuro (Flagship)
1-20-7 East Ikebukuro,
Toshima Ward, Tokyo
+81-3-3988-1351

Daiso (Harajuku) *
Village 107
1-19-24 Jingumae,
Shibuya-ku, Tokyo
+81-3-5775-9641

Mandarake* (Akihabara)
Sotokanda, Chiyoda-ku
Tokyo 3-11-12
Mandarake Bldg. 6F
+81-3-3350-1701

Retro Game Camp
Kowa Electric Bldg. 1F
Sotokanda, Chiyoda-ku, Tokyo 4-4-2
+81-3-3253-7778

Yodobashi Camera*
1-11-1 Nishi-shinjuku, Shinjuku, Tokyo
+81-3-3346-1010

* These shops have multiple locations

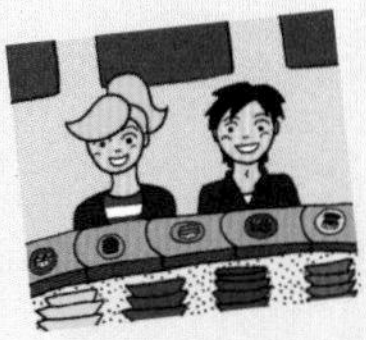

RESTAURANTS

8Bit Café
3-8-9 Q Building 5F
Shinjuku, Tokyo 160-0022
+81-3358-0407
Retro video game-themed bar. Nostalgic fun for grown-up children of the '80s!

Butlers Café
Udagawa KK Bldg 5/F
11-6 Udagawacho,
Shibuya, Tokyo 150-0042,
+81 3-3780-6883
A treat for the ladies! Charming English-speaking butlers will wait on you hand and foot. Reservations recommended.

Café de Copain
16-12 Udagawacho
Shibuya, Tokyo 150-0042
+81-3-3496-5001
Our favorite breakfast spot Shibuya. featuring a huge selection of fresh scones in interesting flavors (like Maple Cream Cheese), all served with cream!

Cambiare
1-1-7 2F Kabukicho, Shinjukuko,
Tokyo Shinjuku, Golden Gai Hanazono 3rd Lane
+81-3-3208-9461
Horror fans will love this tiny bar inspired by the films of director Dario Argento!

Kushiwakamaru
1-19-2 Kamimeguro,
Meguro, Tokyo
+81 3-3715-9292
A popular izakaya open after 5pm.. Their meat skewers and potatoes are great!

Shunsai
Shibuya Excel Hotel Tokyu in the Shibuya Mark City Building
1-12-2 Dogenzaka,
Shibuya, Tokyo 150-0043,
+81 3-5457-0131
A fantastic place to have a kaiseki lunch. Reservations recommended. Be sure to request a table with a view!

Togaden
87 Kyoto Chukyo-ku,
Kyoto Nakajima-cho, 604-8004
+81 075-212-1209
A tofu restaurant with wonderful set meal options.

Warai
1-5-6 Dotonbori Chuo-Ku
Osaka 542-0071
+81 6-6214-8513
A great Okonomiyaki spot in Osaka right by the Canal!

Fukuro no Yakata
Higashi-Tsuchido-cho 15-17
City Onomichi Higashi-Tsuchido-cho 14-17
+81 8-4823-4169
Adorable mountainside café near the cat alley on the 25 temple trail in Onomichi. A magical place covered with owl knickknacks, it's like a Ghibli movie set!

Matsuya
2 Chome-6-12 Saifu
Dazaifu, Fukuoka Prefecture 818-0117
+81 92-922-6125
A lovely teahouse in the Dazaifu shrine area that has a huge garden and Umegaemochi (plum blossom-themed sweet bean cakes).

FESTIVALS OF JAPAN

Japan has wonderful festivals year-round, but my favorite is Shichi-Go-San in November. The elaborately dressed children are so cute!

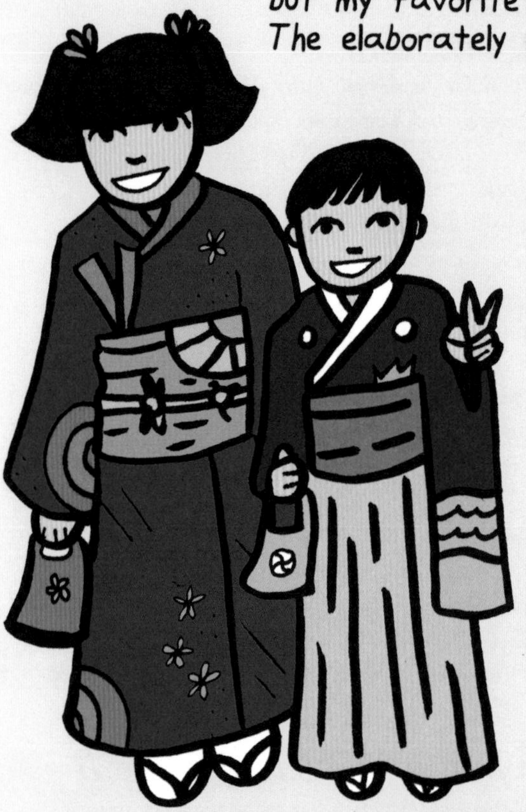

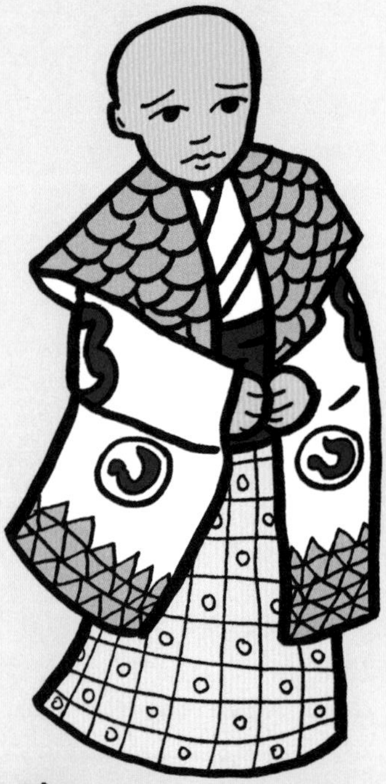

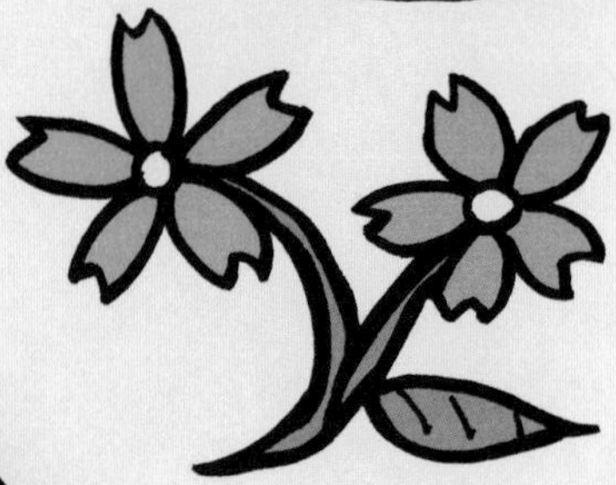

Watch for Sakura in April!

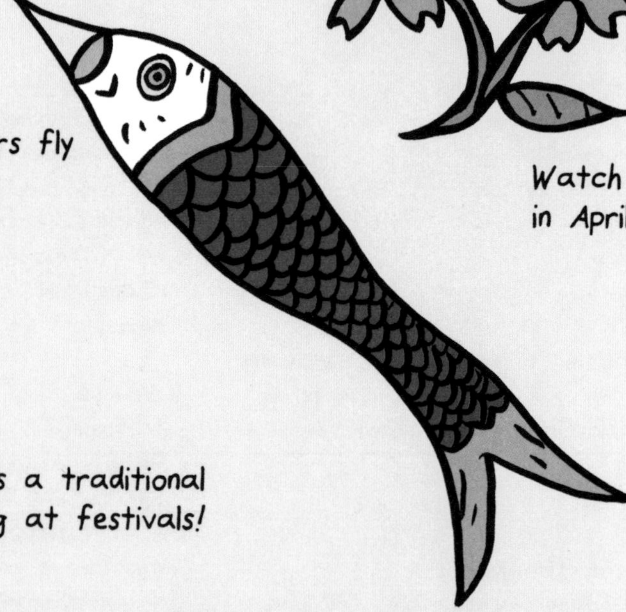

Colorful carp streamers fly during Kodomo-no-hi!

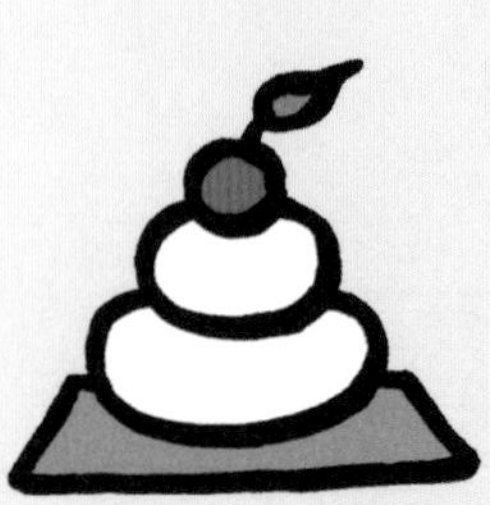

Mochi is a traditional offering at festivals!

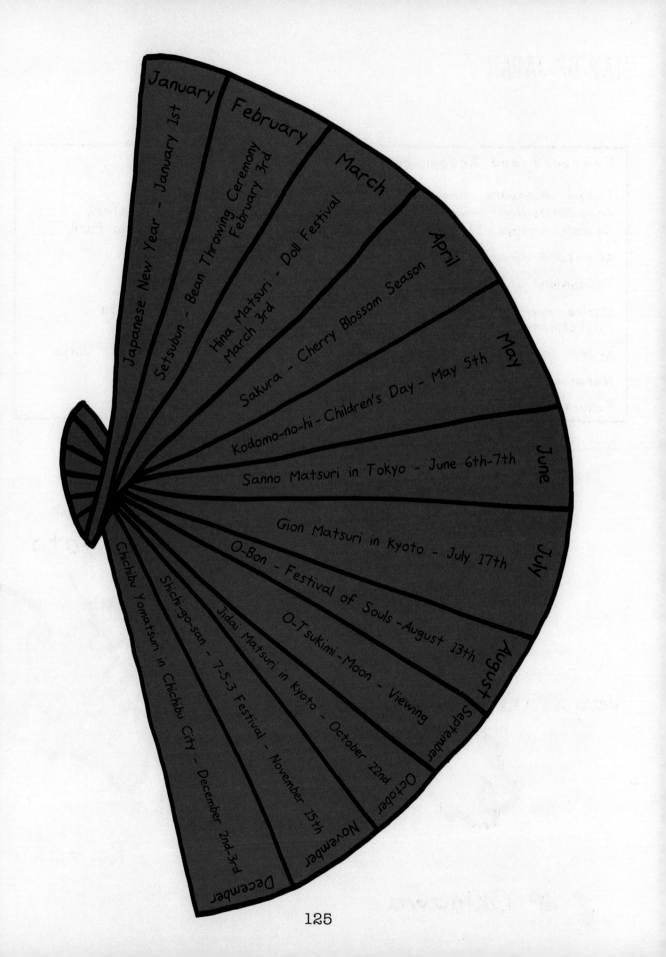

January
Japanese New Year – January 1st

February
Setsubun – Bean Throwing Ceremony February 3rd

March
Hina Matsuri – Doll Festival March 3rd

April
Sakura – Cherry Blossom Season

May
Kodomo-no-hi – Children's Day – May 5th

June
Sanno Matsuri in Tokyo – June 6th-7th

July
Gion Matsuri in Kyoto – July 17th

August
O-Bon – Festival of Souls – August 13th

September
O-Tsukimi – Moon – Viewing

October
Jidai Matsuri in Kyoto – October 22nd

November
Shichi-go-san – 7-5-3 Festival – November 15th

December
Chichibu Yomatsuri in Chichibu City – December 2nd-3rd

MAP OF JAPAN

Featured and Recommended Destinations

Tokyo: Akihabara, Ameyoko, Ghibli Museum, Ginza, Harajuku, Kappabashi-Dori, Nakano Broadway, Odaiba, Ooedo Onsen Monogatari, Sensoji, Shibuya, Shinjuku, Tokyo Big Sight, Tokyo Sky Tree, Ueno Park

Kamakura: Great Buddha, Hachimangu, Hase-Dera

Yokohama: Chinatown, Shinyokohama Ramen Museum

Osaka Area: Dotonburi, Kaiyukan Aquarium, Takarazuka, Tempozan Marketplace, Tsutenkaku Tower

Kyoto: International Manga Museum, Kinkakuji, Kiyomizudera, Yasaka Jinja

Nara: Katsuga-Taisha, Nara Park, Todaiji Temple

Fukuoka Area: Canal City, Dazaifu Tenmangu Shrine

Hiroshima
Takarazuka
Kyoto
Fukuoka
Nagasaki
Shikoku
Nara
Osaka
Kamakura
Okinawa

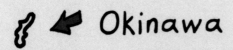

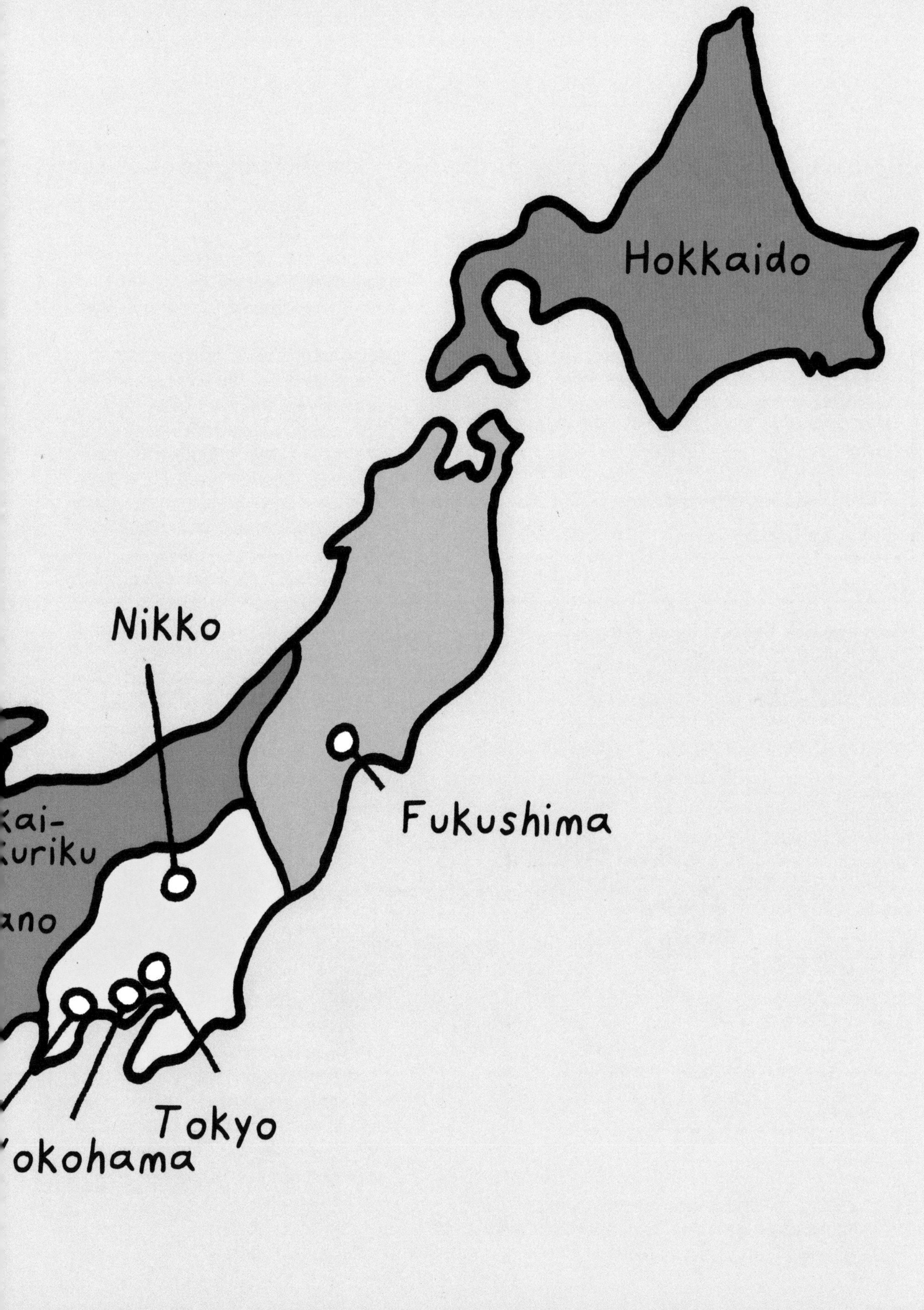
Hokkaido
Nikko
Fukushima
Tokyo

Published by Tuttle Publishing, an imprint of
Periplus Editions (HK) Ltd.

www.tuttlepublishing.com

Library of Congress cataloging in process

ISBN 978-4-8053-1279-7

Distributed by

North America, Latin America & Europe
Tuttle Publishing
364 Innovation Drive
North Clarendon, VT 05759-9436 U.S.A.
Tel: (802) 773-8930; Fax: (802) 773-6993
info@tuttlepublishing.com; www.tuttlepublishing.com

Japan
Tuttle Publishing
Yaekari Building, 3rd Floor
5-4-12 Osaki, Shinagawa-ku Tokyo 141 0032
Tel: (81) 3 5437-0171; Fax: (81) 3 5437-0755
sales@tuttle.co.jp; www.tuttle.co.jp

Asia Pacific
Berkeley Books Pte. Ltd.
61 Tai Seng Avenue #02-12
Singapore 534167
Tel: (65) 6280-1330; Fax: (65) 6280-6290
inquiries@periplus.com.sg; www.periplus.com

First edition
18 17 16 15 14   6 5 4 3 2 1   1409TW
Printed in Malaysia

**The Tuttle Story:
"Books to Span the East and West"**

Many people are surprised to learn
that the world's largest publisher of
books on Asia had its humble
beginnings in the tiny American state
of Vermont. The company's founder,
Charles E. Tuttle, belonged to a New
England family steeped in publishing.

Immediately after WW II, Tuttle
served in Tokyo under General
Douglas MacArthur and was tasked
with reviving the Japanese
publishing industry. He later founded
the Charles E. Tuttle Publishing
Company, which thrives today as one
of the world's leading independent
publishers.

Though a westerner, Tuttle was
hugely instrumental in bringing a
knowledge of Japan and Asia to a
world hungry for information about
the East. By the time of his death in
1993, Tuttle had published over
6,000 books on Asian culture, history
and art—a legacy honored by the
Japanese emperor with the "Order of
the Sacred Treasure," the highest
tribute Japan can bestow upon a
non-Japanese.

With a backlist of 1,500 titles,
Tuttle Publishing is more active today
than at any time in its past—inspired
by Charles Tuttle's core mission to
publish fine books to span the East
and West and provide a greater
understanding of each.